New Theatre Voices of the Fifties and Sixties

SELECTIONS FROM *ENCORE* MAGAZINE 1956–1963

in the same series

New Theatre Voices of the Seventies
Interviews from *Theatre Quarterly* 1970–1980

New Theatre Voices of the Fifties and Sixties

SELECTIONS FROM *ENCORE* MAGAZINE
1956–1963

Edited by Charles Marowitz,
Tom Milne, Owen Hale

With an Introduction by Michael Billington

Eyre Methuen · London

First published in Great Britain in 1965
by Methuen & Co Ltd
Re-issued with new Introduction in 1981
in simultaneous hardback and paperback editions
by Eyre Methuen Ltd, 11 New Fetter Lane,
London EC4P 4EE

Copyright © 1965 Encore Publishing Company
Introduction copyright © 1981 Michael Billington

Printed in Great Britain by
Richard Clay (The Chaucer Press) Ltd,
Bungay, Suffolk

ISBN 0 413 48900 0 (Hardback)
      0 413 48910 8 (Paperback)

CONTENTS

ILLUSTRATIONS

INTRODUCTION

BY MICHAEL BILLINGTON

I suppose a whole generation has grown up for whom the name *Encore* means absolutely nothing. So perhaps one should explain that it was a pugnacious, pocket-sized theatre magazine that appeared every two months from the mid-1950s to the mid-1960s. It was dogmatic, partial, principled, feverish and extremely well-written. I started collecting it, as a Midlands schoolboy, in June–July 1957 (a splendid issue that, with Olivier on the cover, the full text of a Royal Court debate chaired by Kenneth Tynan plus articles from Colin Wilson, Kingsley Amis, Richard Roud and Stephen Joseph) and kept every number until the magazine's expiry in 1965. Indeed, even now, if I want to check on early attitudes to Arden and Pinter, Beckett and Ionesco it is to *Encore* that I inevitably return.

Re-reading the articles that make up this selection, however, I am struck by several things. First, the enviable certainty of life in the *Encore* era. Vital theatre was something that you found at the Royal Court, Stratford East and, from time to time, the Arts: listless, deadly, devitalized theatre was the speciality of the West End. Indeed one almost feels *Encore* writers got bonus points the more knocking references to Shaftesbury Avenue they could include in their copy. David Watt, for instance, tells us in his 1957 piece that the West End was then full of plays that "appear to have been written by the inhabitant of one pent-house in Knightsbridge for the amusement of the girl in the flat below". Reared on such references, it was quite a shock to come to London in 1962 to meet two *Encore* alumni, Tom Milne and Geoffrey Reeves, and be told that one of the best things in town was Noel Coward's *Sail Away*.

But on the whole the magazine pinned its faith in Devine and Littlewood and treated the West End as a citadel in enemy hands; and it was right. From the vantage point of 1981, however, one can only look back with hungry nostalgia to an era when everything was so clear-cut. Now the situation seems much more muddied and confused. On paper, we have the kind of pluralist, subsidized theatre that the *Encore* writers dreamed about; yet the blunt truth is that vast tracts of that theatre (particularly the regional reps) are run on pragmatic, commercial lines. Even the Royal Court, once the focus of so much idealism, is forced to put economic survival before the formation of a coherent policy. As for the West End, it is now a bewildering mix of musicals, comedies, thrillers plus quality imports from the subsidized sector. It is still, in some ways, an enemy citadel; but one that keeps waving a white flag of surrender every time it runs out of ammunition.

I envy these writers their moral certainty (*"Encore* should not be expressing *every* point of view but the *right* one": Lindsay Anderson). I also envy them the flushed idealism that came from being handmaidens to a hoped-for revolution. New writers were being discovered; new theatres were opening; Brecht and Beckett were beginning to exert their influence. Throughout these pages one gets a wonderful sense of a future full of limitless possibilities. Kenneth Tynan, in a dazzling interview, envisions a National Theatre with some fifty productions in a revolving repertory: in fact, the NT has never sustained more than a dozen productions at any one time. Peter Brook dreams of a small, 100-seat theatre *subsidized to the hilt*: we have the venues but they are subsidized as much by pittance-paid actors and directors as by grant-giving bodies. Joan Littlewood, in a touching farewell note, asks "Cannot each district afford to support a few artists who will give them back some entertainment, laughter and love of mankind?" But, although we have a network of community centres, there are all too few Joans to make them magical fun-palaces.

I don't want to give the impression that nothing has been achieved in the years since *Encore*'s demise. As a drama critic, I could draw up a long list of things that make my job worthwhile: the growth of the RSC under Trevor Nunn into a major world-class company, the spread of new writing through theatres like Hampstead, the Bush, the Warehouse, the Half

Moon, the buoyant internationalism of isolated companies like the Glasgow Citizens' and the Manchester Royal Exchange. My real point is that the pages of this book cover a period (1956 to 1963) when the British theatre was emerging from a prolonged post-war slumber and when there was a real scent of dynamic change in the air. In 1963 alone, for instance, one had *Oh What a Lovely War* at Stratford East, Arden's *The Workhouse Donkey* at Chichester (can you imagine that today?), *The Wars of the Roses* at Stratford-upon-Avon, Olivier and his National Theatre Company moving into the Old Vic, John Neville opening up the new Nottingham Playhouse, writers like Saunders and Wood coming up with plays bulging with promise. Those were expansionist times and there seemed no reason to doubt that the British theatre would not go on getting better and better. Well, much has been accomplished. But one also has to concede that genuine experiment is in very short supply, that there has been a steady seepage of good writers to television and cinema and that many of our most pioneering directors (Brook, Littlewood, Jonathan Miller) are either in exile, retirement or other jobs.

Reading these pages, however, takes one back to an era when all things were possible: far more than any academic study, they give off a whiff of danger, excitement and rancorous frustration. But they also remind one of the need for good, intelligent writing about the theatre away from the time and space pressures of daily journalism. *Encore* was congratulated on many things but rarely on the quality of its writing. But look at Peter Brook's review of *Happy Days*: "For Beckett's symbols are powerful just because we cannot quite grasp them: they are not signposts, they are not text-books nor blue-prints – they are literally creations." Or Charles Marowitz on Lenny Bruce: "Bruce is the closest thing we have to a Zen comic; a direct descendant of the madcap monks whose lunacy is depicted in the early Zen drawings." Or Penelope Gilliatt on *The Hostage*: "The English habitually write as though they are alone and cold at ten in the morning; the Irish write in a state of flushed gregariousness at an eternal opening-time."

Today there are very few places left where one can do this kind of extended review or prolonged think-piece. *Encore* in its heyday was always letting off verbal stink-bombs about the Crisis in Criticism and gunning for Fleet Street hacks. But the real crisis in criticism today is that there are so few outlets, so little room for serious discussion. The popular papers give drama a tithe of the space they afforded it in the 60s. Even the quality papers have become victims of the PR machine with columns given over to tedious puff-interviews rather than to serious analysis of plays. And the specialist theatre magazine has all but disappeared. We urgently need a new *Encore* (is there a millionaire in the house?) where the judgements are more considered, the real issues debated and where theatrical practitioners can pitch in.

In the meantime this selection valuably takes us back to an era when the British theatre was alive with promise. Some of the dawns turned out to be false, some of the dreams chimeras. And there is no doubt that the whirligig of time has brought in its revenges. A dramatist like Rattigan, who was far too quickly thrown into the discard-pile, has turned out to have real staying-power while some of the sensations of the hour have quickly faded. But you hear in these pages the unmistakeable sound of the liveliest art loosening the tenacious stranglehold of Mammon and attempting to get to grips with life itself. If, like me, you are an old *Encore*-ite from way back the book should stir some memories. If you were but a child at the time, fall to and feed.

CHAPTER ONE

MURMURS FROM ABROAD

INTRODUCTION

Before the advent of the English Stage Company in April
1956, and the era it ushered in, the theatrical underground
in London was already buzzing with the names of Beckett,
Ionesco, Genet and Brecht. In France, one heard that an
Irish poet, a Rumanian *émigré* and a convicted homosexual-
thief were staking out new ground for the modern theatre. A
legend had begun to gather round the name "Godot"; and
there was constant chatter about a fascinating piece of nonsense called *The Bald Prima Donna*. When *Waiting for Godot*
finally reached London in 1955 at the Arts Theatre Club,
two and a half years after its Paris première, Sean O'Casey
greeted it in the very early pages of *Encore* with characteristic
life-loving rejection: all the same it was abundantly clear that
exciting paths were being opened up. And when Ionesco burst
on London by way of *The Lesson* (also at the invaluable Arts,
in 1955), ideas about the theatre underwent another severe
shake-up. Genet, represented only by an overheated production of *The Balcony* in 1957, was to remain underground a
little longer – though no less powerful as an influence for that.

In East Germany, a Marxist poet, dramatist and director
was breathing new life into the Epic Theatre forms of the
'twenties and into the whole conception of theatrecraft. So
little was known about his work that a few years previously
one of our leading actors, Sir John Gielgud, could write: "I
did not at all care for Mr Brecht's article. It seems to be
obscure, pointless and humourless. Mr Brecht presumably
writes his own scripts, and it might be interesting to see a
performance of one of them . . ." In the 'fifties, reports and
accounts of his work began to filter through, together with a

few groping productions of his plays, preparing the ground for the eye-opening shock of the Berliner Ensemble's visit to London in 1956. The "Ensemble" came to be quickly-understood shorthand for a troupe of actors whose discipline and devotion had created the most formidable permanent company in Europe. Something potent and irreversible had begun to stir on the continent, and as it gathered momentum, it became clear that England was its next point of contact.

One of the most interesting aspects of the English New Wave was that it arrived at the same time as the so-called Theatre of the Absurd and Brechtian-styled Epic Theatre. In the years that followed, these distinctions tended to get slurred, and everyone was lumped together under the title of "Angry Young Men". Writers as dissimilar as John Arden, N. F. Simpson, John Mortimer and Ann Jellicoe were all thought to be representative of some movement. There never was a *movement* in the sense that the popular press tried to suggest, but there was undeniably a new impetus and a formidable output. Only after the flurry of activity had died down did it appear that the sum of these works was considerably more impressive than any of its parts.

THE BERLINER ENSEMBLE
by George Devine

The theatre of Bertolt Brecht has been sharply criticized and Brecht himself accused of narrowing his modern conception of it within a political framework. To many he is a creative artist of some rank, but an artist with an unpardonable bias. What critics overlook is that the theatre and the art of Brecht are essentially of their time and place. The *Berliner Ensemble Theatre* answers a very palpable need.

It is situated, as we know, in a city divided against itself; and there it manages to thrive. To get to it, you must cross from the ghastly glitter of the Western sector, which displays all the crass showmanship of Broadway and Piccadilly, into the vast sadness of East Berlin. Under its red neon sign, the atmosphere of the theatre is quiet and informal. The group appears to function in a natural and unneurotic manner, and by West End standards the kind of theatre they believe in seems carefree and dedicated, but without polish.

To watch a Brecht production is to stumble upon the agreeable chaos of an artist's studio, to have the artist turn up a picture and tell you, "This – this is more-or-less finished." Such an ability to work in a truly artistic manner is unique in the theatre of the world, and most enviable. But underlying the informality, there is something vital and real. The audience makes this a people's theatre. Their participation in the production is a wonderful thing to sense even though the stage management seems careless by our standards. During the performance of *The Caucasian Chalk Circle*, I was escorted backstage to talk with Helene Weigel, Brecht's wife, the principal actress. We discussed the *Ensemble* for twenty minutes, and the curtain was held up for me to return to my seat. It did not seem to matter, for the audience behaved as if it thought itself lucky to be there. Brecht's dedicated public give the production an air of religious ritual. That is the best kind of theatre atmosphere. Although the actors seemed to be like children playing, they gave the impression that they worked because they liked and believed in what they had to portray. Such devotion changes everything that comes off the stage. There was none of the affected *clichéd* acting which is current in our theatre.

The *Ensemble* is clearly sustained by a strong artistic conception. Behind the simplicity, and the beauty of décor and costumes, every aspect of the production had been studied and worked on until it was absolutely polished. Brecht often rehearses his plays for months and if, when the time comes, a production is not ready, another play in the repertory is substituted until it is ready. In *The Caucasian Chalk Circle*, there is a scene in which twenty peasants are gradually convulsed with laughter. The detail of observation and execution of this scene was entirely remarkable and it must have been achieved with much time and care: one peasant in the front started laughing, the mirth rippled gradually then and overcame all twenty of them. In British theatre, either repertory or West End, I imagine a producer taking the same scene: "Right, okay. Off we go. Yes, it starts with you and it goes right through. No, no. You weren't very good, and I didn't believe in your laughter. Try it again. Good, good that time. Try it once more for luck now, and we open on Monday."

I do not wish to give the impression that there is anything stark or austere about the Brecht production. The costumes are unglamorous but very beautiful. Where richness is needed, richness is given by the choice of materials and colours. While there is a lack of strong colour, there is extreme subtlety of tone. Although it is a *popular* theatre, the décor is in wonderful style and of the highest order, with no kind of concession to "popular taste".

I took a note on my programme that the style was "like film acting". The players worked as if under close scrutiny, the stage is very clearly lit, and the style bears some relation to film technique because of the honesty of effort. The heroine in *The Caucasian Chalk Circle* was a girl who would never be employed in any theatre in England, at least not as a heroine. She was plain, she had thick legs and was completely unglamorous. But in her part she was beautiful and alive and entirely the heroine of the play. She acted what the part demanded to the full and did not short-cut her way either consciously or unconsciously.

Much has been said and written about the E-effect.[1] It is really a matter of convention. The concentration of the audience on what was going on before them was like that of a group of friends who have just dropped in to witness the unfolding of a tale. It was not as though they had paid 16s. 6d. for a stall seat, and had just put away a good dinner and were now waiting to be taken into an unreal world where they could forget themselves. A form of poetic reality is presented to them for their consideration. The E-effect reverses the tendency of the actor to impress or hypnotize the audience with his versatility or his personality. During the most dramatic periods of the theatre, it has never been the object to "take people out of themselves", but rather to show what

[1] The *Entfremdungs-* or *Verfremdungseffekt*: translated by John Willett as the 'alienation effect' or 'A-effect'.

was the truth and to let the audience get out of it what it wanted. The actors simply try *to be*, and it adds up to pure theatre. With Brecht, the realism of Stanislavsky is transformed into another world, and it is the real depiction of humanity seen through certain eyes, and for a certain society. As for the plays themselves, they are written in short scenes which serve to break up the normal involvement of the audience, to discourage the kind of hypnosis that is accepted as normal by us. There is no real attempt at illusion. You are not told that this is life, that this is really happening. Rather, these are actors presenting a tale for you to witness, for you to form your own conclusions about.

The *Berliner Ensemble Theatre* has been in existence for seven years. It is Helene Weigel who runs it and Brecht who serves as its general artistic director. The theatre is well subsidized. It is the showpiece of East Berlin and everyone goes there because everyone is very proud of it. Plays which have been worked on for some time go into the repertory and remain there to be revived periodically. But the work on them never stops.

I met Brecht and talked with him. My first impression of him was that he might have been an intellectual peasant. He is both shy and shrewd. He talked about the artistic life of Germany, about the deleterious effect on the theatre of the elimination of the Jews in Germany and in Central Europe generally. He deplored the lack of great actors today, and talked about the days when they were really great.

Brecht admonished all the young actors in the *Ensemble* to go to see Sir John Gielgud and Peggy Ashcroft who were playing in Berlin at the time in *Much Ado About Nothing*. There is no school at the *Berliner Ensemble Theatre*, but Brecht keeps a very large company with many young actors.

The belief that Brecht has narrowed his modern conception of the theatre within a political framework can only be examined in the light of one important consideration. Brecht's theatre is above all a theatre of its time, of its place, and of its nation. This is its exemplary value. It answers a need and is given the means to answer it because it *is* a need. In the light of this logic, all attempts to *impose* a theatre or an art are

basically esoteric. Brecht's art is biased, but all great creative
work comes out of strong prejudice and is not any the less
valuable for it. Brecht's theatre still has a justification towards humanity – any art is bound to which is practised as
humbly and as well as this is.

[APRIL 1956]

IONESCO : THE OPPOSITE OF
SAMENESS *by Richard Roud*

After the première of *The Bald Prima Donna* in 1950, Jean-
Jacques Gautier assured the readers of *Le Figaro* that the
author of this play would never be heard from again. When
The Chairs was first given at the Théâtre Lancry, there were
many nights when the actors outnumbered the audience, and
there are only three actors in this play.

Abroad, the record was not much better: in Brussels, a
first night audience demanded its money back and threatened
to lynch the actors; in Milan, *The Chairs* was booed off the
stage. However, there were the usual few who recognized
Ionesco from the very start as one of the three most important
dramatists now writing in France. Ionesco himself would
name Samuel Beckett and Jean Genet as the other two.

The view – that the theatre of Ionesco is, without a doubt,
the strangest and the most spontaneous to appear since the
war, that Ionesco's characters constantly resemble us, in
profile, and that we recognize a greater truth in them than we
have ever before known – this view has now become more
generally accepted.

The Chairs, after its unfortunate beginnings in 1953, was
revived at the Théâtre des Noctambules in 1954, and again
at the Studio des Champs Elysées in the spring of 1955,
where it ran until July. It was revived once again at the same
theatre and went on tour in the provinces. His plays have
been produced in Ireland, Italy, Spain, Sweden, Finland,
Belgium, Holland, Germany, Switzerland, Mexico and the
United States. His first production in England was *The Lesson*,

at the Arts Theatre Club in 1955, which was followed by *The Bald Prima Donna* and *The New Tenant* in 1956. This year has seen *The Lesson* at Oxford, *The Bald Prima Donna* at Nottingham. May brought *The Chairs* to the Royal Court, and June, *Amédée* to Cambridge. Not a bad record for a man who was never to be heard of again.

Eugène Ionesco was born in Rumania in 1912 of a Rumanian father and a French mother. At the age of one, he was taken to Paris by his mother, and he remained there until he was fourteen. Although often considered a Rumanian writer, French was his mother tongue (he only learned Rumanian on his return to Bucharest in 1926), and he is a French citizen. Nevertheless, he received his higher education in Bucharest, and it was there he had his first literary success, or rather, *succès de scandale*. When he was twenty, he wrote a wildly controversial article attacking the great Rumanian poet Arghezi, maintaining that in the light of poets such as Rimbaud, Mallarmé, and Claudel, Arghezi was of little or no importance. There followed then a flurry of angry letters with various Rumanian scholars and critics. Three weeks later, Ionesco wrote another article defending Arghezi, insisting on his importance in world literature. The article then went on to prove the non-existence of critical criteria, and hence, the utter worthlessness of all criticism. This article was called *The Sameness of Opposites*.

These articles and letters were collected into a volume called *NO!*, together with fragments from his journal concerning the general absurdity of life, the inanity of culture, the uselessness of language as a means of communication. This example of existentialism *avant la lettre* was not generally appreciated.

Ionesco returned to France in 1938, and has lived in Auteuil ever since. Indeed, his ideas and theatrical concepts are strongly rooted in France. Beginning with Alfred Jarry's *Ubu Roi* (1896), the *avant-garde* tradition in France has been characterized by its attempts to express metaphysical ideas in concrete theatrical terms. Like Jarry, Ionesco's plays are largely outside of time and space, a first step in his attempt to achieve universality: *The Chairs* takes place four hundred thousand years after the fall of Paris; *The Bald Prima Donna* takes place in England, to be sure, but only because Ionesco got the idea of writing this play while taking an *Assimil* course in English.

This course taught him many astonishing things, such as that the floor is beneath us, the ceiling above us, there are seven days in the week, that one walks on one's feet, but that one keeps warm with the aid of coal and electricity, etc. From such fascinating bits of information, *The Bald Prima Donna* was born.

Another of his plays, *Jack, or Obedience*, could be imagined to take place anywhere or at any time since the rise of the middle class.

Furthermore, just as Jarry proceeded to a conscious simplification and deformation of language in reaction to the over-refinement of language in much of the drama of the 1880s, so Ionesco, disgusted by the high-flown rhetoric and eternal variations on the triangle of so much of French drama of the past twenty years, has reduced his vocabulary to a bare minimum, and has attempted to "re-theatricalize" the theatre by returning to classical theatrical forms, only in a purified and abstracted state. In Jarry, the deformation of language is a *criticism* of everyday speech, with the cliché heightened to a state of near paroxysm.

But Ionesco goes even further. For instance, *Jack* begins with the usual family group sitting round a table: father, mother, sister, grandparents, and the rebellious son, who does not want to accept his family's choice for his bride. As the play begins, the mother is upbraiding her son for his unfilial disobedience:

> My son, my child, after all we've done for you! After all our sacrifices! I should never have thought this of you. You were my brightest hope ... You still are, for I can't believe, no, I just can't believe, by Bacchus, that you'll be so stubborn...

Amid all the clichés of the boulevard drama, the only hint of anything odd has been the "by Bacchus". But now comes the break. The thin shell of sense cracks, and the language reveals the abyss always present just beneath the conversational level, and Ionesco plunges us into it. As Antonin Artaud has said of Strindberg, "He gives us a feeling of something which, without being at all supernatural, or unhuman, is nevertheless imbued with an interior unreality. We see nothing but what is real, only it is a hidden and a devious reality. The real and the unreal are mixed, as in the brain of a man going to sleep, or a man who awakes suddenly to turn over. We have lived and dreamed all that is revealed in these plays, but we have forgotten . . . these plays are constantly touching on reality, only to depart almost immediately from it." After the calm beginning of *Jack*, Ionesco begins to move *past* reality; the language is broken up, broken down; the thin logic which holds our lives together is destroyed, and we are set face to face with what lies beneath; we are on the other side of the looking-glass:

You can't love your parents any more, your clothes, your sister, your grandmother. Don't you remember, my boy, remember how I bottle-fed you, how I left you to dry in your nappy, just like your sister . . . Didn't I, child? . . . You see, you see, I was the one, my boy, who gave you your first spanking; not your father over there who could have done it better. He's stronger than me. No, I was the one, because I loved you too much. And it was I who made you go without your pudding, and who kissed you, looked after you, trained you, and taught you how to ameliorate, to violate, to articulate, and who brought you such nice things to eat in your stockings. I taught you how to climb the stairs (when there were any), how to rub your knees with nettles when you wanted to be stung. I've been more than a mother to you, I've been a bosom pal, a husband, a hussy, a crony, a goose. Nothing has stood in my way. I surmounted every obstacle, every barricade, to satisfy your childish whims and fancies. Oh, ungrateful boy, you don't even remember when I used to take you on my lap, and pull your pretty little teeth and your toenails out to make you caterwaul like a calf, a lovely little calf. What an unhappy mother I am! I've brought a mononster into the world, and you're the mononster. Here, your grandmother wants to talk to you. She's tottery. She is octogenic. Perhaps she can move you by her age, her past, her future.

People, says Ionesco, must talk to exist; silence frightens them, and it is only when they are talking that they feel themselves alive and secure. But the world of insecurity constantly closes in. Carried on by the flow of their pitiful eloquence, they tumble into the ambushes of reality that language lays for us, and they are destroyed, like the pupil in *The Lesson*, or the Maid in *The Bald Prima Donna*, or are forced to destroy themselves like the old couple in *The Chairs*. Perhaps the point Ionesco is making is that language is an escape from reality, not an expression of it. As the old woman in *The Chairs* says:

It's in talking that one finds ideas, and words; and then ourselves in our own words; the city, too, and the garden; perhaps we can find everything, and then we won't be orphans any more.

But this illusion will prove cruelly false, just as the illusion of Mr and Mrs Martin in *The Bald Prima Donna* that they are Donald and Elizabeth is proved false by the superior logic of the Maid.

In *The Chairs*, the old woman's husband has been working for fifty years on a "message" for the world. All his life he has been nothing, a janitor, when, as his wife constantly reminds him, with a little ambition he might have been much more: "a General-chief, a Doctor-chief, a King-chief, or even an Actor-chief". Instead he is only a janitor, or Chief-Quartermaster, as he likes to call himself. Nevertheless, he has his message and, now that he is 94 years old, he is ready to give it to the world. He has invited everyone to come to his home that night, "the wardens, the gardeners, the bishops, the chemists, the violinists, the presidents, the policemen, the merchants, the buildings, the pen-holders, the chromosomes, etc." The main action of the play starts with the arrival, one after the other, of all the guests; and the guests, who are invisible, constitute a microcosmic picture of society. The first lady and the Colonel begin to flirt politely, as people would do at an ordinary party, but they go on and on until, as the stage direction indicates, "invisibly, they begin to behave improperly". The next guest is a former sweetheart of the old man. She was once beautiful, and he assures her that she hasn't changed at all, except that her nose has grown larger, and longer. Did she do it on purpose? How did it happen? Ah, little by little . . . And so its goes. Each time little conversations start up on a normal level, only to go beyond, behind everyday reality, somewhat in the way that, when we are half-asleep, the exigencies of normal waking life left behind, the mind functions with a logic of its own. Paradoxically, reality is not submerged, but intensified. We reach a level of free association where the essential meaning (or meaninglessness) of life is revealed to us.

Finally, after all the guests have arrived, the Emperor appears. He, too, is invisible. The old couple are at the height of their joy. At last, at last, *He* has arrived. (Considering the remark made by Ionesco to the effect that it is essential for God to appear in some form on stage, and equally essential that he should not be named, can not take the Emperor to be the god-figure of *The Chairs*?)

The old man significantly does not feel that he can give the message himself, so he has hired a professional orator, who arrives just before the end of the play. (He is visible.) When he arrives, the old couple, feeling that now their life is complete, kill themselves by jumping out of the window. The orator clears his throat, and tries to speak. But all he can utter are meaningless guttural sounds; he is a deaf-mute.

But language (or silence) is not Ionesco's only weapon. From Antonin Artaud, he has learned that effective use can be made of props. In Ionesco's plays, props are not only part of the décor, they act directly, modifying, transforming, and creating. In *The Chairs*, for example, the constantly proliferating chairs (by the end of the play the thirty-five chairs leave no room for the couple to move) create a nightmarish effect, their physical presence rendering by contrast the ineluctable solitude of the old couple. After their suicide, the stage remains covered by a jungle of chairs. And it is only at this point that we finally hear the sounds of the invisible crowd – laughter, murmurs, coughs, etc, which gradually grow louder and louder, accentuating the silence which has gone before, a silence only interrupted by the pathetic and senile hysteria of the old couple.

In *The New Tenant*, the furniture with which we clutter up our lives gradually invades the stage, transforming it into a tomb. In *Amédée*, the corpse with its enormous feet and legs gradually forces the protagonists to their destruction. Thus, the impossibility of communication and the essential aloneness of man is rendered by the crushing presence of *things*, which finally stifle the New Tenant, Amédée and Madeleine, and the old couple of *The Chairs*.

Throughout this consideration of Ionesco's plays, we have seen how often he is concerned with the theme of the couple. Indeed, he has carried the drama of the couple to the furthest degree. Like Nietzsche who said that Strindberg's work magnificently expressed his own feeling on the subject of love: love, with war as its means and the deathly hate of the sexes as its fundamental law, Ionesco considers that it was Strindberg who was the first really to attack the theme of the married couple. But in *The Father* and *The Dance of Death*, the couples are shown linked eternally by the bond of hate, and their hatred is as strong a bond as love. But in *The Chairs*, for example, we find the couple practically at the end of their lives: hate has disappeared, and only loneliness remains. The old couple are terribly devoted to each other, but the *marriage* tie has disappeared, and the old woman has become the mother of her husband. They even go so far as to play at mother and son: she takes him on her knees, pets him, rocks him, consoles him over his failures, encourages him, and finally wipes his nose and dries his tears.

In *Amédée, or How To Get Rid Of It*, we have a younger couple, each about forty-five. He is a playwright incapable of finishing a play, and she is constantly nagging him, upbraiding him, insulting him, because in fifteen years he has only written two lines, and is still waiting for the inspiration to write a third line! They have long since ceased to love each other and the corpse of their past happy life is expressed concretely by a dead body which inevitably keeps on growing, invading their flat, until it becomes so big they can no longer go on living there. The terrifying growth of the cadaver is accompanied by the sudden sprouting of giant mushrooms all over the carpet. The action of the play largely consists in their efforts to get rid of the cadaver, trying to deliver themselves from their past. This proves impossible, and Amédée dies, but Madeleine remains a prisoner of their tragic past.

So we find united in *The Chairs* and *Amédée* all the themes of Ionesco's anxieties. Vacuity, failure, transitoriness, the crushing weight of the world, despair, and death. Up until these plays, many left-wing critics in France liked Ionesco because they thought they saw in his plays a satire on bourgeois life in a capitalist society. But with *The Chairs*, they realized their error – it is not simply bourgeois life with which Ionesco is concerned, and it is not simply satire. Behind the absurdities, the laughter, the nonsense, lies a compassionate despair:

> For me, the theatre is the projection on a stage of the interior world: it is from my dreams, from my hidden anxieties, from my obscure longings, from my internal contradictions that I draw the substance of my plays. As I am not alone in the world, and as each one of us is, deep down, everyone else, my dreams, my longings, my anxieties, and my obsessions do not belong to me alone; they are part of an ancestral heritage, an age-old depository, which constitutes the domain of all humanity. And it is that which makes all men one, regardless of outside differences, and it is that which constitutes our universal languages, our profound one-ness.

By this token, the plays of Ionesco are ultimately tragic. Man is the only tragic animal. On the other hand, when he is not tragic, he is ridiculous; that is to say, comic. By denouncing his ridiculousness, Ionesco can also indirectly attain a kind of tragedy, as he has done in what we can call his tragic farces: *The Bald Prima Donna*, *The Lesson*, and *Jack*, where the characters' non-realization of their metaphysical unhappiness, their non-realization of the stupidity and emptiness of their lives creates the double effect of hilarious farce and profound tragedy.

Critics such as Sartre find that this is going too far. They find him too pessimistic; his work is nothing but the product of the internal solitude of the bourgeois. Besides, Sartre feels that Ionesco is too much of an outsider – he is a foreigner, French is not his native language (though this, as we have seen, is untrue) and, worst of all, he is a-political.

But for those who are not concerned with political efficacity as a yardstick for artistic achievement, Ionesco's plays, especially his later ones, bring back to the stage that sense of the mystery of life which the political and propagandist stage has taken from it. Brecht, says Ionesco, has reduced man to a two-dimensional figure by considering him solely from the political point of view. Ionesco realizes that his own plays will not save humanity; on the other hand he is not interested in "saving" humanity. For him theatre is simply the most compelling way of presenting his view of the "human condition". That is his only aim.

[JUNE 1957]

REALITY IN DEPTH *by Eugène Ionesco*

This is part of an address given by Eugène Ionesco, as an introduction to his play Amédée ou Comment s'en Débarrasser, *which was presented for a short run at The French Institute in 1958.*

A theatrical work does not need to be produced. It should simply be allowed to happen. And so I am not going to try to explain the play that you will see and hear in a few minutes. A play cannot be explained or demonstrated, it must be acted, it is not a lecture but a piece of living evidence. If it fails to be this, it fails to be a play.

All I am going to do is tell you that this play – *Amédée ou Comment s'en Débarrasser* – is a very simple play, quite childish and almost primitive in its simplicity.

You will find no trace of symbolism here. This play simply

relates an incident from any newspaper, a sad commonplace adventure that could happen to any of us and that has certainly happened to many of us. It is a slice of life, a realistic play.

So, if you can accuse this work of being ordinary you certainly cannot condemn it for its lack of truthfulness. For example, you will see mushrooms growing on the stage and this must be evident proof that these are real mushrooms, altogether normal mushrooms.

Of course it is obvious that not everyone thinks of reality in the same way as I do. There will certainly be people who will say that my idea of reality is unreal or surrealist. But personally I object to that sort of realism which confines itself to the so-called social realities. I believe that this is not real enough. It is only a sub-realism because it stops short at a limited and impoverished human reality which has only two dimensions where it should have three. Depth is the third and indispensable dimension without which man seems to be incomplete. What possible value can there be in this sort of realism which fails to recognize the most obvious realities of humanity, love, death, surprise, suffering and dreams?

Our dreams are hardly ever concerned with social reality, which surely proves that this particular reality is much further from our hearts than we imagine. Still, I have no intention of debating these problems in public. It is not my business. All I am trying to do is make you aware of the complete objectivity of my attitude towards the characters whom you will shortly see speaking and moving on the stage. I am in fact powerless against those objects, images, events and creatures which come from within me. They do as they wish, they control me, indeed it would be quite wrong for me to control them. I am convinced that I must give them complete freedom and that I can do nothing but obey their whims. The writer with a thesis (the thesis which has to be demonstrated is the opposite of the evidence which does not have to be proved because it is undeniable) such a writer alienates the freedom of his characters. He tries to mould them to his own ideals and in so doing makes them appear false. He makes them into preconceived ideas. And when they do not fit into his private political framework or into a world view, which does not spring from basic human truths but is simply a borrowed ideology, he will destroy, caricature or disfigure them. But creation is not the same thing as dictatorship, not even an ideological dictatorship. It is life, it is liberty, it can even be counter to the conscious desires (these are seldom fundamental desires) and to the prejudices of the creator. The creator is not the master of ceremonies. He has only one duty, not to interfere, to live and let live, to allow his obsessions, his sufferings, his fine sense of truth to rise up, take shape and live.

I hope I have foreseen the questions you will want to ask. If you have anything further to ask, write to your dramatic critics, to Messieurs Harold Hobson and Kenneth Tynan. It is their job to explain. I wish you a pleasant evening.

[MAY 1958]

EXCERPT FROM *ENCORE* EDITORIAL

In the matter of Jean Genet *v* Arts Theatre Club, let us take as our text: *Puris omnia pura* – "To the pure all things are pure". M. Genet, speaking apparently from an even more celestial balcony than we do from our position in the "gods", has called the wrath of his own personal and private gods down upon the unsuspecting, frightfully English production of his raw and ready play. Left to his own passions, he might well have ripped the self-imposed chains holding the tiny Arts together quite asunder – a veritable Samson bellowing his disgust with a brothelful of scantily clad Delilahs. We were spared the grim spectacle. Instead we had *The Balcony* in a production not entirely sanctioned by author, gods, or even Mr Harold Hobson – though the latter explained kindly that the misunderstanding is all because we damned English persistently refuse to be French.

But what were the points at issue? We learn from lowly placed spies that M. Genet couldn't care less about English stomachs or libidos: he simply maintained that by cutting

the obscene four-letter words from the text, by dressing and/
or undressing actors and actresses in a basic and literal
manner, the play was curiously distorted by looking and
sounding sordid where nothing filthy was intended. We all
know how much more enticing and suggestive a thinly veiled
lady is than a stark naked one.

Let us assume, however, that M. Genet's objections are
arguable, if only because his last-minute demands were quite
unreasonable. The Arts, after all, has been one of London's
most responsible theatrical institutions in recent years. What
then does the incident indicate? The strange fantasy of a
club theatre partly in existence to put on the mature plays
that the censor won't permit without cuts, then proceeding
to act as its own censor!

Where, oh where, does timidity end if the Arts Theatre
turns out to be afraid of offending the sheltered sensibilities
of a few offensive customers. If *they* won't respect writers,
challenge censors, and do more than merely titillate audiences,
who will?

A mild, slightly bitter British cheer for M. Genet then. He
is reported to have flown out of London with a characteristic
wish on his lips: he would have liked to have left behind a
small punching machine that would regularly poke the producer of *The Balcony* in his ... *Puris omnia pura* ... What is
that word again?

[JUNE 1957]

IS THERE MADNESS IN THE METHOD?
by Tyrone Guthrie

The Method is now the most talked-about approach to
acting in the American theatre, its temple is the Actors'
Studio, its high priest is Lee Strasberg. The Actors' Studio
has attracted some distinguished adherents; some extrava-
gant claims for it are advanced with ardour and as warmly
rebutted. It has been a valuable force for thought and discussion about the art of the theatre, about the craft of acting

and about the philosophy and technique of self-expression. Its influence is widely felt in contemporary acting, not just in New York, but in every English-speaking theatre. That cannot be questioned. The value and the performance of this influence are a matter of controversy.

Let me begin by saying that I have no first-hand experience of the Method. I have met and worked with zealous Methodists; I have heard descriptions of rehearsals and demonstrations of the Method; but I have never attended any of the Gospel Meetings.

I am under the impression that Lee Strasberg, a wonderful teacher, is inculcating an approach to acting derived from that of Stanislavsky, the founder and director of the Moscow Art Theatre. The basis of this is that the actor must derive his characterization from his personal experience. He must imagine a given situation so strongly that he can "feel" himself in it. His own experience being necessarily limited, he must also feel it legitimate to derive at second-hand from the real experience of other people, but not from other acting.

With little of this could any sensible person disagree. My own disagreement with the Method is limited, and under two heads: theoretically, it is in rebellion against conditions which have ceased to exist and, consequently, is out of date. Practically, it places too much emphasis upon self-analysis and too little upon technique.

First, let us consider the theoretic side. The professional context in reaction to which Stanislavsky founded the Moscow Art Theatre and his own acting method belonged to the *fin de siècle* and the very early years of the twentieth century, and no longer exists. It has been liquidated by the social, political and economic revolutions which have occurred all over the world. Stanislavsky was reacting against a theatre which was still in aim very much concerned to please an audience of the socially élite and its imitators; a theatre very concerned with inherited conventions, largely derived from the artificial comedy of manners of the eighteenth century, transmitted through the Parisian Boulevard comedies and dramas, which had dominated Europe for more than a century.

Stanislavsky preached a method based upon first-hand observation, rather than upon imitation of other acting. He also advocated the production of plays which reflected contemporary Russian life in a real way, rather than as a romantic image of elegant manners abroad. The Moscow Art Theatre, while not at all political, was nevertheless strongly nationalist.

Although it was never of any great popular or commercial account – the theatre was tiny and by no means always full – the Moscow Art Theatre became the most powerful influence on the stage of its time. The "poetic naturalism" of Chekhov, in supplement to the prosaic and didactic quality of Ibsen and Shaw, has been the dominant influence on serious playwrights of the last fifty years, not only in Russia but all over the occidental world; and the acting and direction at the Moscow Art are still the dominant models, although possibly a little less so now, since the impact of Bertolt Brecht.

Stanislavsky did not really hit the American theatre until after the publication in English of his book *My Life in Art*. He then found enthusiastic disciples in Mr Strasberg and Harold Clurman, founders of the Group Theatre. The Group, like the Moscow Art before it, found itself in reaction against the theatrical *status quo*. It was opposed to the conventional themes and methods of the commercial theatre, which to the young people of the Group seemed extremely reactionary. It was opposed also to foreign domination of the American stage, particularly by London's West End, with its insistence upon elegance and gentility to the exclusion of almost all other content.

This was the period of depression, the end of one epoch and the beginning of many radically new political, social and economic ideas. The Group Theatre was in the *avant-garde* of this ferment; and I hope that a non-American may be forgiven for emphasizing something which in subsequent political ferments has been either overlooked or misinterpreted: this literary and theatrical movement was an earnest and conscious expression of American nationalism. The Group was trying, early in the comparatively brief history of the American theatre, to look at indigenous American problems and characters through American eyes, and to express them in an indigenous way, not in a manner imitative of dominant – and imported – conventions.

Harold Clurman in *The Fervent Years*, one of the best books of theatrical reminiscence which I know, has described the aims, impact and some of the inner stresses and strains of the Group. Its activity, compared to that of the Moscow Art Theatre, was confined to a very brief period. Its artistic achievement has been less than its influence. The Group, I venture to believe, has been an all-important influence in the evolution of the Method. The ideas which brought the Group into being are the source of the Method's greatest value; but I suggest that they still express youthful revolt against a social and political environment which has now ceased to exist.

In 1930 there was some point in young actors and actresses proclaiming by their dress, speech and bearing that they were of the Proletariat. In 1930, there was some important political and social purpose to be served by depicting faithfully the efforts of the inarticulate American masses to express themselves. In 1930, this required some serious political faith, not in Leninism, but in the future of American democracy. Artistically it was ground which, outside Russia, had hardly been trodden, and demanded a serious effort to evolve a new technique because the current fashions in acting and directing were no guide.

But today the burning issues of 1930 are ashes, and other issues burn. Even in America, comparatively so little affected by the events of 1939–45 (a fact which is to many Americans bewilderingly hard to grasp, so accustomed are they to believe themselves in the vanguard rather than the rearguard of historical context), the political, social and economic changes have been immense. Meantime, the young iconoclasts of the early Odets period are now middle-aged; the prominent ones are well-to-do and securely seated upon the very thrones under which twenty-seven years ago they were placing the dynamite.

But the Method-ists do not seem to have quite got around to this. In blue jeans, with dirty nails and wild hair, they are busy proclaiming themselves Proletarian – but members of a vintage Proletariat. While in 1930 it was new, and even dangerous for artistes to announce that they were also Proletarians, it is now cliché; especially when more than one prominent associate of the Method has been at pains to dissociate this type of Artistic Proletarianism from any taint of political subversion, from the faintest tinge of red. In 1930, adequately to present an inarticulate proletarian upon the stage required some innovation of acting technique; but this too has now become cliché.

This brings me to the second issue on which I part company with the Method: technique. In 1930, it was necessary to seek new means of expressing new ideas about people whom it was a novelty to see depicted on the stage. Until then, stage conventions had required that, with amazingly few exceptions, plays were about the Upper Orders. If members of the Lower Orders appeared at all, it was as character parts – Faithful Retainers, Roughs, Prostitutes, Little Matchgirls or, most frequently, just "Comics". Then plays began to have as their chief figures Taxi Drivers and Boxers shown, not as the expression of natures more rough and inarticulate than their former "betters", but as people who had been denied the privileges of the more fortunate.

It can readily be seen that the new school of playwriting required a new school of acting, less conventional, less romantic, less elegant, but, in compensation, more "real". Now, oddly enough, most of us in the theatre, as in other avocations, are nearer in environment to the Proletariat than to Grand Dukes. Hence, when the new school required of the actor that he unlearn a lot of fancy ways and fancy speech, which had been thought necessary in the portrayal of Grand Dukes, it seemed as though he were being required to revert to "behaviourism", to just Being Himself.

Incidentally, isn't it just middle-class sentimentality, and a very "superior" attitude, to imagine that it is more "real" to be rough than to be genteel, more "real" to wear blue jeans than a neat Ivy League number, more "real" to look like a whore than a Junior Miss? Surely it is not more real, but less expensive. The proletariat does not dress and speak and behave as it does, nor live where it does, from choice, but because it cannot afford to do otherwise. In America today it is only eccentric "intellectuals" who are "prole" by choice.

In 1930, however, the Group believed that good acting consisted in Being Yourself and, consistently enough, aimed to make its members better actors by making them more Aware of Themselves. Remember that this epoch coincided with the first great popular impact of psycho-analysis. At the confluence of two rivers – popular psychology and "behaviourist" acting – like Pittsburgh, stood the Group. At the same confluence stands the Method. But twenty-seven years have passed and the waters of both streams are now less turbulent, but also far less clear and fresh.

In my opinion, the Method now means Behaviourist acting, which is cliché, and which is inadequate to express any wide range either of character, environment or style. It is suited only to express the very limited field of the actor's own, and his friends' experience, and in a naturalistic style. It is stylish acting (by which I do not, of course, mean merely elegant) which now needs cultivation.

The search by actors for the Truth Within Themselves has now gone too far. They are in grave danger of forgetting two more objective elements of truth which no artiste should dare to ignore: first, each of us is not only himself, but a member of the Human Race; second, it is the duty of an artiste to develop the Means of Communication of the truth within himself, so as to share it with fellow members of the race.

The Method-ists overprize the Search For Truth as opposed to the Revelation Of Truth. They have neglected the means of communication. Now the actor's principal means of expression is the voice. The expression of eyes, of the whole body, is important, too; but it is on the breathstream and by means of sounds and, more particularly, the organization of sounds into, first, syllables, then words, then sentences, that the most subtle and the most articulate communication occurs between human creatures.

Until recently the Actors' Studio has tended to pay but little attention to matters of technique. But now Mr Strasberg has said that this has been a mistake. Lessons in Voice Production and Diction are now part of the curriculum. No reasonable person but will applaud when error is admitted and amendment begun. But amendment has only just begun, so it is rather too early to look for the fruits of this Revised Method. Also it is a radically new idea that anything so self-conscious and artificial as Vocal Technique, so unspontaneous, so remote from the animal life of the individual, or the social life of the group, should be admissible as part of the Method. And so influential has the Method become in the contemporary theatre that it is going to be very hard to eradicate the notion that any cultivation of this Craft can only be to the detriment, not only of an actor's Art, but of his Psyche.

This notion has led the Method-ists into one very awkward dilemma: none of the great classics of the theatre – the Greek tragedies, French tragedy, Shakespeare, Molière, Schiller or Goethe – can be adequately performed without a real battery of technical accomplishment. An untrained beginner, however gifted, just cannot do justice to great rhetorical poetry any more than an untrained beginner in music can sit right down and play a Bach fugue. So far the Method has not suggested that it aims beyond a very highly developed Behaviourism. I am not denying that in this field remarkable results have been achieved. But mere Behaviourism will not take an actor far on the way to King Lear, Andromache or Faust.

A world-famous and justly eminent director, who is also a supporter of the Method, has avoided this dilemma by declaring that the classics are all bunk; that he, thank God, has never directed a classic; and, please God, never will. This rather immature point of view is certainly not that of Mr Strasberg.

I guess that a great deal is talked and written about the Method by persons, including myself, who have only been indirectly concerned with it. And while this is not quite fair, it is absolutely inevitable. The Method is a popular talking-point and, as such, has gained extraordinary prestige. But fame and success carry their own penalties as well as rewards. That Marlon Brando, Marilyn Monroe, and so on, have been associated, has been, in one sense, a great boost for the Actors' Studio, but in another it has been detrimental. Neither of these gifted alumni could be described as an accomplished actor; their fame rests upon other qualities. And the sort of publicity which their connection has generated has blown up a serious professional effort into a sensational stunt, with many of the stigmata of quackery.

To sum up: it is my opinion that Mr Strasberg is a serious teacher and no quack. The Actors' Studio is genuinely and laudably trying to break away from theatrical clichés, but has gone too far in the direction of self-analysis, and away from a sensible pursuit of craftsmanship, particularly vocal technique. The great professional and popular success of the Method has resulted in a rather grave lack of humility on the part of many of its adherents. Statements on the lines of the classics being all bunk are not unusual; and there's a tendency to forget that people of my age do not find anything new in the theory. On the contrary, we remember when it was new to us in the mouth of Stanislavsky; people a little older remember the same theories being applied still earlier at the Abbey Theatre in Dublin and in the folk theatres all over Europe; still older people recall the Quintessence of Ibsenism. And so on, back and back.

Looking forward, I see reason to believe that, like every popular craze and like so many Progressive Movements whose adherents become unduly excited by success, today's Method may all too easily become tomorrow's Dodo.

[NOVEMBER 1957]

A WRONG DIAGNOSIS *by Eli Wallach*

Since I first wrote an article for *Encore* on the Actors' Studio in 1954, it has grown from a tiny note in a theatrical programme to become a real force, a power whose influence is widely felt. Take the straw from the straw-men set up by the Studio's erstwhile critics and you could stuff half the mattresses in London.

Last November *Encore* printed an article by Dr Tyrone Guthrie – "Is There Madness in the Method?" – well, let us see. First off the Doctor admits he has never seen the patient – "I have heard descriptions of rehearsals and demonstrations of the Method, but I have never attended any of the Gospel Meetings." The Studio has been imitated, condemned, condoned, blasted, mocked and rocked by people who have never attended these "Gospel Meetings".

First let me say that a torn T-shirt, dirty nails and a blue-jean mutterer do not make a Studio actor. Hamlet, through the genius of Shakespeare, put what the Method stands for most succinctly: "Speak the speech, I pray you . . . trippingly on the tongue," etc. . . . "suit the action to the word," "to hold, *as t'were*, the mirror up to nature." It is the "as t'were" which is vital and important in acting.

Actually the Method was and is in rebellion against posturing, singing orators, and technically polished and emotionally empty actors. Dr Guthrie states that the "Methodists" have neglected the means of communication – the voice. Perhaps so – most iconoclasts in rebellion attack the *status quo* and in turn leave themselves open to attack. In the beginning – in the search for truth – the important stress lay in having *something* to communicate . . . then came the study of the means of communicating. Oh yes, Brando muttered (as once Garbo spoke) so a whole generation of imitating juveniles followed suit – but don't attack the Studio for this. London and New York are full of quack schools, each professing a panacea, a cure-all, a method – but don't attack the Studio for this.

Dr Guthrie mentions a director, a supporter of the Method, who declared that the classics are all bunk. The director should have his head examined – but isn't Dr Guthrie being just as smugly superior about the genteel, Ivy-Leagued Junior Miss who drifts daintily across the stage dropping her pearshaped tones in a phonetically lilting manner – or about the precise Prince Hal all resonant and yet strangely hollow? I merely suggest that good speech does not a Hamlet make – any more than muttering and back-scratching make him more real.

Perhaps the most important statement of Dr Guthrie's was that the Method is out-dated. It is true that we have not donned cloak and dagger, nor played with fans or snuff boxes in the classics. It may take our producers a while to realize that until we are given this challenge, our theatre will remain a limited, naturalistic one. But the search for truth will never be out-dated – and the classics can be livelier and more exciting when actors capture their essence rather than just their style.

To sum up, we young actors in America have taken a *Look Back in Anger* at what we disliked in theatre and acting. We turned our anger into concrete and constructive work. Our "blue-jeans" are only the first of many costumes we may don before we complete the character. We are still searching, still learning. Our restlessness has spread to other countries, other theatres – we have made a ripple in the mirror-like pool of staid, convention-ridden, cliché-clad theatre. Come on in – the water is fine!

[JANUARY 1958]

CHAPTER TWO

RUMBLES OF DISCONTENT

INTRODUCTION

The arrival of new plays and new preoccupations only sharpened the discontent that many felt with the established theatre. A false but persuasive distinction was drawn between the "kitchen sink" school (embracing the Royal Court group and Joan Littlewood's Theatre Workshop) and the tea-tinkling bourgeois entertainments of Shaftesbury Avenue.

The discontent was both social and aesthetic. The prevailing theatre, archaic and elegant, mirrored only a fraction of the contemporary society, and seemed wilfully to ignore the new social strata emerging all around it. The fashionable style of acting, forged in the 'twenties, was still suave, facile and external; wholly insufficient for the purposes of the new writing. (Little by little, this style changed and, curiously, it was the writers rather than the acting-schools who changed it. The drama instructors of the "new realism" were Osborne, Pinter, Wesker, Delaney, Behan and Owen – the very writers whose work compelled actors to interpret the gritty realities of working-class life.)

The cry was for "vitality", and it came from a theatre which was clearly debilitated by makeshift comedies, turgid melodramas and endless whodunits; a theatre in which top honours were shared between Terence Rattigan and Agatha Christie. The language of those years was couched in battle terms. Readers were constantly being urged to *run to the barricades, store up ammunition, invade enemy territory*. There were fisticuffs in the Royal Court foyer when a play by Stuart Holroyd produced a wrangle between Colin Wilson, Kenneth Tynan and others. The Sunday newspapers were crammed with fulminations and retorts. Ionesco challenged that view of reality which confined itself to social and political considerations. Noël Coward came to the defence of the nineteenth century. The Method and its attributes became stigmata, and the application of Stanislavsky principles, tantamount to subversive foreign intervention.

On November 18, 1956, *Encore* held a symposium at the Royal Court Theatre. Its title was "Cause Without a Rebel", its subject the state of the English theatre. The speakers included Benn W. Levy, Wolf Mankowitz, Arthur Miller, John Whiting and Colin Wilson. Kenneth Tynan was in the chair. In its mood and undercurrent – and occasionally in its comments – it expressed the discontent of those years. The following brief extracts are from the verbatim account published in *Encore* No. 9:

"I sense that the British theatre is hermetically sealed against the way the society moves."

ARTHUR MILLER

"The fact is that until we have some possibility of intelligent planning of productions with relation to groups of actors being used in some constructive and consecutive way, this seasonal fluctuation in the theatre – whether on Broadway or in the West End – will be inevitable."

WOLF MANKOWITZ

"How is it that political plays aren't being turned out in England at the present time? How is it that in fact we have no tradition of political theatre?"

KENNETH TYNAN

"*Look Back in Anger* to me is the only modern, English play that I have seen. Modern in the sense that the basic attention in the play was toward the passionate idea of the man involved and of the playwright involved, and not toward the surface glitter and amusement that the situation might throw off. That play – and I'm not judging it now in terms of aesthetic fact – seems to me to be an intellectual play . . . and yet it seems to have no reflection elsewhere in the theatre."

ARTHUR MILLER

"It's no use saying the English people don't want to pay money to go to the theatre; it's not true at all. You talk to movie technicians, they wouldn't be seen dead in a theatre. They've got money enough to go to the theatre. They're not interested because the theatre is dead."

GEORGE COULOURIS

"You can't have an *avant-garde* composed of dramatists only. You've got to have an *avant-garde* on the receiving end as well. . . . What we are really suffering from is the loss of a serious little theatre movement, of the kind that proliferates in Paris, and gives opportunities for difficult playwrights to put on difficult plays without involving some management in very serious loss."

BENN W. LEVY

"As a human being on this planet, it doesn't seem to me possible that, in a free society such as this is, there cannot be rebellious people."

ARTHUR MILLER
[JUNE 1957]

VITAL THEATRE? *by Lindsay Anderson*

I start this article with hesitation. Try as I may, I cannot help feeling that for me to write anything about the theatre at this stage – as a director anyway – is rather absurd, and even impertinent. One Sunday night "Production without Décor" at the Royal Court does not constitute a very large body of experience on which to construct generalizations. And to write as a critic is likely to be even less rewarding. It has all been said. Yes, of course our theatre is moribund – like our cinema. For a variety of reasons – social, economic, and just through plain lack of vitality. But there's no point in going on sneering at Shaftesbury Avenue (or Pinewood) for ever. Only two courses are honourable: shut up – or do something.

And here you seem to me to have a distinct advantage in the theatre. With all the difficulties of costs, materials, premises, etc., it is still easier to put on a stage production than it is to make a film. Take the *Free Cinema* films, for instance. They look simple enough, I know: some people even call them primitive. In only one of them (*Every Day Except Christmas*, where we had sponsorship from the Ford Motor Company) is there any direct sound recording. And even there we didn't have enough money for a blimped camera: if you listen hard enough, you'll hear the camera noise. For the rest (*O Dreamland*, *Together*, *Momma Don't Allow*, *Nice Time*, *Wakefield Express*), the sound was all recorded separately, and laid afterwards. No dialogue. Yet a twenty-minute film of this kind, shot on 16 mm, will cost you between four and five hundred pounds. And if you make it in your spare time – as you'll have to, since no one will pay you for it – it's likely to take you between eight months and a year. And all to what purpose? So that a National Film Theatre audience can come in, and sit down, and then go out again saying: "what interesting faces. . . . Tomorrow night a Japanese version of *Macbeth*. What a RICH cultural life we're leading."

In the theatre surely the business is a bit easier, or so I'd have thought. It can't cost so very much to put on a play at the Theatre in the Round. *The Waiting of Lester Abbs* cost the English Stage Society about a hundred and fifty pounds. And quite a lot of that was presumably recovered from the receipts of the audience. But even more encouraging than the number of people who turned up to see the play, was the number of people ready to act in it. And delighted to find they were going to get even a couple of guineas for their trouble. When I started casting the play, I was distinctly timid. It seemed outrageous to be asking people to work for a fortnight for virtually nothing. Yet I found that, in general, they were happy to be asked; and to do it if they could. They even volunteered. And what a pleasure they were to work with! With so much idealistic talent around (and don't let anyone tell me that actors are *all* opportunistic egotists), why isn't more of it used? Why doesn't it flower in odd places, in little theatres, jabbing and stimulating?

This is the fundamental question. But before I attempt to pursue it, let me say just a few words about my experience in producing a play instead of making a film. "How did I adapt" (I am asked), "what I had learned in film-making for the theatre?" Now this – as I was forced to reply to that nice young Moscow girl who asked me what the British People are doing for Peace – now this is rather a naïve question. I associate it in fact with the disapproving comment of Mr Henry Adler, in the last issue of *Encore*, who remarked that "Mr Lindsay Anderson did not use his film experience to employ the kind of rhythmic cross-cutting and use of fades which this sort of theatre calls for." This, to be honest, is the sort of thing that makes you see purple. Such references to "cross-cutting", to begin with, imply a conception of the cinema that has congealed after an early, traumatic experience with *The Battleship Potemkin*. I should be distinctly sceptical of any director who approached a *film* with this type of superficial, "applied" idea of technique. To try to impose it on a play would be ruinous. It is not the "sort of theatre" that is important – this is the cliché idea of "Production without Décor", which brings with it Mr Adler's hankering for Vilar-type lighting and "lozenges of colour".

As I say, though, what is important is not the "sort of theatre" – but the PLAY. (It seems odd to me that a film director should have to say this to a theatre critic.) *The Waiting of Lester Abbs* may have been Mrs Sully's first work for the stage, but there is nothing tentative or uncertain about it. As in her books, she knows exactly what she is doing, and the effect she requires. The mixture of simplicity and sophistication is perfectly calculated, and there is only one possible style in which it can be played. I mean with directness, austerity, and an utter rejection of conventional methods of "dramatizing". From the actors, humility before the words, truthfulness to character, complete purity of feeling. This is what we worked for; and I don't think we did badly. But it was what I felt about the play, and not any previous experience with the cinema, that guided me.

And yet – I won't pretend that, as we worked, cinematic parallels didn't present themselves to me. It is perhaps even true that at times the tensions I tried to create derived consciously from films – not the conventional, film-society, "montage" idea of cinema, but the anti-dramatic poetic concentration on the everyday which has characterized some of the later developments of neo-realism. Lester comes into the pub, orders a glass of beer, makes a remark to nobody in general, drinks his half-pint, orders another one, drinks again . . . all this before there is any real action, any real dialogue even. Now what do you do with a scene like that? Jog it along with a lot of irrelevant business? "Cross-cut" with some fatuous piece of character-play in a corner? Or just cut it short? I preferred to take my cue from *Umberto D.*, from that sequence where the little serving-maid gets up in the morning, wanders blankly round the kitchen, sprays some ants off the wall, and sits down, and starts grinding the coffee . . . Can't we try, in the theatre, too, to break away from the tyranny of words occasionally? From the tyranny of "construction" and "technique"? *The Waiting of Lester Abbs* is a poetic play, as for instance *Together* is a poetic film (the themes, indeed, are related; and I wonder if anyone noticed that the music we used between the scenes was in fact from the sound-track of *Together*). I wanted the pace to be equally deliberate. I remembered how Lorenza Mazzetti used to insist, when we were editing *Together*, that she wanted it to be the most *boring* film ever made. Of course she meant she wanted it to be a film whose beauty and significance would be expressed precisely in those elements of style (extreme slowness and austerity) which the desensitized, conventionalized audience would fail to understand – and therefore be bored by. This was the kind of lingering, poetic concentration I tried to create on the stage.

"The play was directed with extreme sluggishness . . ." When an intelligent critic makes a comment like that, I don't feel – "Oh what a pity, it didn't come off, I should have made the whole thing brisker . . ." On the contrary, I feel I should have made the whole thing *really* slow – caricatured the effect I was after – ruined the play perhaps, but at least in the process *boring* the audience into a realization of what they were seeing – into an acknowledgment that they come to the theatre to work – not just to sit, and be "absorbed", made to laugh or cry by an expert machine, being "entertained" . . . Not school of Vilar, you see, but school of Brecht. The same attitude towards construction (story-telling rather than play-making); the same shifts in style of dialogue (between semi-formal and naturalistic); and above all the same relationship between audience and play, the same objectivity, the rejection of "identification".

This question of the audience is perhaps the most important; and it returns us to the fundamental point I mentioned earlier – that of the overall deadness of our theatrical atmosphere. In nothing is this more apparent, or more depressive, than in the prevailing conception of the passive audience, the audience as sheep, hungry for "entertainment" or vicarious emotion, or the audience as amateur, Third Programme critics, which conceives of its superior function as being one of "judgement" – and whose only standards are subjectively emotional, or platitudinously "literary": i.e. "profoundly moving" – "curiously unmoving" – "witty, compassionate" – "too episodic" – "the second half isn't as good as the first" – "the characters don't develop" – etc., etc. Success, according to this view, is more important than significance; manner provides a richer (certainly an easier) topic of discussion than meaning. This is where I join issue with my friend Kenneth Tynan, when he writes a "selling" notice of *The Chalk Garden*, and a distinctly chilling one of *The Good Woman of Setzuan*. All right – so the first London production of a straight Brecht play didn't have the high polish of the Berliner Ensemble. All right – so the leading lady was not in all respects successful. But let's keep our eye on the ball.

For effort to be creative, response must be creative too. The development of a new kind of theatre (what *Encore* calls "vital theatre") is intimately bound up with the development of a new kind of audience. But this, of course, cannot just be achieved by slanging existing audiences and critics, and telling them to pull their socks up. It carries us further – to the need for a new conception of the relationship between art and audience, a total change of cultural atmosphere. And in this respect particularly, to produce a play for the English Stage Society gave one food for thought. For these are supposed to be laboratory productions. They can only really fulfil their function with audiences who come, not with the passive expectation of "entertainment", nor just with mouths wide open for another slab of minority culture, but themselves prepared to give something, to work, with minds open and alert, themselves creative. (*Judge Not* should be inscribed on the programme.) But this kind of audience – I am driven to conclude – does not exist in London.

If it did exist, you would surely expect to find it at, or around, the Royal Court. No single management (nor all the others put together, for that matter) has given us such intelligent stimulus in the last eighteen months as the English Stage Company. Yet it remains a significant fact that instead of being able to develop as a theatre with a permanent company, in pursuit of a definable and consistent tradition, the Royal Court has become (or been forced to become) just a theatre run by the most progressive management in London. There is an essential difference. An "intelligent" theatre which chooses its presentations on a basis of "quality" is one thing (and a thing for which one is grateful) – but what we need now are *ideas* even more urgently than "quality", and a theatre which relates itself to life rather than to culture.

In other words, what we run up against is the economic and social framework within which we have to practise our various arts. Working within the established framework of the West End, upper-class theatre, the English Stage Company has accomplished wonders. Yet this framework is also a prison. Theatre Workshop tries to work outside it: yet the penalty they have to pay, of exclusion, of an audience just as ungrateful, of finally a certain inverted snobbery, is equally frustrating. The framework, the system remains, corrupt and killing; and I doubt whether, within it, the vital theatre for which *Encore* wishes to speak, or the lively and aspiring talent which I encountered in my brief experience, will ever be able to find a satisfying means of expression.

Is an alternative tradition possible? *What* ideas are the

ones which will revitalize our theatre? Is there a new public that could be attracted to, or reached by, a progressive theatrical company? What do we mean when we talk about a relationship between theatre and life? These fundamental questions are, it seems to me, the ones which should be engaging us at the moment, the ones which young writers should be discussing instead of pulling Lucky Jim faces at themselves in the Beaverbrook Press. Only criticism written in this perspective is going to be of any value to us. To this extent my experience of the theatre leads me to precisely the same conclusions as my experience of the cinema.

And may I make a final, specific point? I notice that the last issue of *Encore* was praised by one critic for "not being afraid of letting every side have its angry say . . ." I believe that this is precisely the attitude we need to escape from – the assumption that all ideas are equally valuable, that intellectual discussion is an end in itself, a superior diversion for the cultured, instead of being a hunt for the useful truth. The opposition has plenty of organs of its own: *Encore* should not be expressing *every* point of view, but the *right* one. You see – the question of commitment raises its obstinate, contemporary head. You can't get away from it.

[NOVEMBER 1957]

CORRESPONDENCE

The Editor, ENCORE

Dear Sir, – Mr Lindsay Anderson gets more intellectually disingenuous – not to say dishonest – every time he puts pen to paper. In your last issue he writes:

> "I notice that the last issue of *Encore* was praised by one critic for 'not being afraid of letting every side have its angry say . . .' I believe that this is precisely the attitude we need to escape from – the assumption that all ideas are equally valuable, that intellectual discussion is an end in itself, a superior diversion for the cultured, instead of being a hunt for the useful truth."

Now, the critic's simple remark does not by itself – and could not possibly – carry the *assumptions* which Mr Anderson twists into it. It is his own temperament – not to say neurosis – which imagines that to put more than one side of an argument means that you think all ideas equally valuable: or that if you argue you can only be indulging in "a superior diversion for the cultured". You may quite equally, if you are an old-fashioned liberal, be hunting for the useful truth, which is what, in the liberal tradition, argument is for. How else would he hunt for it? With police dogs, or unilateral decisions by Central Committees? *"Encore,"* Mr Anderson concludes, "should not be expressing *every* point of view, but the *right* one." If Mr Anderson really thinks that he or you or any one other single person is in possession of the one and only right view, he is not only as silly as he sometimes makes himself seem on paper; he is mad as well. Even the Communists admit argument (thesis: antithesis: synthesis) in theory at least.

Yours faithfully,

T. C. WORSLEY

[JANUARY 1958]

The Editor, ENCORE

Sir, – The comment aroused by my piece "Vital Theatre" (which I note you have retitled for me – rather well – "On Being Right") is encouraging. Some of the discord obviously results from conflicting beliefs, uncompromisingly held. But there seems also a good deal of misunderstanding in the air – the result, no doubt, of overcompression on my part. May I try to dispel some of this? It seems clear at least, from the emotion generated and the space devoted to it, that we are stumbling here on a problem that is basic.

The problem, as I see it, is not merely one of ideas – of "what should we believe?" It is equally a question of the *effectiveness* of those ideas – of their "reality" in a practical as well as a philosophical sense. Part of my contention is that, in the cultural sphere at least, ideas have pretty well ceased to have this kind of reality. Hence the artificial, inbred, hot-house (pick what metaphor you please) atmosphere of our Sunday Paper, Week-end Review, Third Programme culture of the moment. The pseudo-liberal tradition, which abstracts art and culture from their economic and political environment, which accepts the social *status quo*, and restricts itself almost entirely to formal and aesthetic criticism, has gone a good way to deprive art of any contemporary function at all. Our problem is to reassert that function. And this means not merely finding some new ideas, but making them effective. Now is it possible to be effective, and to be undiscriminatingly tolerant at the same time?

This, I guess, is where trouble begins. For in this age of fugitive and cloistered virtue, tolerance has become the one absolute, unqualified Value, and any suggestion that other people's ideas are not as good as one's own lays one open immediately to charges of Fascism, Communism, Bestiality, or What-have-you . . . Mr Worsley sees me hunting him down with a pack of police dogs, and Groundling shrinks from the "massive limitations", the "blinding conformity" which he supposes I wish to impose on *Encore*. Surely the confusion here is obvious? I believe in freedom (which I think is a more positive concept than tolerance); but I also believe in responsibility to analyse one's situation, come to conclusions, and to act according to those conclusions. Other people may come to different conclusions, and will so be led to different actions. The conflict of such actions, under law, is democracy. Nobody need be ashamed of believing he is right, or of trying, as forcefully as he can, to convince other people of the rightness of his views – of trying in other words, to make them *effective*. It is a very recent heresy to suppose that either democracy or true liberalism oblige one to allow that the ideas of people who oppose one are as "right" as one's own.

This attitude does not seem to me to justify accusations of *political* intolerance. Of course we all have every reason to be aware of the evils of political authoritarianism; but if as a result we allow ourselves to become too scared to express our own convictions without compromise, we will find ourselves speedily reduced to ineffectiveness. Which is, in fact, precisely what has happened to cultural intellectuals in this country. Mr Worsley says that I am "mad" if I think that I, or anyone else, am "in possession of the one and only right view" about anything. This kind of scepticism makes it impossible for anyone ever to act on right principle. It is on principle, for instance, that I consider that *Encore* is right, and the Treasury is wrong, about the National Theatre. And I deny that there is any true democratic or liberal principle which can require me to accept the equal validity of the Treasury view.

Mr Jerome Clegg of Brooklyn says that "the world just isn't built this way" – i.e. by people formulating their beliefs in an uncompromising way, and by acting according to them. How else has the world been built then, or any of the enlightened institutions we enjoy today? Not, you may be sure, by people who felt it safer to sneer at belief than to subscribe to it. "Truth, One and Indivisible, revealed in that Immaculate Entirety to Certain Persons (according to themselves)."

Of course I do not suggest that the "right" viewpoint – a viewpoint that an adequate number of us can subscribe to and effectively campaign for – has yet been formulated. What I hope very much is that people are beginning to think in these terms, and to understand that solidarity is not merely a polite way of disguising the horrors of conformity. Don't think that I underestimate the difficulties either. As an illustration, we have only to examine Groundling's attempt to define the position (or the objective) of *Encore* in your last issue. The heart is evidently there, the tentative idealism and the liberal aspirations: but how little courage – and how little *thought*! You can see his essential lack of conviction in the way he continually falls back on what he obviously intends to be the style of the detached, sophisticated *litterateur*. "Mr Anderson in characteristic punching form" . . . "A commitment is a sometime thing" . . . "There are indeed more things in heaven and earth than are dreamt of in his philology." This sort of thing is not merely tiresome: it is positively damaging, because it evokes the atmosphere of smartness and sceptical flippancy which is exactly what we need to escape from. And what conclusion is reached? Is that quotation from Harold Clurman expressive of anything beyond a familiar, innocuous, eye-washy idealism which we can all say yes to easily enough, but which is quite incapable of actively inspiring anybody? Groundling thanks God that he and you are "Young and unresolved". But is irresolution really such a wonderful quality? I would thank God for you with much greater fervour if you could announce yourselves "Young and resolved" – or at least bent on resolution. That young character whose portrait appears at the end of Groundling's article – is he just exhausted? Or is he praying for strength? That would be good. But I like to imagine that he is *thinking* too.

And finally, in case I have still not made myself clear, let me end with a specific illustration. There was once a magazine called *Scrutiny* which, operating in the field of literary criticism, set itself to oppose contemporary fashion, and to stand for certain clear, consistent and defined principles. The magazine ran for some twenty-five years and exercised a great and salutary influence. Now would *Scrutiny* have achieved as much, and would Dr Leavis have achieved the eminence that he has, if he had printed articles from every point of view – if, in other words, he had been intimidated by the accusations which were continuously levelled at him from Right and Left, of arrogance, intolerance and illiberalism? As Eric Bentley has remarked (and Messrs Spelvin and Clegg might return with profit to the earlier work of their distinguished fellow-countryman):

"The uniformity of attitude which some object to is the defect of a quality without which there could not be such a magazine at all: unity of purpose. If it is to have character a literary review has to stand for something. It has to fight."

I believe this to be true.

Yours sincerely,
LINDSAY ANDERSON
[MARCH 1958]

THAT UNCERTAIN FEELING
by Edwin Morgan

Have you felt it too? A suspicion that the present vigorously stirring situation in drama, exciting and praiseworthy though it is, must be greeted with some reservations? This feeling has grown on me, and it might be useful if I try to define these restless doubts.

The liveliness and theatrical power of the plays of John Osborne, Tennessee Williams, and Arthur Miller derive mainly from two things; vivid dialogue, and a choice of situations that are emotionally very raw and exploitable. Mr Osborne has remarked how "we need a new language", and already this new language – racy, close to common speech, unafraid of contemporaneity, inventive in a spoken not a literary sense – is making its impact. It is brilliance and pace of dialogue that save Samuel Beckett's plays from sharing the tedium found in his novels; and the relative deadness of the dialogue in John Whiting no doubt contributes to the muffled impression his drama has so far made.

Dialogue isn't everything, but add powerful emotional situation to it and what more could anyone want? The long probing smouldering scene between Brick and Big Daddy in *Cat on a Hot Tin Roof*; Archie Rice singing the blues when he hears about Mick's death in *The Entertainer*; Eddie's agonized taunting and embrace of Rodolpho in *A View from the Bridge* – if these are not real theatre, you may ask, what is? Yet good scenes and great moments don't make a play, and for all the theatrical effectiveness of these passages, and of others that could have been instanced, there is clearly *something* wrong with the plays themselves, something that fails to satisfy, fails to convince.

Let's look at it first from John Osborne's point of view. In various pronouncements (e.g., in *Declaration*, and *International Theatre Annual No.* 2) Osborne has stressed the importance of a theatre of *feeling*. He attacks the stiff upper lip, and prefers working-class garrulousness to bourgeois reserve, just as Jimmy Porter keeps trying to sting Alison into the outward liveliness of retaliation. "I want to make people feel, to give them lessons in feeling. They can think afterwards." He is not afraid of being charged with sentimentality, and says that if this desire to crack open the British Way of Feeling is sentimental, he'll "go on working towards a sentimental theatre" for the rest of his life. Now the ability to *move* an audience, a mixed audience of unknown composition, to move it and leave it shaken, is a great gift, and Osborne has this gift, to an extent that (for example) neither Eliot nor Fry has been able to show. But it's a gift that carries obligations and responsibilities. Osborne says we "can think afterwards". Supposing we don't make the effort – or we do make the effort and find that no very definitely formulated theme emerges – or that a theme emerges which doesn't deserve our approbation? In *Declaration* he warns us "I shall simply fling down a few statements – you can take your pick". This might be said by some weary verse dramatist knee-deep in symbols, but as the attitude of a prose dramatist who is professedly concerned with modern society and its ills, it shows an alarming dislike of clarity. I say "alarming" because social and moral clarities are, above all, what we are needing, and what we are not getting. *Pathos* we get in full measure – even *Look Back in Anger* is essentially a play of pathos – but if our cheeks are all begrutten with tears and we're not sure afterwards what we've been weeping for, or we do know and feel we oughtn't to have been weeping for it, how are plays of this sort going to help change English society?

O Brecht, where art thou? But let me go further east than Brecht. In that uneven but sometimes revealing olla podrida, the 1957 Yearbook of the Big Soviet Encyclopedia, the article on British literary life contains an appreciative reference to John Osborne and other young writers for their "sharp critique of contemporary bourgeois reality", but reproaches them in that this critique is "uncommitted, anarchic, and tinged with individualistic bolshiness". I am not concerned here with the "uncommitted" aspect, but rather with the "anarchic" and "bolshy". Jimmy Porter's anger expends itself impotently, and we can't really believe that anything is changed at the end of the play. Archie Rice's final "Why should I care?" theme-song simply hands the tangle of thematic material the play had thrown up into the lap of the battered audience with a wonderfully dismissive "*You* sort that out!" *The Entertainer* succeeds as a play of feeling, but fails as a play of ideas. The last scenes – the death of Billy, and the whole Canadian business – are badly managed, and the play loses its grip; it is saved at the end only by a return to pure pathos and a Chaplinesque fade-out. Both this play and *Look Back in Anger* are immediately stimulating, but on reflection ("they can think afterwards") depressing, because they assume human failure and frustration as the norm and are pervaded by strange hankerings after a gauzy Edwardian past instead of some intimations of the better society Osborne presumably (as a socialist) hopes we'll live to see. A comparison with Chekhov (whom he has referred to with respect) would remind us that Chekhov has this whole dimension – his positive vision of the future of society – which so far is absent in Osborne.

"Human failure and frustration as the norm" applies even more strongly to Tennessee Williams. *Cat on a Hot Tin Roof* is a play without an ending, a play that just hasn't worked itself out, a play that seems like a giant excuse to enable the author to write one marvellously intense scene, after which he loses interest. Williams is concerned with a very real problem – the waste of character which accompanies human loneliness, especially the loneliness that grows where normal and abnormal natures are thrown together. But once he has made it plain to us why Brick is an alcoholic and why he has no interest in his wife, he doesn't know what to do with any of his characters. The play is a failure in action, or if you like in plot. Williams has himself referred to his "more or less static" plays (*Four Plays*, p. xii), and he often relies a good deal on poetic atmosphere and subtly changing mood to replace action and development of character. All right: this is one way of doing things. But when your plays issue in such an acutely personal key as Williams' do, involving such a profound distrust of man's freedom to act, such a deliberate foregathering under a "No Loitering" notice – you take great dramatic risks, and chiefly the risk that people must ask themselves a new question at a Williams play, not "What will happen now to these interesting characters?" but "What has got them all that way?" Like Osborne, Williams looks back; most of the dialogue is devoted to recollecting the past. The *really* interesting situation of *Cat*, from any central human point of view, is the situation with which the play ends, and which the author has not thought it worthwhile even to foreshadow convincingly.

The emotional hyperaesthesia which gives dramatic force to Williams and Osborne seems at times to be cherished to the point of moral anaesthesia. This can hardly be said of the earnest Mr Miller. Yet Miller's plays share the same concern with frustration, impotence, and defeat, and the same central vacuum, the lack of any bodied vision, any spur of hope whether social or metasocial, anything against which defeat and squalor and disappointment can be measured. The gloomy and ambiguous closing speech of the lawyer who acts as "chorus" in *A View from the Bridge*, coming as it does after the passionate events of the play, is surely a most inadequate send-off. Is it even true that Eddie the longshoreman had "allowed himself to be wholly known"? And granted that it is at least partly true, is it important? Is it *enough*, in a "social play" of the kind he discusses in his prefatory essay?

My reservations, then, are largely moral reservations. I have reached them without examining Beckett, Genet, or Ionesco, where the problem becomes even more acute. I haven't mentioned *Cards of Identity* or *Don't Destroy Me*, where the same moral bolshiness is at work, though in different ways. My general feeling is that the vigorous plays of the 'forties and 'fifties, entertaining and striking as they are, achieve their impact at the expense of very important things – themes that have been really brooded over till they issue from the plot like light from fire, and images of something positive and inspiring (*we* never, for example, see Jimmy Porter as Alison first saw him, when "everything about him seemed to burn, his face, the edges of his hair glistened and seemed to spring off his head. . . .").

Arthur Miller writes in his essay "On Social Plays": "Our society . . . is so complex, each person being so specialized an integer, that the moment any individual is dramatically characterized and set forth as a hero, our common sense reduces him to the size of a complainer, a misfit." This is untrue. It is not "our common sense" which does this, it is despair, or failure of nerve, or cynicism. What playwrights can do is to help to make any such despairing point of view obsolete, by reinvesting characters with more heroic qualities than at present they seem willing to dare.

[MAY 1958]

CLASS REPORT *by David Watt*

Now is the summer of our discontent. We have acclaimed, during the past twelve months, what most people have hopefully, almost pathetically, described as a "Renaissance of the English Theatre". We boast Mr John Osborne, we mention Mr Nigel Dennis, we take a little reflected glory from Mr Ray Lawler and we pat ourselves on the back for not having booed *The Chairs* and *Fin de Partie* off the stage in sheer incomprehension. With such a playwright, with such discriminating and intelligent audiences the English theatre cannot be dead. So they say.

But it is only now, in the doldrums, that we begin to realize how tenuous a hold on life the patient really has. It is small consolation to the exasperated playgoer as his trembling finger goes slowly and hopelessly down the entertainment column of the newspaper to know that some talent has fled to the Festivals, or to be told by Francophile critics that London theatres should close in July and August as the Paris ones do. London is swarming with tourists, notebooks poised and thirsty for English culture, the streets are crammed with country cousins their eager faces aglow with excitement, there are even a few Londoners with nothing better to do than go to the theatre and they all need entertainment. Yet there are at least four plays now running in the West End which must seem as remote to them as an evening's recitation in ancient Rome and not quite as convulsing. There are about half-a-dozen others (including two musicals) which appear to have been written by the inhabitant of one pent-house in Knightsbridge for the amusement of the girl in the flat below. One has heard nothing lately as helplessly funny as that line in *The Reluctant Débutante* which was always such a success – "I first met him in the Cromwell Road" (My dear, *fancy* meeting anyone there; can you imagine it?) but there are some pretty good ones. At *Silver Wedding*, for instance, you will hear the sonorous and reassuring names of Marshall and Snelgrove, Fortnum and Mason, the Café de Paris, even Harrods, flung like talismans across the footlights to an audience, small but enthusiastic, only too delighted to answer "Pass friend and all's well."

Now no one, I suppose, is going to be so grudging as to say that if you can induce people to pay for the privilege of being allowed to share your private joke you should not be entitled to do so. It is also going to be a long time before the Lord Chamberlain is empowered to blacklist any play in which the words "Martini, darling?" appear more than once, or in which there is a view of the roofs of Chelsea from the window; but the fact remains that this type of play monopolizes as many London stages as it did when there were twice as many people interested, and that unless something radical happens before long the English theatre will be receiving a hygienic, expensive and exceedingly tasteful burial at whichever crematorium is most fashionable.

We have heard with monotonous regularity the obvious answers to all this – and it is easy enough to recommend that people start writing about other sections of society. It is not easy to get an adequate response. A quick mental review of recent plays about "other sections of society" produces the depressing conclusion that they are nearly all written by, and for the amusement of, the same people as those aforementioned.

There are two archetypal characters now recognized by long usage. The first is the old-fashioned comic charwoman who, I suppose, with her salty apophthegms is descended in various degrees of bastardy from the nurse in *Romeo and Juliet*. She is, however, unless handled with great care, a fearful old bore and she has now had to make way for even more improbable creatures (all uproariously funny, of course) – the mentally deficient parlour-maid (how many people, incidentally, have parlour-maids these days?), the grouchy gardener who turns out to have committed the murder, and the boorish student from the provinces who makes a ridiculous pass at the hero's daughter. The second character is the simple British sailor (or, in civvy street, pub-keeper), the salt of the earth, the guardian of the British sense of humour, sturdily independent, kind to children and animals though not averse to a pint here and there. Mr Coward used to have rather a corner in him but we don't see quite so much of him on the stage these days; he has taken to the films, I fear. Both these ways of looking at the British working man are intensely comforting; after all, who, in *Reluctant Heroes*, is ever likely to go on strike? what butler ever turned teddy-boy? what charwoman took to Communism? They are too busy being funny or responsible to cause trouble, and if anything is to be avoided in the upper middle-class theatre it is the uncomfortable feeling that trouble is brewing somewhere. If someone wishes to point out that this sort of working-class character is beloved by its originals, that forces farces are crammed to the doors with all sorts and conditions, and that you can always get a real charwoman to play Mrs Crump in the WI play, let him consider the irreducible tendency of all sections of British society to simper in front of anything which holds the mirror up to them, be it as dark as a shop window or as distorting as a play.

All this reacts very noticeably with the English style of acting, and not always for the best. Arthur Miller remarked not long ago on the difficulty over here of casting a "common man" play like *A View from the Bridge*. In New York, it seems, you scratch a longshoreman and you get an actor. Try scratching a London docker and you get a scratch in return, if nothing worse. Most English actors are forced by the segregations of their birth, education or training to rely on observation rather than instinct for roles in lower reaches. While instinct is generally realistic, observation is apt to be satirical. There has therefore grown up a race of "character" actors, or rather, "caricature" actors, often technically brilliant but never wholly sympathetic and a standing incitement to char-mongers to write parts for them.

What I have so far been inveighing against is often called the class-consciousness of the English theatre but this is really a mis-statement. To be class-conscious the English theatre would have to be self-conscious and that it is most certainly not. It clings by implication to an out-dated picture of the way English society works; explicitly it says little about it. It is England through the eyes of the Deb's Mum, who is super-bly indifferent to class unless something regrettable forces it under her nose, unless for instance someone quite impossible applies for her daughter. There are signs, perhaps, that class will soon become a popular hunting ground for playwrights, as it has recently become for novelists. The picaresque school of Amis, Wain, Braine, Donleavy and Co (to lump together a number of very unequal talents) is obsessed by the anomalies of class, the fact that one of the most intelligent sections of society is excluded from the birthright to which it thinks its intelligence entitles it, and the possibility of changing the existing order by means of animal noises, rude faces, and sharp kicks at the entrenched backsides of the upper middle-classes. The first and so far almost the only drop in the equiva-lent theatrical deluge has been *Look Back in Anger*, probably the most acutely class-conscious play (in the true sense) in English since Galsworthy. But it is not the class-conscious-ness of *Look Back in Anger* which is important. Its real signi-ficance is that it reached an entirely different class of play-goer from the Knightsbridge enclaves. This new audience was not (as Mr Osborne evidently hoped) the "ordinary working man" or "monster in the ashcan" as he picturesquely calls him – the ordinary working man was just as likely to want to take a strap to Jimmy Porter as any retired Brigadier was; the new audience was a small, lower middle-class intel-ligentsia whose frustrations and bayings were reflected in the play. This was a triumph but it was also, in a way, a failure. It was indeed something to have breached the barrier; and if others follow they may help save the English theatre, for here, at any rate, are new audiences ready to pay good money to hear someone put problems to them in terms they can understand. They may not have gained true representation but they will stand taxation.

But they, too, will have failed unless they realize that two things are still missing. The first is a lower-class tradition. Mrs Dale is desperately genteel and the Archers are mere straw puppets; the caricature-acting school is still in full cry. More important, though, is the fact that even if this tradition could be built up it would only be a second best. Suppose for an instant that a perfect balance could be reached; two London theatres for Mr Douglas-Home and the nobs; half-a-dozen for Mr Osborne and the espresso bar egg-heads; a dozen for the yet unborn genius from Harlow and his friends from the housing estates. There would still be no playwright to transcend the class barriers, to write a classless play in the sense that it should be for, and about, Everyman (that after all is one of the chief requirements of tragedy). Now it might be said that this is a disease for which there is no cure except the development of English society in a classless direction, but in these days of the Welfare State it is just as well to plan against such an eventuality and to consider its probable effects on the theatre. Anyone interested in the possibility ought to read Arthur Miller's essay *On Social Plays* with which Cresset have prefaced their edition of *A View from the Bridge*, for in spite of some characteristically tortuous thought it gets to the point.

Mr Miller's thesis is slanted, almost twisted, to deal with the state of the contemporary American theatre but it is, briefly, as follows. The great periods of the theatre have occurred when a homogeneous moral outlook has informed a whole society. The most obvious example (a cynic might amend, "the only example") is Greek tragedy. In the city-state and in particular in Athens in the fifth century B.C., there was a community of interest and belief within a whole social unit which has never been equalled since. What it produced (quite apart from a unanimity at certain crucial historical moments) was a belief in the destiny of Athens which was common to all parts of society (following general usage one leaves slaves out of consideration for these purposes), and a well-established and widely spread belief in a moral order applicable to the whole of a (largely) classless society. This enabled the three great tragedians, at least, to concern themselves in their plays with the greatest questions, for whatever applied to an individual could be seen to be exemplary because it obviously applied to all; an all-embracing morality is by definition no respecter of persons.

Mr Miller is complaining of the lack of such a social consciousness in America which, he says, has resulted in a wholly detrimental "personality" cult, neurotic, introspective and rebellious, and a preoccupation with the individual of which the "Method" is merely the latest manifestation. He is able to end on a note of some complacency: "We have developed such a culture that in America neither the speech of a man nor his way of dressing nor his ambitions for himself inevitably mark his social class. The decks are cleared."

There are really two things at stake here, though Mr Miller has run them together a little. The more important contention, and the one which seems to me more likely, in fact almost certain, to be right is that playwrights need a background of belief, communal belief, against which to set their ideas; further, that such a background does not exist in England at this moment. The second part of the thesis, the more arguable and, unfortunately, the more relevant to this discussion, is that this kind of background is more likely to exist in a classless society, or, to put it in a way that is perhaps more acceptable, the less class-ridden a society is the better defined, and the more homogeneous its morality and its beliefs become.

Suppose for a moment that it is true and that the whole syllogism holds good, what does it mean for the English theatre? It does not mean that we must at once start trying to write plays in which everyone mingles gaily in a classless paradise – no one outside doctrinaire circles would insist that all good plays are *about* such a society. Nor does it mean, unfortunately, that we should try to create a morality or act as if we belonged to a classless society; it cannot be done. If the theory is right then the time will produce the playwrights, not the playwrights the time, and one cannot subtract social cubits from one's stature merely by taking thought.

Until the day dawns here as it may be dawning in America as Mr Miller implies, and as *Summer of the Seventeenth Doll* gives hope that it may have done in Australia, we must concentrate upon making the English theatre more representative within the structure we have. It may not be great theatre, or tragic theatre within living prospect but it could at least contain something for everyone. We owe a great debt to the English Stage Company for beginning the process; it doubtless needs something with the force of a pneumatic drill to implant into the skulls of most West End managers the fact that there is money in the country which is not banked at Coutts, and it is just possible that the sight of it being poured out to see *Look Back in Anger* and *The Entertainer* may have had some effect. Unless they do the English theatre will die with the words, "Martini darling?" on its lips.

[SEPTEMBER 1957]

TAKING STOCK AT THE COURT
by *Tom Milne*

In the moneyed wilderness of the London theatre, the English Stage Company shares with Theatre Workshop – and perhaps the Arts Theatre Club – the distinction of being the only management interested in good theatre before good box-office. And that, quite apart from the genuinely high standard of its productions and the emergence of John Osborne as a dramatist potentially of the first rank, is enough to make it a cherished possession. Since its opening in April 1956, the Company has produced nineteen plays (including one-acters), housed the homeless *Fin de Partie*, and produced a further eight plays in single performances without décor. Bearing in mind the commercial servitude, and therefore inanity, of the English theatre today, any playgoer seeking validity – seriousness/insight into contemporary problems/commitment/good theatre (call it what you will) – must remain eternally grateful to the English Stage Company for its work.

God help the English theatre if this Company dies. But, for such a theatre to survive, there must be an audience which wants it; if there is no such audience, it must be created, and must be kept together by the knowledge that it will get good theatre *all*, and not some, of the time. A recent survey in *The Times* justifiably pats the English Stage Company on the back, adding however, that a cynic might well be suspicious of the "commercial flair" evident in the presentation of the bawdiness of *Lysistrata* or *The Country Wife* conveniently at the Christmas season, and in the lacing of its casts with such names as Joan Greenwood, Sir Laurence Olivier, Robert Helpmann and Laurence Harvey. "That is about as far", the correspondent continues, "as criticism of the English Stage Company's policy can effectively go" (given the vulgarization of the theatre today). This is true only if you believe that the function of a theatre is to present distinguished plays on a distinguished level, reaching a wider public than is usually considered possible with "uncommercial" plays, but without having any distinct artistic personality of its own. That this is not the English Stage Company's view of its function is evidenced by the early publicity material, which centred on the stimulation of new playwrights seriously concerned with the world today, their plays to be performed in repertory. And a note in the programme of *Look Back in Anger* (September 1956) records, "In the spring, we will present two or more new English plays from the group of writers we are gradually collecting round our theatre." In other words, the Company considers that it is (or should be) the central link in a chain of writers whose aim is to write valid comment on the world around us. An admirable aim.

An analysis of the plays presented at the Court, however, is both interesting and disturbing. Only seven of the nineteen plays presented were premières (including *Epitaph for George Dillon*, already produced non-professionally, and the one-act *How Can We Save Father?*); three others had been previously produced in the provinces, seven were foreign plays, two were classics. The premières involved only four playwrights – John Osborne, Nigel Dennis (a successful novelist), Ann Jellicoe (discovered through *The Observer* Competition), and Oliver

Marlow Wilkinson (hardly an unknown playwright). Further-more, of the 139 actors employed in these productions, eighty-six appeared in one role only, twenty-one in two. These figures suggest that the English Stage Company, with its self-set goal of new plays and a repertory company, has resorted very frequently to established foreign plays with specially engaged "West End" casts. Of course, valid plays do not grow on trees, but if the Company's five play-readers could turn up nothing, it is a little difficult to understand why the promising work of such playwrights as John Whiting, Leo Lehman, Robert Shaw, John Hall, Brendan Behan, Derek Monsey, Ian Dallas and Bernard Kops has apparently been ignored.

Where does the establishment of a "group of writers . . . round our theatre" come in? The answer, presumably, lies in the Sunday evening performances, where eight young play-wrights have had the enormously valuable experience of being able to see their work in production. Several points may be noted. One, a query: to what extent are these Sunday even-ings a subconscious bolthole for the directors from the neces-sity of producing a play in the raw? – by an unknown dramatist, or without Sir Laurence Olivier in the cast, or without backing by Messrs Schweppes. Surely at least the plays by Michael Hastings and Doris Lessing had sufficient textual quality to warrant full production immediately? Two: it is a pity that of the eighty-five actors employed in these performances, only seventeen appeared (before or afterwards) in regular productions; this drives a further wedge in the "permanent company" goal. Three: Tony Richardson told me that as a result of these try-outs, plays had been commissioned from four of the playwrights con-cerned – which augurs well for the future. *But* – if, in the meantime, the Company persists in its policy of giving polished "West End" performances of established plays, where the pill is sugared by star actors (*Nekrassov*, *The Country Wife*, *Lysistrata*, *Requiem for a Nun*), then these commissioned plays will find it hard to gain an adequate hearing on their own merits, because after two years the English Stage Company still has no audience on which it can

1. The New Wave, *circa* 1958
Left to right (*back row*): Arnold Wesker, Errol John,
Bernard Kops, David Campton
(*front row*): N. F. Simpson, Harold Pinter,
Ann Jellicoe, John Mortimer

2*a*. John Osborne

2*b*. John Arden

rely. (This last is not a merely personal opinion, but a statement by Tony Richardson.) It is, in a sense, an indictment of those two years that a play so brilliantly acted and produced, and with such a challenging first act at least, as *The Sport of My Mad Mother*, could not find an audience – even a small one. That an audience has not been built up is not perhaps surprising: there are too many anomalous chinks in the English Stage Company's otherwise excellent armour, quite apart from the pill-sugaring already mentioned, which cause doubts about the Company's policy. Why, for example, was *The Apollo de Bellac* produced, a play which has been stone-dead from birth (and, of all things, why accompanying *The Chairs*)? Why were *Don Juan* and *The Death of Satan* given the unwarranted honour of production? Why a production of *Lysistrata* which turned a wildly funny, but quite serious, comment on war into a mildly amusing, glossy sex-war play?

The answer to at least some of these questions lies in the failure to establish a repertory, so that each production is a separate entity, not linked to what has gone before or what is to come, by either the actors, producers, or aim of the playwright; they are, in fact, governed by the laws of the commercial theatre. The advantages of a repertory are obvious. Here, a play need not descend into limbo merely because we are burdened with incompetent critics, or a bone idle audience: it can be nursed gently with occasional performances, or revived after an interval. More specifically, a repertory company has the great value that it provides a unity from which individual productions may be viewed. For its first six months (and for brief intervals thereafter), the English Stage Company did, in fact, run a repertory season, and nearly foundered. But during that time, the work of its principal and highly individual producers (the solid, rather stolid good qualities of George Devine, the delicate, nervous tension of Tony Richardson) appeared as the expression of a single belief in the aim of their theatre, strengthened by the use of a permanent company. Later productions, with special casts, such as *Requiem for a Nun* (Richardson) or *Nekrassov* (Devine), might have sprung from any enterprising West End management.

The idea of a full repertory season may well be a pipe-dream, involving, as it does, immense storage space for scenery, the carrying of plays which do not draw, difficulty if a play must be transferred with its cast, etc. But if a repertory season is not practicable without solid subsidies, a permanent company is. And the great benefit to actors in being members of a permanent company must be borne in mind. Tony Richardson told me of the difficulties involved in keeping actors – high salaries, the attraction of television and the cinema as soon as an actor "emerges", paying an actor when he cannot be used. Three points may be made. Firstly: if you catch 'em young and train 'em hard, salaries are not crip-pling. Here, the Sunday productions could be of immense value both in training and discovering actors. Secondly: if you contract an actor, there need be no question of the attrac-tion of television or the cinema. The case of one actor, who was much praised in the lead of a Sunday production and is now appearing very successfully in the West End, is illumi-nating. After the try-out play, he was offered a small part in the next regular production, but no contract. He refused. When I asked him if he would have accepted a contract, so as to have both security and the possibility of development, he said: "Wouldn't any actor? I am thinking of going to Notting-ham to do just that." Thirdly: you can almost always use a good actor (special circumstances excepted, e.g. coloured characters) *if* you believe that an actor is an actor and not merely an exponent of the art of playing variations on a character. One of the most exciting features of the Theatre Workshop seasons of 1954 and 1955 was the extraordinary development of Harry H. Corbett and Maxwell Shaw, within a permanent company, in varied and often unexpected roles in such plays as *The Long Voyage Home, Arden of Faversham, Volpone, Mother Courage, Androcles and the Lion* and *The Good Soldier Schweik*. There was no question of engaging a "suitable" actor for certain roles. The permanent company had to meet the challenge and the results were stimulating, often exciting. This challenge in being invited to play roles apparently rather outside his existing scope is the only way in which an actor can really develop. The English Stage

Company, however, like the commercial theatre, tends to cast an actor well within his usual scope. The performances, for example, of Joan Greenwood in *Cards of Identity* and *Lysistrata*, George Benson in *Nekrassov* and *Lysistrata*, John Moffatt in all his roles, Yvonne Mitchell in *Epitaph for George Dillon*, though excellent, were all largely predictable. Again, Joan Plowright, one of the Company's "developments", has been seen in eight plays at the Court, including three major roles: while praising, the critics are now beginning to remark that she relies too much for her effects on one amusing regional accent. This is, of course, short of the truth, but it is true to say that her parts in *The Country Wife*, *The Making of Moo* and *The Chairs* seemed to be variations on a theme, and none of them was so testing, or in a small way so memorable, as her Pip in Orson Welles' *Moby Dick* (1955). Tony Richardson told me that Miss Plowright wishes to return to the Company, and that they are having difficulty in "finding a play for her". Why not simply *cast* her, and extend her range? If – let us suppose – *The Sport of My Mad Mother* remained to be cast, why not as Greta, the Teddy-girl leader, rather than the obvious casting as the pathetic but amusing waif, Dodo, which she could play blindfold, and from which she would learn nothing?

Harold Clurman, in his history of the Group Theatre, has a very relevant passage: "We had chosen our actors before we knew what plays we should do. They were our actors, and they would have to suit our plays. That is what we directors were there for." It is worth remembering that the Group Theatre, in its ten years' existence, always maintained a permanent company, many of the actors remaining throughout the Group's existence; and that, by its exclusive concentration on the production of new plays dealing with the problems of people in society (by Odets, Irwin Shaw, John Howard Lawson, etc.), the Group welded a link which made it possible for such writers as Arthur Miller and Tennessee Williams to exist in America when none such existed here.

[MAY 1958]

OH FOR EMPTY SEATS! *by Peter Brook*

It is popularly believed that the West End theatre is controlled by iniquitous people; men without courage, greedy,
unidealistic, power-mad – and it is thought that if something
could be done about *them*, then a new theatre would emerge.
I live amongst *them* – and can report to you your suspicions
are partly true: villainy does abound; there is much cupidity
and little imagination: but side by side, however surprising it
may sound, there is a touching, absolute wish to do good.
Many successful West End managers, most leading actors,
and almost all directors have a great desire to do the unexpected, the sensational, the vital (because these elements
are somewhere in the make-up of anyone connected with
theatre), they all share a desire to provoke discussion and to
be hailed as pioneers.

It is said, repeatedly, that masterly plays lie around the
country unread. This is rubbish: there has seldom in history
been such a vested interest in finding scripts – by managers,
actors, directors – by the small theatres, by the few art
theatres, by the television people. In fact, talent has never
had such an easy opening. Let anyone write a play with a
glimmer of ability and with a quarter of a sou's worth of
talent and it is almost inconceivable that he won't be snap-
ped up at once. This applies as much to actors, for now – with
television – it is almost impossible to keep an actor with a
fingernail of personality out of work.

Why then is the theatre so bad? Because, let's face it, it is
on a catastrophically low level: weak, watery, repetitive,
drab and silly. Why are there no plays that reflect the excitement, the movement, the change, the conflict, the tragedy,
the misery, the hope and the emancipation of the highly
dramatic moment of world's history in which we live? Why
are we given the choice between colour and poetry in the
classics, or drab prose in contemporary drama? Why has no
one followed on Brecht's track? Why are our actors lazy and
passionless: why do so few of them do more than two hours a
day: why do so few of them think theatre, dream theatre,
fight for theatre, above all practise theatre in the spare time

at their disposal? Why is the talent in this country – and the goodwill – frittered away in a mixture of ineffectual grumbling and deep complacency? I think that to find the causes one must not look for individual villains or for a race of villains: I think the villain is deeply buried in the system: it lies in laws that operate at almost all levels.

Once upon a time, in an evil, tyrannical world, there was a monstrous but clear-cut gulf between the wicked *them* and the virtuous *us*. For instance, there were two distinct types of theatre. There was the faded boulevard theatre, synonymous with the frivolities of an idle class, and there was the *avant-garde*, where the serious artist worked. This serious artist, this man-with-something-to-say, found that the barriers into the other world were virtually impenetrable – he found this along with his comrades from other arts – and all of them by force of true outsidership acquired true anger – and true anger in turn forged true identities – true identities manifested themselves in passionate utterance: utterance that was its own reward as it could never in the nature of things bring riches or social acceptance.

Today, all worlds intermingle. Now, in liberal, broadminded England the Archbishop of Canterbury can sit beside an atheistic author at the Queen's luncheon table – and each man can be genuinely delighted to meet the other. The author emerges from the bosom of his family, his shoulder spiked with chips and he charges at society as at a hated dad. To his amazement, the enemy retreats, disappears and like a man with a battering ram encountering no resistance, he falls flat on his face. Else it welcomes him with open arms, but this hug of welcome, the warmth of this bosom carries with it a kiss of death.

For England destroys artists. This is a peculiar property of our social system. In England the edge (and what else matters?) is rapidly knocked off an artist – not by a concerted and wicked policy of the *them* – but by the artist's best friend. Social snobbery in England takes many forms, infinite in their variety, subtle in their invisibility, powerful in the illusion of total freedom they seem to give. No one presses the artist to do anything – all they do is to create a climate in which he only too readily will castrate himself. In England artistic success brings with it the entrance into one of a million little worlds – and the odd feature of English life is that these worlds rarely overlap. In New York, everyone on the same level of financial success seems to meet: in London the private worlds may have a few outsiders, the artist may conceivably meet a few specimens of different views and backgrounds from himself – but on the whole a strict auto-conformity will characterize his group. This "style" of his world may be one of good taste, good furniture, prettiness and queer gossip – for so long the typical marks of West End parish life – or it may be a world of duffle coats, coffee bars, socialism and nonqueer gossip. The fact remains that each group will find some things vital and others boring; in one group politics will be taboo, in the other, chi-chi will be – and gradually the group will exclude the things that irritate it: the private jokes, references and private slang will slowly bring about a state in which certain things are "in" and other things are "out". A group keeps its integrity neither dramatically nor excitingly – nor even visibly: it puts what it dislikes into Coventry, into that "dull" category to which no one ever aspires. The artist who has made a success realizes intuitively that his position is based on certain characteristics in his work for which he was accepted in the first place. He realizes that these characteristics have brought him the praise of his circle – and he finds that what his tiny circle praises also makes money. There is no conflict, only reassurance. How can he turn his back on money when all the people he admires confirm that it is truly earned? It takes an unusually independent spirit to venture further.

This, then, is the problem. The dramatist has a desire to create, a desire for success and a desire for money. In the olden days the three were irreconcilable and the true artist of course chose the first of them. But today starvation is out of date; the garret is merely a romantic setting at the opera house: the artist can have his cake and eat it – at the price of a set of compromises each one so tiny that he is probably oblivious of their existence. *And no one any longer can take a flop*. Once a failure with the crowd served to confirm the artist's inner convictions. But today a true flop in England or America cannot possibly be interpreted defiantly as a sign that one is ahead of one's times; such a variety of nearly good, nearly true works succeed that an author with any humility is found to put his own failure down to his own lack of skill. Think where painting would be if a painter failed in his own estimation when at these early exhibitions his canvas hung in empty galleries, unseen. This to him is no failure; the buying of a picture is positive and gratifying, but the non-buying is no denial of his worth. Of course, people will say, he knows his picture will be around for ever – the unsuccessful play must close. That is the trouble. Empty seats are always the crowning argument. They humiliate the playwright, they assault his ego – above all they close his play. Thus its failure is his failure – and failure is a boring, unglamorous, unchic, unstimulating, negative state: it is an experience from which some writers never recover; which all vow in their hearts never to repeat. Instead they dig in their hearts to discover the causes for this failure – they contrast it with their previous success – and intuitively they turn to imitation of their own formula – and if the need to say what was once said is no longer there, their technique enables them to manufacture a false emotion to take the place of the original urge.

All of this is because the yardstick is "Full or empty seats". This is now sincerely believed by the best managers and actors and directors and writers to be a sort of artistic standard. It is maintained honestly and sincerely that a good show should *pay its way*. I think it can often pay its way: it is very agreeable when it does. I think furthermore that in our system, every theatre *must* pay its way – because no one however idealistic can remain in business at a permanent loss. So while those who want to make money may say crudely, "We're only interested in the profits", the best that anyone can say is, "We want to cover our costs". And this is wrong. The theatre that covers its costs is the true theatre with its edge knocked off.

Where has there been the most experimenting in the English theatre in the past ten years? At Stratford-on-Avon. What are the most exciting theatres in Europe? The TNP.

The Komische Oper of Berlin. Glyndebourne. The Berliner Ensemble. Theatre Workshop. What have all these unlikely bodies in common – some classical and formal, some revolutionary and proletarian? They have only one thing in common – they are totally independent of the box office, the Press, the audience. The need to make a "reasonable success" does not exist for them. To take the case of Stratford, which I know so well, there is no box office pressure as there is no risk – more reliable than any Government subsidy is the guarantee that comes from Shakespeare's name: this is such a draw in Stratford that seats sell whether the notices are good or bad, whatever the word-of-mouth says. In theory this could lead to complacency on the part of the people running it. But does it? Not a bit. There has been more vitality, more freedom, more experiment, more youthfulness at Stratford – and since the war more achievement – than in any other theatre in England. Except perhaps Theatre Workshop – and for the sake of this argument Theatre Workshop is in the position of a subsidized theatre – by reverse – because it despises money totally (not "somewhat", as in the cases of the Arts Theatre or the Royal Court – semi-artistic theatres that must still pay their way, for whom "good notices" or "a West End transfer" are vital to keeping alive). Martha Graham keeps the whole ballet world in her debt – and maintains a standard for other choreographers to imitate – by being so ahead of her time that she regularly plays to empty houses. But she is subsidized – and as a result she works harder than anyone. The quality of the Moscow Art Theatre comes from the absolute and total divorce between the artists' work – and money. The quite enormous achievements of the BBC over the years, of the atomic research laboratories all come from subsidy. Pythagoras could experiment at his own expense: nowadays to experiment with moon rockets, giant subsidies are needed: logically without subsidies the bold dramatic enterprises of our time cannot be considered. The theatre has become expensive. The artist has acquired a standard of living. The clock can't be put back.

National theatres, many of them, of different shapes and sizes would be part of the answer. Of course, we won't ever get one – because the Government will never spend the money. And anyway it would be such a cumbersome organization, inevitably in the wrong hands, bound to pass through so many ghastly years of teething troubles, that it could not affect the scene as far ahead as we can look. No, I think we should clamour for the big National Theatre, as a thorn in the flesh of successive governments, but actually hope for something more realistic. I would like to see a start made – and the principle established – with one tiny theatre with a hundred seats, even fifty seats, but *subsidized to the hilt*. By this I mean that the subsidy should cover all that such a theatre could lose even if every seat were empty at every performance. If we think of a small theatre this would be still a reasonable sum, one that a rich television company, a mineral water manufacturer, or even a government department could furnish. This subsidy would then be a *total subsidy*. It will be run by a director and a new sort of committee. This committee will applaud the director if he announces that he has lost every penny – he is entitled to do this. It will chase him with furies, however, if he has failed to keep his theatre alive. It will hound him if his theatre becomes consistently group-y or clique-y; if it seems to belong too much to one type of person, to one set of experiments. Its appeal must be that it can *dare completely*: that it can *dare* offer any author with a completely uncommercial idea, a stage *immediately*. It would be an actors' studio of writers, it would be our *avant-garde*.

I believe that a healthy theatre has three divisions: a national classical theatre kept alive by a continually revitalized tradition: a boulevard theatre kept alive by its zest, its gaiety, by diffusing a sense of happiness and fun through music, colour and laughter for their own sakes; and also an *avant-garde*. Through the easy passage of the artist to big commercial success we have lost the *avant-garde*. In music, there are serial composers, electronic composers, concrete composers, working far ahead of their time, yet opening the way for the broad middle stream of their art to follow. In painting, there are action painters, experiments in every form of shape, surface and abstraction. Where is the vanguard of the theatre? Where can one see disastrous experiments from which authors can develop away from the dying forms of the present day? To face new audiences we must first be in a position to face empty seats.[1]

[1] The idealized theatre Peter Brook described in 1959 became a reality in 1963 when the Royal Shakespeare Company established a fully-subsidized, experimental company at the LAMDA theatre in London. The theatre, under Brook's direction, was in no way obliged to show a profit or even break even, and if the company played to empty seats, the management were still committed to full support.

[JANUARY 1959]

CHAPTER THREE

THE GOOD YEARS

INTRODUCTION

From 1958 to 1961, the English theatre was quickly and unalterably transformed by what in 1956 had been only portents. New plays, new directors and new actors came thick and fast. The "New Wave" was no longer isolated at Sloane Square or Stratford East. The West End managements began to pay court. Hard-headed managers, brought up to respect the matinee audience and the library bookings, were obliged to acknowledge a change in public taste. John Osborne, Harold Pinter, Arnold Wesker, N. F. Simpson – all found their way into West End theatres, and after twelve years in the relative obscurity of the provinces and East London, Joan Littlewood's Theatre Workshop invaded the mainland and triumphed there with Brendan Behan and Shelagh Delaney.

This troupe, bred on Stanislavsky technique and now assimilating Brechtian tactics, gave a new vigour to English acting, dynamically mixed social matter and cockney farce, and, in passing, revitalized the English musical. Harold Pinter, after the success of *The Caretaker* and the agonizing reappraisal of his first play *The Birthday Party*, emerged as a heavyweight talent. Arnold Wesker hammered out the first social trilogy ever to be produced on an English stage, and John Arden – despite wounds sustained in *Serjeant Musgrave's Dance* – continued to cultivate a talent which made him at once the most fascinating and controversial writer in the country. Even so, Tradition had its little victories, and the tragedy of the period was Joan Littlewood's departure (temporary, fortunately) from Theatre Workshop, tired of fighting a running battle with critics and audiences, and tired of trying to maintain a permanent ensemble whose personnel was constantly being dispersed in the long runs which became necessary in order to pay the bills.

THE BIRTHDAY PARTY
Review by Irving Wardle

Reviewing a production after everybody else has had a crack at it is like entering a magnetic field; protesting, qualifying, rephrasing, you are swept off to belittling embrace with whatever positive or negative pole has exerted the strongest pull. Only occasionally can you saunter out on the field and find it still littered with iron filings.

Mr Harold Pinter's *The Birthday Party* offers this rare pleasure. When the play flared up briefly at the Lyric Opera House in May it provoked such anarchy of opinions, all very dogmatically held, that you have to look towards French government before finding a fit comparison. Nowadays there are two ways of saying you don't understand a play: the first is to bowl it out with that word "obscurity", once so popular in poetry reviews; the second way is to say that the seminal influence of Ionesco can be detected.

Mr Pinter received the full treatment. As well as standing for x in the formulae outlined above, he was described as inferior N. F. Simpson, a lagging surrealist, and as the equal of Henry James. Remembering James's melancholy affair with the theatre this last one carries a nasty sting; and, within a couple of days of receiving it, *The Birthday Party* was over.

The comparison with James is quite baffling. Far from being a cautious verbal artist struggling to "throw away cargo to save the ship", Mr Pinter has no difficulty in putting theatrical requirements first. No matter what you may think of the contents, the ship is afloat. And it is his very instinct for what will work in the theatre that has prompted hostility. One character in *The Birthday Party*, for instance, is given to tearing up newspapers: we are not told why. But the spectacle of John Stratton, as the inflammable McCann, holding his breath while rapt in the task of tearing each strip of paper to the same width, took on a malevolent power perfectly in key with the play and requiring no explanation. This device is an extreme example of the playwright's habit of introducing an intrinsically theatrical idea and letting it find its own road back towards common sense. Mr Pinter's way is the opposite of setting out deliberately to embody a theme in action.

All the same a theme does emerge, closely resembling that of *The Iceman Cometh*: the play demonstrates that a man who has withdrawn to protect his illusions is not going to be helped by being propelled into the outer world. Stanley, the man in question, is an obese, shambling, unpresentable creature who has moved into a dilapidated seaside boarding house where, as the only guest, he is able to lord it over his adoring landlady and gain recognition as a concert pianist of superhuman accomplishment. But even in this protected atmosphere there are menacing intrusions: he cannot banish the memory of arriving to give a recital and finding the hall locked up; there are enemies. And when they arrive – in the persons of a suspiciously fluent Jew and his Irish henchman – they seem as much furies emerging from Stanley's night thoughts as physical characters. His downfall is swift. Scrubbed, shaved, hoisted out of his shapeless trousers and stuffed into a morning suit he is led away at the end in a catatonic trance.

Theatrically the play loses its grip only when the two intruders appear alone. They have no need to keep up the mystery, but they do keep it up arbitrarily and begin to reveal distressingly human weaknesses which undermine their power to shock. John Slater, as the leader, almost redeemed these scenes by handling them with operatic licence – treating the lines as cadenced gibberish and alternating blandly honeyed rhetoric with a savage stamp of the foot or a chilling facial contortion. In company, however, the intruders had no need to adopt extraordinary practices: the wink, the muffled threat, the ogrish leer carried them effortlessly through scenes of introduction, accusation, and through the nightmarish birthday party in which Stanley sat bowed and speechless, as his guests, ludicrous in paper hats, worked themselves from giggling gentility into a frenzied *totentanz*.

Peter Wood's production, which seized tigerishly on the play and left it picked clean, contained two major performances – Beatrix Lehmann's Meg (the landlady), and Richard Pearson's Stanley. How these came to be cold-shouldered in the Press is a puzzle more unfathomable than any set by Mr Pinter.

[JULY 1958]

A TASTE OF HONEY
Review by Lindsay Anderson

To talk as we do about popular theatre, about new working-class audiences, about plays that will interpret the common experiences of today – all this is one thing, and a good thing too. But how much better even, how much more exciting, to find such theatre suddenly here, suddenly sprung up under our feet! This was the first joyful thing about Theatre Workshop's performance of *A Taste of Honey*.

A work of complete, exhilarating originality, it has all the strength, and none of the weaknesses, of a pronounced, authentic local accent. Going north in Britain is always like a trip into another country, and *A Taste of Honey* is a real escape from the middlebrow, middle-class vacuum of the West End. It is real, contemporary poetry, in the sense that its world is both the one we know and read about every Sunday in the *News of the World* – and at the same time the world seen through the eyes and imagination of a courageous, sensitive and outspoken person.

Just how far Josephine, the plump, untidy schoolgirl who moves into a Salford attic with her flighty Mum, just how far she is Shelagh Delaney, we cannot, of course, say. But the play belongs to her just as unmistakably as *The Catcher in the Rye* belongs to Holden Caulfield. She learns about life the hard way. Her mother goes off again, this time to marry a peculiar, drunken upper-class boy with one eye and a weakness for older women. She spends Christmas with a charming Negro sailor, and ends up pregnant. She shares her room with a brisk, affectionate, vulnerable, queer art student, who knows pretty well how to manage her and likes the idea of babies more than she does. Pretty well anything could have been made of this material, which is written in vivid, salty language and presented without regard for conventions of dramatic shape. In fact, so truthful is Miss Delaney, so buoyant in spirit, and so keenly alive to what is preposterous, vulgar and ruthless in human beings (as well as to what is generous, creative and warm), that she makes us forget about judging. We simply respond, as to the experience itself.

The world has always been a corrupt and disappointing place; but the total commercialization, the deadening over-organization of the big societies of today make us prize more than ever the naïve, spontaneous, honest visions of youth. This is where this play compares interestingly with *The Catcher in the Rye*. Like Holden, Josephine is a sophisticated innocent. Precious little surprises her; but her reactions are pure and direct, her intuitions are acute, and her eye is very sharp. The little kid she watches, out in the yard, with hair so dirty it looks as though it's going to walk away – "He doesn't do anything, he just sits on the front doorstep. He never goes to school. . . ." Holden would have noticed him; and he would have made the same right moral and social comment. Mothers like that shouldn't be allowed to have children. But Josephine is luckier than Holden in some ways: she is tougher, with a common-sense, Lancashire working-class resilience that will always pull her through. And this makes her different too from the middle-class angry young man, the egocentric rebel. Josephine is not a rebel; she is a revolutionary.

One of the most extraordinary things about this play is its lack of bitterness, its instinctive maturity. This quality was emphasized by Joan Littlewood's production, which seemed to me quite brilliant. Driving the play along at break-neck pace, stuffing it with wry and humorous invention, she made sentimentalism impossible. The abandoning of the fourth wall, the sudden patches of pure music hall, panto-style, were daring, but completely justified by their success. No soppy "identification" here; just the ludicrous, bitter-sweet truth, a shared story. And so, when the lyrical moments did come, we could credit them, knowing the reality from which they sprang.

Grateful (as actors always seem to be) for first-rate material and production, the company played together splendidly, with the complete rightness of tone that alone could bring off the most startling and difficult transitions. Frances Cuka, as Josephine, had exactly the right, adolescent fitfulness, the abrupt rages and tendernesses, the concealed longing for affection, and the inner, unshakeable optimism. As her mother, Avis Bunnage managed most skilfully to combine the broadest, eye-on-the-gallery caricature, with straightforward, detailed naturalism. Surely this was real Brechtian playing. John Bay made a most exotic grotesque out of the seedy boy friend; and as the art student, Murray Melvin gave a performance that was a miracle of tact and sincerity. John Bury's set was bold, simple and effective as usual; and the jazz interludes by the Apex trio gave the whole evening a friendly, contemporary and hopeful air. The movement continues.

[JULY 1958]

ART IN ANGEL LANE *by Tom Milne*

In the thirteen years of its existence, Theatre Workshop has produced some seventy plays, a catalogue of which reads remarkably like the repertory one would hope to find at our hypothetical National Theatre: Aristophanes, Shakespeare, Marlowe, Jonson, Molière, Webster, Marston, Lope de Vega, Ibsen, Chekhov, Lorca, Pirandello, O'Casey, Synge, Shaw, Gogol, Brecht, etc. The standard has been consistently high, and since the company took over the Theatre Royal at Stratford in 1953, its productions of *Edward II*, *Arden of Faversham*, *The School for Wives* and *A Taste of Honey* may be ranked with the finest seen in London during that period, with another nine or ten treading closely on their heels. In spite of this, Theatre Workshop has rarely been able to

3a. Encore Remembrance Service for a National Theatre, 1958

3b. Right: Albert Finney (aged 21)

3c. Far right: Peter O'Toole (aged 24)

4a. Peter Brook

4b. Joan Littlewood

command a full house in London (although, unlike the
English Stage Company, the audience it does have is faithful).
And still the critics patronize, giving praise where praise is
inevitable, but with an air of surprise that this enfant terrible
(a *Leftist* enfant) should actually have produced something
worthy of mature consideration, needing no excuse or special
allowances.

The point is, of course, that Theatre Workshop commits
a double sin. The first is that it believes that the theatre must
be in direct contact with life. Recently, after a performance
by the Belgrade Theatre of Arnold Wesker's *Chicken Soup
With Barley* (a Theatre Workshop-style play, and one which
would have benefited from the strong hand of Joan Littlewood), an elderly lady remarked disapprovingly to her companion: "It may be propaganda, it may be documentary, but
it's not a play." In other words, Arnold Wesker came too
close to life, dealt with actual problems, felt strongly about
them, and wanted to impel the audience to do something
about it. But the business of the theatre – as the old lady felt,
and as box-office receipts confirm – is to construct a protec-
tive shield of fantasy between the audience and the crude
realities of life, not to open the audience's eyes to life itself.
Not only does Theatre Workshop sin thus by picking its new
plays exclusively from those which attempt to say something
constructive about the world we live in, but it adds the unpardonable corollary of having no respect for the classics as
classics (i.e. as vehicles for star performances, formally
beautiful productions, historical reconstructions, careful
textual readings, etc). Instead, Theatre Workshop produces
Shakespeare or Marlowe as though the play had only just
been written, and the playwright were commenting on life
as we know it today. Their modern dress *Volpone*, complete
with bicycle and spiv-Mosca, was accepted by the critics, a
little grudgingly, as being only Jonson, and only a satire on
spivs, hangers-on and other undesirables. *Macbeth*, on the
other hand (finely conceived but indifferently acted), was
greeted with dismay and muttering about political overtones:
it was Shakespeare, and, moreover, the modern dress lent a
touch of satire to the army and (most horrible) to royalty.

Modern dress, however, is only a small part of this contemporaneity and, in fact, Theatre Workshop's most successful Elizabethan revivals were in costume. More important is that the actors are made to consider their characters firstly as human beings, and only secondly as characters with beautiful lines to speak or gestures to make.

In *Edward II*, for example, we witnessed not merely the downfall of a king, but of a living person, behind whom lay the tragic king; only too frequently Elizabethan plays in production are awe-inspiring or abstractly beautiful, but unmoving, because they make no contact with our own lives. Here, Joan Littlewood's rehearsal method (essentially, like the work of the Actors' Studio, a development of Stanislavsky's system) is invaluable. In her rehearsals for *Macbeth*, for example, the actors began by playing at cowboys and indians, moving gradually to an improvised battle, and finally to the opening scene of the play, using Shakespeare's text. This may sound crude, but it undoubtedly ensures a completely unstereotyped attitude to the play. The actors are given several valid angles of approach to their characters, and are forced to consider their lines, not merely as lines, but as expressions of emotions or situations within the compass of their own personal experience: a production such as Benthall's recent Old Vic *Henry VIII*, where three stars were brought in to give "performances", and the remaining actors were present merely to give cues, fill gaps and declaim the text, becomes impossible. This method is invaluable, too, for the inexperienced playwright: in the case of a great play, the original words will inevitably be used, as the best expression of the author's intention, but a young author may find in the improvisation, clarification of certain falsenesses in his writing (as was the case with Henry Chapman's *You Won't Always Be On Top*), or of the whole construction of the play (as with Shelagh Delaney's *A Taste of Honey*).

Theatre Workshop's second sin is that it believes that the art of the theatre lies in a fusion of the work of the writer, actor, dancer, painter, musician: in other words, what is important is the meaning of the play as conveyed to the audience by the combined talents of a number of artists in different media, while the brilliance of the actors, sets, costumes, or production is merely secondary. Audiences love to applaud a showy piece of acting, even if the meaning of the play is not clarified by it (Vivien Leigh and Claire Bloom in *Duel of Angels*): or a pretty set, for its intrinsic prettiness and not for its particular relevance to a scene (Reece Pemberton's Riviera set for *A Touch of the Sun*): or a bravura production (Peter Brook's Stratford *Tempest*). Harold Hobson unconsciously summed up this attitude when he wrote of Theatre Workshop's visit to the Paris Festival in 1955, complaining that no West End company or knighted actor, and neither Stratford nor the Old Vic, was going: ". . . The solitary English representative in Paris will be Theatre Workshop, honourably known near Bow and on the fringes of the Edinburgh Festival, but a stranger to the central tradition of the English theatre. It is fortunate for the theatrical reputation of this country that, in the face of strong competition, Theatre Workshop will be able to show so fine and interesting an actor as Mr Harry Corbett." The Parisian critics and audiences, strong in the Copeau-Baty-Jouvet-Dullin tradition, of which our theatre knows nothing, knew very well that what matters is not an actor's fine solo performance, but the presentation of a play so that it rocks the audience back in their seats. Theatre Workshop did exactly this with *Volpone* and *Arden of Faversham*, and received the acclaim of Paris, to the mystification of English critics.

There is, of course, no positive merit in shoddy acting or designing, and shoddiness, particularly in minor acting roles, is an accusation frequently thrown up against Theatre Workshop. The accusation is undoubtedly justified, but largely irrelevant, in view of the company's preoccupation with the play rather than with fine performances: I can think of no example of a play produced by Theatre Workshop in which the meaning of the play was obscured by indifferent acting. Kenneth Tynan, in spite of his warning in *Declaration* that "an ear for a well-turned phrase, an eye for a good performance and an entire absence of convictions" is not enough, was guilty of false values in his review of the simultaneous productions in 1955 of *Richard II* by Theatre Workshop and the Old Vic. Joan Littlewood's production had rough edges in the minor roles and costumes, but the core of the play was thrust forward with passionate conviction, and it was impossible to fail to be excited, to think about the play and what it meant. By contrast, Benthall's production, elegantly dressed and spoken, remained quite dead. Yet Mr Tynan awarded the laurels to the Old Vic – on points.

Unable to offer attractive money prospects, Theatre Workshop finds much of its acting personnel in relatively raw material, to be moulded and developed by Joan Littlewood herself: and this is the material she prefers, considering established actors to be too set in their ways to be of use to her. The result has been a body of young actors with a bold, vigorous approach, free of mannerisms and falsity, not given to "poetic diction" or posturing, and the astonishing development within the company of such actors as Harry H. Corbett, Maxwell Shaw, Gerard Dynevor, Barbara Brown, Howard Goorney, Dudley Foster, Olive MacFarland, Murray Melvin, Peter Smallwood and Frances Cuka, is a strong argument in favour of a permanent company, where actors can not only extend their range in a constant variety of roles, but are under the firm control and direction of a master of the calibre of Joan Littlewood. London is full of young actors who have given proof of outstanding abilities, who are not yet fully developed, and who drift from part to part, allowing their development as actors to be subject to a mere accumulation of roles and years: Brian Bedford, Michael Bryant, James Kenney, Jeremy Brett, Peter Woodthorpe, Joan Plowright, Dudy Nimmo – to name only a few. Yet I can think of no example of a young actor, having achieved some recognition in the West End, who has then joined Theatre Workshop. Why? Lack of interest? Not enough money? Fear of a theatre which has avowed Leftist beliefs? Desire to become a virtuoso?

Of the accusation of shoddiness in its settings, Theatre Workshop is gloriously free, possessing probably the finest designer and lighting director working in the English theatre today. John Bury has a complete understanding of what Joan Littlewood is trying to do, and his settings, in their starkness, are platforms from which her productions are launched at the audience. Their bareness is not a merit rising out of material necessity, but a merit in itself, using the whole range of the stage, vertically and horizontally, to frame the play without detracting from it by unnecessary trappings. The naturalistic lamp-posts and railings of *The Quare Fellow*, emphasized by leaving the stage open to the back wall, so that its bricks and central heating pipes underlined the bleak solidity of the prison; the five narrow black curtains hanging to a chequered floor – the entire set for *The Duchess of Malfi* – formed a dark maze from the depths of which Bosola wove his Websterian villainies; and what could lend more richness to any play than the set for *Edward II* – a vast map of England stretched across the tilted floor of the stage, the extent of Edward's kingdom, and across which he dies. John Bury's lighting, too, becomes a positive element in the play, and not merely an illumination of the actors' faces, or a suggestion of sunset and sunrise: in *Arden of Faversham*, lit almost entirely from the back of the stage, the acting area contained unspecified depths which gave a nightmarish quality to the play. And lighting, particularly in the Elizabethan plays, is used to ensure smooth and rapid continuity: actors emerge into a pool of light, or disappear into a barrier thrown from the wings, so that scene can follow scene rapidly and without confusion, distinctions of time and locality being blocked off by light.

Now, after five years of achievement in the East End, Theatre Workshop is faced with an indifferent public, and a refusal by the Arts Council to continue its subsidy under present conditions. What next? Henry Adler, in a letter to *The Times*, suggested that to remain at Stratford was merely romantic, and that the company should move to Chelsea or thereabouts, where its audience was to be found. (A curious parallel may be drawn here with Brecht's failure to impose his theatre on the working classes of East Germany, but success with the Western intellectuals.) Joan Littlewood has stated that her aim is to create a popular theatre, giving as examples the Shakespearean theatre and the travelling theatres. Though little enough is known about the conditions of the Elizabethan theatre, it seems evident that the plays were addressed primarily to the Court and nobility, while the groundlings were thrown the sop of the clowns; in the travelling theatres, the plays demanded and offered were of the cheapest thrill-and-sob stuff. The point is, perhaps, that you cannot create a healthy theatre for one section of the audience only: at one end you have West End cups and saucers, at the other, nude revues. Brecht's experience seems to indicate that in the theatre, as in the political field, revolution begins with the intellectual and works downward. Nevertheless, even if, in terms of his own aims, Brecht's enterprise might be said to have been a failure, the enormous influence of his work and ideas throughout the world is indicative rather of success. At the moment Theatre Workshop is an East End oasis of theatrical vigour, integrity, enterprise and excitement. If Stratford is impossible, perhaps there is much to be said for a move into town, where, provided it could preserve its own qualities intact, Theatre Workshop might begin to impose those qualities on the West End theatre, driving out the Old Vic-ery, *Dry Rots* and *Touch of the Suns*, and establishing the *Taste of Honeys* and *Arden of Faversham*s.

[SEPTEMBER 1958]

COMEDY OF MENACE *by Irving Wardle*

The past three years have witnessed the arrival of several playwrights who have been tentatively lumped together as the "non-naturalists" or "abstractionists". They are an oddly assorted group: among them there is one established novelist, a schoolmaster, and an actor; only one bread-and-butter playwright. They are separated by age, occupation, political opinion and experience of the stage. But their works are all, in one sense or another, comedies. And it is the common drift of several dissimilar talents which has given rise to this article: the writers have set up a theatrical climate without getting involved in anything you could call a movement.

I want to discuss four of them – Nigel Dennis, David

Campton, N. F. Simpson and Harold Pinter. This list is not exhaustive. I am excluding Ann Jellicoe because I have not seen her work; and John Mortimer whose recent arrival as a dramatist (even though it was immediately tagged with the Ionesco label) has nothing to do with the prevailing theatrical climate. Mr Mortimer's wryly compassionate studies of failure and loneliness could have been written, and would have been welcomed, at any time in the past forty years.

Evidence of the comic trend peculiar to the present experimental theatre is also supplied by playwrights who – either through reticence or as an interruption of an otherwise profitable career – have turned out a solitary play of this kind. Such plays are David Bird's *Tom*, Giles Cooper's *Mathray Beacon*, and a piece of significant juvenilia by John McGrath called *A Man Has Two Fathers*.

This ramshackle allegory forms a useful starting point. Although there are no major writers among the quartet I mentioned, each of them is too pronounced an individualist to turn out a play that can be exhibited as an introductory specimen of a theatrical trend; but when you come across a straightforward piece of derivative work, such as *A Man Has Two Fathers*, it is plain that the trend is there.

Mr McGrath is a third-year undergraduate who seems to have seen everything, and when his play appeared at the Oxford Playhouse in June, one's first impulse was to write it off as a ragbag of other men's work. Mechanically anticlerical, it contains a money-spinning Catholic novelist, and a priest who delivers a sermon on spitting; its most positive figure is a tramp-philosopher whose chief delight is to retire to his dug-out and assume a pre-natal position. However, in atmosphere the play was wholly consistent. In its exhibition of fluctuating identities, its satire, its comic preoccupation with cliché, and its surrealist action, a note of menace is constant. And when foreboding is resolved in an otherwise inexplicable holocaust, the quality of the comedy remains undisturbed.

"Something is going to go, baby,
And it won't be your stamp-collection.
Boom!"

This squib of Cyril Connolly's, more quintessentially Audenesque than any couplet written by Oxford's present Professor of Poetry, epitomizes the habit of oblique, doom-laden irony that has been carried over from the 'thirties into the experimental theatre of this decade.

Coming to inspect the four exponents of the comedy of menace that I have chosen, close stylistic affinity is apparent between Campton, Simpson, and Pinter – so close that it may seem arbitrary to have brought Nigel Dennis into their company. But in fact he is the arch-abstractionist; his plays, like those of David Campton, are parables that invite you to gaze at a naked theme through the transparencies of plot and character. Both writers are moralists whose habit is to take a short cut to generalized statement. We have yet to find out whether Nigel Dennis is a dramatist at all, for his inventiveness is tethered so slavishly to the business of illustrating an argument that the resultant work is more a rhetorical exercise than an organic growth.

Cards of Identity, all the same, bubbles over with engaging eccentrics and intellectual callisthenics which keep the play from sinking. But in *The Making of Moo* argument is all, and you are confronted with the spectacle – depressingly common in satire nowadays – of a writer shooting down characters without bothering first to bring them to life. This is the penalty Mr Dennis pays for writing in a realist idiom; and – box-office considerations apart – it is hard to understand why he ever adopted the idiom at all, for it requires a respectful curiosity about individual behaviour; he has yet to display any such curiosity.

A more successful practitioner of dehumanized comedy is David Campton, though admittedly in the plays of his that I know he is not hindered, as Mr Dennis is, by having anything out of the ordinary to say. The Campton plays are easily reduced to brief statements – the bomb is coming; politicians are dangerous fools; the English? well, just look at them – and so on. Simplification is no drawback in the theatre, and Mr Campton is an uncommonly resourceful craftsman. His language, which is largely a satiric distortion of cliché, never becomes so smart that the ear cannot follow it; he is, in fact, the only writer I know of who has adapted Joyce's verbal techniques for the theatre. In *Out of the Flying Pan*, for instance, almost every line of the text turns another diplomatic platitude upside down, but whenever word-play approaches obscurity ("grasping swine" for "glass of wine") it is repeated in a way that drives the meaning home and intensifies the irony in doing so.

Non-naturalism of this kind begins when its subject is well enough understood to be communicated in dramatic shorthand. It occurs at the turning point between criticism and satire; consequently it is obsessed with cliché, and tends to be practised by lynx-eyed verbal stylists. Its chief limitation is that when it takes an unfamiliar object of attack it declines into impenetrability. As Mr Campton's target is usually a barn door he is not hindered by the limitation: his plays are brief, elegantly constructed, and they accomplish what they set out to do.

N. F. Simpson and Harold Pinter, though their handling of language resembles Mr Campton's, are not limited in the same way. They are not concerned with putting over a message; and in their plays it is impossible to detach what is said from the way in which it is said. They seem to work, this is to say, like poets – beginning with a *donnée* and developing the action by a process of exploiting internal clues. Their characters possess a more complex consistency than do the facile abstractions of Campton and Nigel Dennis.

There is no point in pressing any exceptionally close affinity between these two writers; but, considering that Mr Simpson is a schoolmaster in his forties and Mr Pinter an actor not yet thirty, the similarities that do exist between them are worth noticing. Consider their handling of a parallel situation. In *A Resounding Tinkle* the craziness of the dialogue is arrived at by inventing a series of outlandish conventions and treating them as entirely normal. In *The Birthday Party* Mr Pinter goes to work in a similar way. He presents a threateningly melodramatic action and allows two of his principal figures to remain totally unresponsive to its atmosphere. Technically both writers are masters of the heightened cliché; and in their plays comedy of menace is arrived at without explicit theme or the intercession of the dramatist as *raisonneur*.

From their plays you might get the idea that both writers are saying the same thing – that people, the lower-middle class in particular, get used to anything, and that this is dangerous. But the very scorn implicit in that statement demonstrates its inaccuracy, for the figures in the plays are too richly idiosyncratic to have been born of contempt. The texts are not susceptible to any single interpretation, and once we begin to consider the real components of the plays – distinct from themes which can be plausibly foisted on them – the close resemblances between Mr Simpson and Mr Pinter are at an end.

In *A Resounding Tinkle* the playwright evokes menace by representing a state of mental attrition. Nothing can surprise any of the characters because they have lost all powers of deduction – what happens is accepted as a fact without cause or implication. Uncle Ted arrives having changed sex; someone knocks on the door and asks the husband to form a government. These events meet only with the verbal recognition that they have occurred. As it happens they are innocuous; but the response would be the same if plague broke out, or if the zoo had sent scorpions instead of a docile snake curled in a cigar box.

Highly entertaining though the verbal inventiveness of the play is, it suffers by its very consistency; its underlying clarity is manifest in the characters, each of whom view the world in precisely the same way, and consequently they cannot impinge dramatically on one another – they are confined to executing verbal arabesques which make the same point over and over again.

In *The Birthday Party* Mr Pinter goes to the opposite extreme with a violence approaching anarchy – but even at its most dislocated there is more theatrical bite in the work than in Mr Simpson's unbroken suavity. One of the accusations against *The Birthday Party* when it arrived in London was that it lacked Simpsonian wit. The objection was not sensible. Wit of that kind emerges only when characters share a pattern of behaviour and are devoted more to con-

versation than to action; *Tinkle*, in fact, is an exotic exercise
in the comedy of manners. In *The Birthday Party* characters
are drawn together by the action and by nothing else; there
are three groups – the assailants, the victim and the by-
standers. It is in the relationships between the groups – not
how they behave in isolation – that the play's force resides.
Each group views the action in a different way; for the assailants it is a smoothly handled job; for the victim it is the
realization of his constant nightmare; and for the landlady
it is the agreeable visit of two nicely spoken gentlemen.

The Birthday Party is the only play of Mr Pinter's that I
have seen; but to judge from descriptions of his other plays,
The Room and *The Dumb Waiter*, he is a writer dogged by
one image – the womb. His main characters tend first to
appear entrenched in a secure retreat from which they are
eventually torn by some agent of external malignancy. Mr
Pinter acknowledges three literary influences – Beckett,
Kafka and American gangster films; and *The Birthday Party*
exemplifies the type of comic menace which gave rise to this
article. For in the play, menace, itself a meretricious and
easily manufactured fictional device, stands for something
more substantial: destiny. Comedy enables the committed
agents and victims of destruction to come on and off duty;
to joke about the situation while oiling a revolver; to display
absurd or endearing features behind their masks of implac-
able resolution; to meet, as Mr Pinter allows them to do, in
paper hats for a game of blind man's buff.

Destiny handled in this way – not as an austere exercise in
classicism, but as an incurable disease which one forgets
about most of the time and whose lethal reminders may take
the form of a joke – is an apt dramatic motif for an age of
conditioned behaviour in which orthodox man is a willing
collaborator in his own destruction.

[SEPTEMBER 1958]

CHICKEN SOUP WITH BARLEY
Review by John Arden

Arnold Wesker (in *Chicken Soup With Barley* from the Belgrade Theatre, Coventry) has written about vanishing virtues. Tolerance, enthusiasm, and warmth of heart are his message: but he is under no illusions as to the difficulty of achieving them. This play has been widely praised, and I have space to do little beyond remarking that this is the way "Social" plays ought to be written. The decline of his Jewish family is excellently rhymed with the loss of faith (in Western Europe anyway) in the ideals of International Communism, and at nearly every point in the play the personal situation is reinforced by, and reinforces, the public one. There was a most happy lack of the normal "Family Chronicle" plot clichés. No one went out of the house to be murdered by a mob, run over by a bus, have a miscarriage or whatever – all the big events happened a long way off, in Spain, in Russia, in Hungary – and hurt all the more for that. The central role of the mother was miscast and lacked the full warmth she should have had: but Frank Finlay as the father was so real that the rest could have acted in Swahili and still the play would have convinced. It demands a full London production, with all the rehearsal time and selective casting that Coventry could not hope to provide.

[SEPTEMBER 1958]

LIVE LIKE PIGS *Review by Richard Findlater*

What happens when a clan of vagrant "mumpers", evicted from the comfortable, anarchic squalor of their slum tramcar, are directed into a council house on a new urban estate? That is the starting-point of John Arden's *Live Like Pigs*, recently staged at the Royal Court, in which the author contrasts the Welfare State's misfits and its prisoners, as the wild animals defy the recently tamed. To pick holes in both play and production is easy enough. By employing Mr A. L.

Lloyd to appear before the curtain every now and then, hollering a few meaningful snatches of loaded balladry, the Court tagged the play with a misleading, folksy sermonizing. Such MacColleries belong to another play and another platform. Mr Arden should also be persuaded that some of his text is expendable: the play needs pruning. More significantly, he overwrites in depth as well as length; the fatal fluency of O'Casey seemed to me to overshadow some of this prolix poeticizing on a first mishearing. (Can't something be done, (a) to insulate the back stalls of the Court from the thunder of the Square's traffic and (b) to reconcile Mr Wilfrid Lawson to the limitations of the human ear?)

By going for his characters, moreover, to such extravagantly lower depths, Mr Arden runs the risk of being charged with romanticizing The People and dodging one of the modern dramatists' main problems – making the inarticulate talk. Wooden-legged sea-captains (a proletarian Shotover?), gypsies who hiss with anger and howl in the night with loneliness, tarts who discuss the pox with Elizabethan dread and humour – these are scarcely typical specimens of the Opportunity State, tinged blue or pink. But does this matter? What *Live Like Pigs* reveals is an exciting, formidable talent for putting flesh-and-blood people on the stage with a racy, poetic, turbulent vitality that recalls Mr Arden's Elizabethan models. Breaking through the class-barrier, he also breaks open genteel conventions about language and love on the stage for the underprivileged.

Inside this play there is the tide of that Orwellian sentimentality about the non-bourgeoisie which washes over so much new writing. Inevitably, it surges up in the theatre when, at long last, plays reach the stage which treat the lower orders neither as stooges nor puppets but as human beings with the stuff of drama. Yet in Mr Arden this smoochy cult of the no-collar man is under control; and his people are projected with the help of excellent casting. Admirable performances came, in particular, from Alan Dobie and Anna Manahan, whose blazing, brooding power helped to cover up some of the worst mock-Tudor patches in Mr Arden's rhetorical philosophizing. I want to hear most of the play again;

and I want to see Miss Manahan in action. Who will write a part for the nearest thing to Magnani on the English stage?

[NOVEMBER 1958]

THE HOSTAGE *Review by Penelope Gilliatt*

"The IRA's out of date because of the H-bomb. It's scaring all the little bombs." Brendan Behan's tragic-extravaganza, *The Hostage* (Theatre Workshop), is about the IRA skirmish, but the larger lunacy of the Bomb keeps breaking through. A young member of the IRA is due to be hanged by the British in Belfast, so an eighteen-year-old Cockney National Serviceman is taken as a hostage and smuggled to Dublin. He is parked in a rotting old carcass of a house that has dwindled from a revolutionary HQ into a brothel. The vestigial elements who live there perk up gratefully. A prisoner about the place again is a shot in the arm to the old caretaker, whose last shot, in the leg, was during the Troubles. ("Here are your instructions. After you've committed them to memory you'll destroy them," says a brisk young IRA officer. "I'll *swallow* them," says the caretaker, thrilled but haughty.)

The game soon gets confused and out of hand. As an Imperialist image the hostage lets them down. This etiolated rabbit – a good, cheerful, expectant performance by Murray Melvin – fails to fill out the symbolic figure of the enemy. In the end he is shot, by mistake, and even the hottest rebels know the fruitlessness of it.

The Hostage is constantly swivelling into the reflexive, knowing itself, mocking itself, and occasionally washing its hands of itself. It is less coherent and less cohesive than *The Quare Fellow*, but the plea is clear. No follow-my-leader games. Innocence is no excuse. Apart from its shape, which keeps on throwing out a thrashing new limb in spite of Joan Littlewood's strong-willed production, *The Hostage* is Dublin's *Dreigroschenoper*. It is abrasive, obstreperous, funny, and serious. Instead of Kurt Weill there is a fiddler who plays any tunes he can lay his hands on – a hymn, *Auld Lang Syne* – as a setting for the impudent lyrics. (The licensing of this play may be a penance for the Henry Chapman affair. Lines of no reverence about such figureheads as the Queen, Dulles, Peter Townsend, Uffa Fox and the Virgin Mary are all there intact.) The set of the house is just skin and bone and works admirably, with a raised room for the progress of the story, and a space downstage for the characters to turn on themselves and sing the interjections.

The house is crawling with dodos. The head of the band is Monsewer (Glynn Edwards), an English bishop's son who learnt an impeccable Irish at Oxford that baffles the locals. There is a queer in a satin dressing-gown who is known as Princess Grace, a twittery religious maniac called Miss Gilchrist ("the ghillie of the Lord"), an arachnoid secret-service agent, and a Negro in a kilt. They are played respectively by Dudley Sutton, Eileen Kennally, Robin Chapman and Roy Barnett, all eccentrically and some frenetically. As Meg, the only balanced whore in the place, Avis Bunnage has an Irish accent that comes and goes but a steady grip on the specialized morality of the character ("Take your hand off me. I keep that for me business"). Celia Salkeld, a grave beauty with the low forehead and cygneous neck of a pre-Raphaelite, plays the maid who falls for the hostage. Their love-duet – "I will give you a watch and chain If you will marry me" – ends pragmatically with "But first I think that we should see-ee If we fit each other," and a run for a bed.

Language hasn't had an outing like this since *The Quare Fellow*. The English habitually write as though they were alone and cold at ten in the morning; the Irish write in a state of flushed gregariousness at an eternal opening time. "There are two kinds of good men," says the caretaker (Howard Goorney). "There's the earnest religious kind and there's the laughing boys." *The Hostage* is a huge belly-laugh that secretes enough morality for a satire. It puts politics where they belong: in the midst of life, where they seldom appear in English theatre.

[NOVEMBER 1958]

LET BATTLE COMMENCE! *by Arnold Wesker*

After many years of writing I have written something which has been accepted. After burrowing in the dark I emerge and look around. It was a play I wrote, I am in the theatre. It could have been a volume of poetry, a novel, a book of short stories or a film script, but it seems I was destined to say best what I wanted to say in a play. For the moment, at least, I am a playwright.

I have arrived knowing exactly what I want to do, but how I am to do it, or whether I can, is the challenge my art presents. The "what" and the "how" and indeed the "why" are the purpose of this article.

I want to write about people in a way that will somehow give them an insight to an aspect of life which they may not have had before; and further, I want to impart to them some of the enthusiasm I have for that life. I want to teach.

I want to write my plays not only for the class of people who acknowledge plays to be a legitimate form of expression, but for those to whom the phrase "form of expression" may mean nothing whatsoever. It is the bus driver, the housewife, the miner and the Teddy Boy to whom I should like to address myself.

There we have three statements which, when I think about them from one point of view, seem pretty outrageous. But do not let us assume a cynical air too soon, let us think about them. I was brought up in an atmosphere where the bus driver, the housewife, the miner and the Teddy Boy were the people that mattered. Later on, as I came to meet others whose education and social background separated them from the people I'm talking about, I was regarded as a romantic – the ineffectual angel type, you know. But what was worse I was accused of audacity! For consider, who was *I* to teach the man in the street, and what the hell was there to teach him anyway? Was he unhappy, did he need teaching, or did he want me to poke my nose into his life? – which is one way of looking at any art: an intrusion of the artist's personality into your life. How dare I assume that what I believed was life was any better than what they believed was life. So I paused and considered this, and felt duly ashamed of my pomposity.

There was Mr Smith. He was married, he had children, a home and a good job. He went to the pictures once a week, to the pub twice a week, a football match, a whist drive or a darts tournament. He has his friends, he could laugh and make people laugh, and in the summer he had a good three weeks' holiday at the seaside or in a caravan. What more could I give him, what more did I want of him? I did not then, nor do I now, consider any of those activities lamentable, unworthy or a waste of time. This was human activity, Mr Smith was happy. Why should I want him to be interested in politics, history, music, art or literature?

And then I left school and found that I was working and living among them. (God! I wish one did not have to talk about "them" and "us"). And I discovered that there were aspects of character beyond the cockney's humour and the farm-labourer's phlegmatic contentment. One day, Mr Smith had a row with his wife, something was going wrong with married life and he could not understand. All he could do was shout abuse and accusations at her. He was not equipped to handle the situation. Then there was a dispute at work and he was asked out on strike, he went but was not sure why. Suddenly one of his children did something wrong and was taken to court; Mr Smith woke up to find a human being who was part of him by all that was natural, but yet, who was this human being? Why had his child done this? He could not understand it. Shortly afterwards he found himself unemployed, there was a slump, the papers raved about an economic crisis, he did not know what this was or how it came about. But then these things were not to be understood by the likes of him. When the war came he was called up and his son was killed. Now who was responsible for this? Oh well it's all over, home again. But home wasn't the same. Everything was broken up. Funny how things changed. There were his friends, the pubs, the holidays – but he was bored more easily now, quick to take offence and row with his wife. The jolly things were a little stale – but then that was life, stale and depressing. The new generation don't think so though –

still, we never could teach them anything. Mustn't grumble – make the best of it – any sort of best. And so he died, not having had a glimpse of anything that might have told him what it was all about, not having understood much. At each crisis in his life, somehow, he had found he was not equipped to handle it – and not only that, he had never understood the nature of that crisis. It was not simply that no one had given him tools for living, but no one had told him he *needed* any tools beyond a job that would earn him money to fulfil responsibilities.

"Tools", perhaps, is the key word. I think that is how I look upon art – as a tool, equipment for the enjoyment of living, for its better understanding. And it is with this definition that I shall approach my writing.

But equip him to deal with life? Surely that is the job of education? Right! It is! But one of the fundamental concepts in art is that all great art is a product of its own time. Now, I feel that our time is one where education is not merely scant and inadequate but is bankrupt of any values; therefore the art we must produce is one that struggles to fill that gap in education, that struggles to rouse interest in the world and persuade one to have faith in life. An art, in fact, that establishes values. After all, what is valued today, what is sacred? The Queen? A football coupon? Even the home and family is dying of nervous strain. Life certainly is not valued, the last war numbed the senses of us all. The function of art changes – when education is doing what it should then we shall write about other things and in a different way. *So we are agreed that there is a general malaise.*

Perhaps Osborne, Tynan, Anderson or Logue want to do it and are not capable – but somebody must be. Is John Berger the man, with his programmes on ITV talking about Léger and workers on a building site? Perhaps it needs the *Daily Mirror* to sponsor a "Public meet your artist" programme on the television screen. I'm not sure. But it must surely be obvious that it is not enough simply to write our little bit and trust to luck it will reach someone, somewhere. We must pick up our poems, our plays and films, tuck them under our arms and go out to the public and do battle with them. It should not be necessary, I know, but it is, these are our sort of times. Perhaps it is our bad luck – it is also our challenge.

Now let us go a little deeper. Here is a long extract from a letter from a writer friend, Dai Vaughan. Apart from the fact that he has written better prose than I have done he seems to me to have stated the issue so well as to need no further embellishment from me:

"Just look into your own experience," he tells me, "and I think you will agree that one of the easiest ways of arousing someone's hostility is to try – from the most selfless motives imaginable – to introduce him to some experience from which you have derived great enjoyment. Talk to a concert-goer about the pleasures of jazz, or to a jazz-lover about the pleasures of concert music, and you will meet not with gratitude or even with 'enlightened interest' but with a tremendous barrier of resentment. Why is this? It is because our cultural tastes are an expression – almost the most public expression – of our fundamental values; and such values are expressed not only in what we like but also in what we choose to reject. If a man dislikes jazz, this is not some accident which has befallen him; it is something essential to his coming to terms with life in the way he has chosen. Let us be clear about the use of the word 'enrichment': it is quite OK for me to speak of the arts enriching my experience (since they do so in so far as I have accepted them); but to speak of my enriching someone *else's* experience *through* art is false, since what I am doing is to attack the very roots of his being.

"So let's be honest about it. Let's not regard ourselves as scattering grain to chickens, but admit instead that what we want to do is to undermine people's existing values and impose our own upon them. (If we believe in our own values we will accept this as a responsibility – as part of the struggle for survival, conducted on a new plane.) Let's drop the air of philanthropy and the talk about 'broadening people's horizons'. If we respect men, then we must respect them enough to be willing to fight them and not be upset if they don't come to heel at the cry of 'enrichment'. And if this thought intimidates us, then for God's sake let's admit that what we really want is an esoteric culture."

And then further on in the letter: "But with the working class you encounter people who have learned through a couple of hundred years of bourgeois culture to equate all thought and intellectualism with the ivory tower. You face the man who says, 'I don't understand long words' and implies thereby that long words are irrelevant. There is no mental defect here. The same man will have the clearest understanding of the permutations necessary for filling in a football coupon (a thing no one has ever succeeded in making intelligible to me), and he would understand long words soon enough if you could convince him that they *weren't* irrelevant. But this is just the problem. And it is not just a case of confronting a class which mistrusts the intellectual. You are confronting a multitude of individuals for each of whom anti-intellectualism is an inextricable element in his adjustment to life, so that what you are attempting for each of these people is something of the magnitude of a religious conversion."

I agree. It is rather frightening when put like that – a religious conversion. Yet are not the values an artist holds his religion? Surely each work of art is an attempt to convert anyway? Ought we not to acknowledge this? But even so this is only a beginning. What now is to be our action?

Looking at it personally I see two problems. Firstly how is this to affect my actual writing; secondly how do I attempt to establish this kind of contact with my audience? Let us look at the first problem. My play, *Chicken Soup with Barley*, is about a family who, all except the mother, lose faith in an ideal. It is also about the relationships between the people of that family. The family relations part of the play will be easily understood, but with the question of ideals it is a case of convincing the audience that to be concerned about disillusionment *is to be concerned about anything worthwhile anyway*. I accept that the language has to be a language they understand – and because it is art it has to be ordinary in a way that is poetic and not banal. But beyond that it has not merely to assume values which are foreign to them but to assume values in a way which suggests that values are worth assuming *at all*. I must not use the arguments of a bourgeois society but the facile, blind arguments, the platitudinous phrases which are the barricades of the man in the street to anything new, and break these down one by one first of all. In other words, I cannot simply *write* plays, I have to write them in such a way as to suggest a play is worthwhile writing for something more than telling a tale. Consider half a dozen words like irony, satire, enrichment, commitment, fulfilment, cultural bankruptcy. These are fields in which we wander at ease. But writing in the way I want to write means that I cannot assume the power of these words, I have to explain them somehow. It is as basic as that. And at the same time it has to be art. I do not say I have succeeded in my first play, but I have learned in time for my next one. And so we come to the second problem.

Having tucked my plays under my arm and stepped out – where do I go? Well, we are in the midst of a new movement, ideas are stirring and the artist is beginning to realize that the man in the street affects his life so he must affect theirs. I know there are always new movements, that they fade out and that new ones appear. I do not take this as a sign of the fickleness of the intellectual or as a sign of the inherent thick skin of the ordinary man. Rather I take it as a sign of inevitable human activity. There will always be problems to solve, but it is when there are no new movements to meet the problems that I shall be sick, for then we shall have stagnated and poisoned ourselves. Where then is the new movement and what has it produced?

It has produced the Universities and Left Review Club, Free Cinema, The Royal Court Theatre, our Civic theatre, *Encore* magazine and various resistance groups up and down the country. In addition to this we have the diverse products of our own industrial and commercial society. Namely: television, the co-op societies, blocks of council flats with community centres *and* committees of those communities, trade unions and the *Daily Mirror*. Frankly, I despise the *Mirror*. It claims to be a paper of the people and yet, apart from shouting loudly in a language everyone can understand – which is all right, don't misunderstand me – yet it doesn't shout about things which can benefit the life of any one member of the public. Nevertheless it claims to be a paper of the people, for and by the people. We could call its bluff. Let us challenge it to spend its money on sponsoring a film by Lindsay Anderson or a play at the Royal Court Theatre for its own readers. Let it open its pages to the Royal Court writers' groups or the new and young politicians of the Universities and Left Review Club. It can get together its own Deb's ball, let it call youth together on a conference about problems concerning themselves. Well, why not? We have called the *New Statesman* to account, why not the *Mirror*?

Next we have the trade unions – rich and powerful. Primarily the purpose of the union is to protect and further the interests of its members. But what can be the virtues of protecting the interests of people who are apathetic to living because no one involves them in living? Could not ULR send its speakers to union members in order to discuss industrial problems? Or could not the Royal Court suggest to the AEU that it sponsors a play for its members? Why not a film about them? Ford does it, and Shell, and Schweppes have financed a play. And what of the communities of people living in blocks of flats? Who will approach the LCC to help organize a series of film shows or one-act plays in the community halls where the artist can go and talk and discuss his art with the people? What about those bastions of working-class people in the co-op societies? Here exist groups waiting for us. Discussion groups, film societies, drama and literary circles; we could be using them, we should be using them. And lastly there is television – well, if we can be exciting enough, television might have us, and there is our public, so hungry that it cannot wait to switch on its set.

There, has it sounded like high-class snobbery? But why should it? There is nothing wrong with rock 'n' roll, there is only something wrong with it every day; three cheers for the whist drive and the football game, but God help the man who cannot enjoy something more – just as the man who likes the classics only and closes his ears to all other music is a bore and is only half alive. Have I made it sound easy? Of course it is not. The greatest problem, even when the principle is agreed upon, is the one of organization. Who can do it?

Are we capable? And having set my vision I may not be big enough for it. I do not know. I shall learn as I go along. It means starting from scratch and breaking our hearts again and again, but at least something would be happening. And England would know that its community was alive and kicking and critical and eager.

[NOVEMBER 1958]

THE WORLD OF PAUL SLICKEY
Review by Charles Marowitz

After the boo-bellowing, razz-riddled opening night of *The World of Paul Slickey*, John Osborne probably suspected he had dropped a great big brick of a musical. What he may not have suspected was that the following day the British press would collectively take hold of that brick and methodically beat his brains out. This, in point of fact, is what they did.

The great point about *Paul Slickey* is not that it is a badly hashed, anti-musical comedy, but that it is a weapon, naïvely provided by *the* angry young man himself, with which a fed-up British bourgeoisie can clobber that surly, intellectual movement which has been razzing it since the end of the war. In knocking *Paul Slickey*, the press is knocking the raucous Ban-the-Bomb enthusiasts who flocked to Trafalgar Square and "made such a bother"; is knocking the anti-royalist Royal Court clique who glory in plays about proletarian conflicts set in working-class kitchens; is knocking, in fact, that whole young and vital stratum in British society which has given new life to this battered old Empire.

That is why one cannot simply review *Slickey* as an ill-fated musical by England's most important new playwright. *Slickey* has triggered the reaction against the anti-Establishment agitators, and the Establishment has responded with all the venom and spite which has been accumulating since the concept of an almighty Establishment was first attacked.

Social furore notwithstanding, *Paul Slickey* is a bad musical. Impudent, satirical, profane, revolutionary, unique and bad. Bad because it is generated by the kind of passion which can best be realized in a straight prose-drama. Bad because this passion has already *been* realized in *Look Back in Anger*, *The Entertainer* and *Epitaph for George Dillon*. Bad because in loading it with too much ammunition, Osborne has spread his gunshot and inflicted flesh-wounds where he should have been lethal. And, primarily, bad because the newness and originality is totally peripheral. The stock conventions of musical comedy are all here, and they are dutifully observed though theme and treatment would have us believe Rodgers and Hammerstein are alien to its progeny. The boldness is nothing more than a tasteless audacity (one number is aesthetically titled "I Want to Screw, Screw, Screw the Income Tax Man"); an audacity which resembles esoteric University revues so strikingly that *it* and professionalism are about as far apart as Oxford and the West End.

In this morass of a musical in which lyrics are so over-elaborate that putting them to music becomes a kind of wrestling match between singer and composer, it is a little pointless to note that Kenneth Macmillan's choreography is usually brisk and generally superior to the songs it follows; it is a little pointless to report that Marie Lohr, by dint of a miraculous neutrality, moves through the mire and emerges unblackened. As for Slickey himself (played by Dennis Lotis with a kind of Pal Joey stringency), this appears to be the fulfilment of Osborne's surgically artistic policy. The process of castrating his heroes began with *Look Back in Anger*. Jimmy Porter merely suffered an injury; Archie Rice lost *one*, and George Dillon came close to losing both. Paul Slickey, miraculously, is totally unencumbered – which proves if nothing else, that artistic consistency can exist without artistic accomplishment.

The essential failing in *The World of Paul Slickey* is rooted in a confusion of form and content. What Osborne wanted to do could not be done in the musical-comedy form; mainly because that form condenses and confines whatever material is placed within it. The musical-comedy form can be likened to a great valise; you fill it to capacity at the risk of not being able to lift it. The straight play was too narrow for Osborne's

multifarious purposes, and the straight comedy, too emotionally restricted for a malice that did not always lend itself to
satire. A Piscatorian Epic Play might have held it, or, if such
things were still being written, an expressionist-drama. But
Osborne's artistic inclination was towards the musical; the
tragedy is that his material did not share that inclination.

Since the opening night fiasco, many segments of an out-
raged public have taken *Slickey* to be the death-knell of some
vaguely defined, overly vocal movement. This is wishful
thinking. A thousand fiascos of the same dimension as *Slickey*
will not turn the tide of the British theatre. The drawing-
room set and its concomitant mentality is permanently
threatened by what is implicit in *Paul Slickey*. The shallow
playing of literary shallowness which has maintained the
British theatre for almost a century, still stands in danger of
immediate overthrow. The murmurings in Chelsea, Stratford
East and a number of other outposts much less publicized,
will not abate because of *Paul Slickey*. Unexpected raids
from unfamiliar quarters will continue to upset the composure
of the Shaftesbury Avenue citadel.

In an art movement, there is no such thing as a leader.
Every artist is his own leader and every work its own personal revolution. And in mid-twentieth century England,
with a handful of writers and only two or three theatres, that
revolution has begun and nothing in the world can stop it!

[SEPTEMBER 1959]

AT EASE IN A BRIGHT RED TIE
by John Whiting

Mr Gaitskell, who wore a bright red tie and a large red carnation,
spoke persuasively and was at his ease throughout. Report in
The Observer, July 12, 1959.

I am not a Marxist. Karl Marx, towards the end of his life.

The main engagement took place in Sloane Square. There was

a complementary action in the far east, at Stratford. These separate forces were never co-ordinated. The east relied very much on mercenaries recruited from another country. The west, although at one time there was an uneasy and short-lived alliance with France, employed the natives. The west once occupied the Palace and the Comedy, but these were not held. At this moment the east has taken Wyndhams and the Criterion. The situation is now confused. What exactly is written on that banner which the winds of expediency will so irritatingly fold? What are these charming business men doing on *this* side of the barricades? Is it true that some of the insurgents have been decorated by the enemy? They say the social-realists and the experimentalists have fallen out. There are ugly rumours of unholy alliances. Even the citadel itself, the curiously named Royal Court, is threatened.

Come home, Ken Tynan![1]

It is permissible, I think, to write in these terms, for we have been told so often that what has happened in the theatre is a revolution. The theatre is a small world, the revolutionary theatre in particular, existing as it does in two centres and between the covers of this magazine. The failure of such a movement need not cause great concern, but for one thing: it reflects the failure of a whole way of thought among young English men and women today.

A revolutionary movement should have some reasonably defined principles, but it was never easy to understand the common cause which bound the Royal Court Theatre playwrights. They undoubtedly understood each other, but their dissension often seemed frivolous to an observer. Of course, the Left has always believed that public argument within its ranks is a sign of virility. There is the famous story of Lenin and the man of the centre, and there are the recent Labour party statements to prove this. Such behaviour has considerable entertainment value, but it is doubtful if it has ever produced a sound political idea. It has certainly failed so far to produce an influential theatrical movement.

One thing was clear, however, and the playwrights engaged

[1] During this period, Tynan was in America, as dramatic critic on *The New Yorker*.

in the Royal Court group were definite about it. Their political philosophy was socialism. This usually had to be gathered from personal statements, as the political ideas in the plays have rarely strayed beyond the parish pump. All these writers, with the possible exception of Mr John Osborne, who has the universal appeal of misanthropy, were firmly committed to parochialism. This, of course, was not admitted.

The danger in revolution is not losing, but winning. By a successful revolt the movement puts itself in power and so relinquishes the possibility of further revolt. Revolutions can only evolve beneath power, never downward. It is this simple fact which more than once has embarrassed the Labour party. Are the fruits of revolution always conservative?

Something of the kind seems to have happened in the recent theatrical revolt. There is a sudden awareness that the natural evolution of man, even revolutionary man, may be from radical to conservative. The idea, which is by no means new, has caused great despondency. Again, I must assume this from conversations, and more especially from a curious article by Arnold Wesker in the last issue of *Encore*. Mr Wesker writes this sentence: "Free Cinema has come and is going, the attendances at the Universities and Left Review Club are dropping, the faith people have had in a theatre like the Royal Court is gradually being lost, and the men and women who spoke to us two years ago with such concern and intelligence are now bored with our company and our groups." This is certainly the voice of disillusion.

Mr Wesker's absentees can be divided into two groups. The first is made up of people who will hang around when any fight is going on in the hope of seeing someone get hurt. They sometimes believe that by cheering and booing they are engaging in dispute. They are not, but it is a fair enough game. The second group is composed of people who were genuinely sympathetic to the ideas and progress of such things as the Royal Court, Free Cinema and the ULR. The absence of this group is the real concern.

The defection has occurred in the past two years, Mr Wesker suggests. In that time we have seen the decline of socialism as a political ideal in Western Europe, and a contempt for all that it stands for. Two men, de Gaulle and Adenauer, have made a mockery of the whole structure of republicanism. The French Socialist Party has demonstrated once again the danger of riding the tiger. Weak, good-hearted and foolish, it has been eaten up. The German Socialist Party has been revealed as a cipher, an invention, a sop to liberals. There has been the failure of both black and white democratic forms of government in Africa. Internationalism, outside the expediency of a military alliance, has died on its feet. Here in England we have the less violent but no less frightening possibility of trade union delegates being recalled after a conference resolution to vote and vote again until the answer comes out right.

Everywhere, faced with the conflict between principle and policy, socialism is backing policy, and losing.

It is against this background that we are asked to accept and approve the plays which are put before us by young socialist writers.

The dictum, "It is not enough to be simple. It is not even enough to be what simple people call good. The simplicity of a darkened mind is no better than the simplicity of a beast," applies perfectly well to politics. I am not suggesting that the writers under discussion are ignorant, but I do suggest that their minds are darkened in the theological sense.

Their concern with humanist values is admirable, but it is so often expressed merely by a sort of kindness, Saroyanism, as it used to be called, which is not enough. Their criticism of class distinction is more applicable to feudalism, and not the highly complex society in which we live today. And their sympathy for minorities and the under-privileged is apt to become sentimental, and end up with no more than the handing round of tea and buns in St Pancras Town Hall.

The supreme problem of socialism has always been that it is essentially a militant philosophy which is largely committed to pacifism. This apparent contradiction has sometimes made it appear foolish, and sometimes simply inert. It is not a new problem. It has exercised individuals and split parties for a long time now. I can find no mention of it in any play written in the last four or five years.

It may be said that the theatre is compelled to present its conclusions more in terms of feeling than of reason. But if this is so it must not assume a didacticism beyond its powers. Large claims have been made for the Royal Court movement by critics such as Mr Tynan, not merely for artistic achievement but for such matters as social reform and change. The movement must expect to be judged on those claims.

I do not underestimate the difficulties facing these writers. They are working at a time when the influence of the art of fiction in both the novel and the play has declined. They may have the zeal and social passion of Zola and Dickens, but their instrument has far less effect. A live two-minute television interview is often more revealing than the most exhaustive reconstruction in fictional terms. All the same, it remains factual and inconclusive. The power to reach and present conclusions is the writer's sole prerogative over mere reporting. The Left Wing writers completely fail to understand this.

In the matter of style the movement is largely committed to realism. Reality, I suppose, may be defined as applying to any one person all that comes within that person's experience. For example, the spiritual experiences of a saint seem to many a form of fantasy, but to the saint they are reality. The substitution in literature of the bed-sitting room for the drawing room, and the dustman for the duke is not an achievement for realism. And an insistence on the universal realities, such as eating, drinking and making love, is only tolerable if such things go on, as they do in most people's lives, in a wider context.

So, with their failure to come to grips with the political philosophy they profess, and working in a style which is deteriorating into the most trivial reporting of fact, these writers can hardly expect the revolution to continue. Set against a play such as Robert Ardrey's *Shadow of Heroes* their work seems tame, but at the same time shrill. It is interesting to note that Mr Ardrey's play caused little stir in Sloane Square circles. Yet this play attempting a documentary style far removed from realism, with its dialectic, its passionately cold concern with the problem of allegiance to an idea, was perhaps the only truly political play we have seen in this country for years. Why was it ignored? It would be unkind to suggest that it was too explosive to be touched by our home-made revolutionaries. Equally unkind to suggest that their liberalism made it impossible to recognize the play because it was produced in the West End by a commercial management.

The struggle at the Royal Court and elsewhere, it would seem, was for the theatre to take on a greater social and political responsibility. Crying "Forward", it is dwindling from our sight. Plays are being produced which rely for their effect on a false naïvety. The problems they present are being simplified to a point of non-existence. We face the prospect of having nothing in this kind of theatre but plays for peasants. Mr Osborne uses his considerable power of invective to wither things that are unimportant. Socially, the whole way of thinking is out of date. And, I say this without malice, out of touch.

From the political point of view the movement means nothing at all. Like the leader of the party it seems content to wear the proper symbols, so that it has always looked right. (I mean, of course, that its appearance was correct.) And the movement has a heart. No doubt about that. All the throbbing emotionalism proves it. We are asked to admire its virility. I am pleased to do so. It is that little tiny head which worries me.

[SEPTEMBER 1959]

SOMETHING TO LIVE FOR *by Stuart Hall*

Anyone who has had to live through the past three years and who is gifted with Arnold Wesker's sense of life, will feel deeply about his article in the last issue of *Encore*. Where *are* we going? How long will it take us? How many will fall by the wayside? I am sure Arnold Wesker was right to draw a distinction between those who *reacted* to the break-up of the cold war truce in 1956, and those who tried to *respond* to it. The people who reacted rushed here and there, committing themselves to one position after another for fear of being left behind in what they took to be the latest turn of the *avant-garde*. They interpreted the new spirit after Suez and Hungary as, primarily, a literary and aesthetic experience, and indulged their tastes with the fervency of the convert. There are plenty of those people in first nights at the Royal Court, and at the National Film Theatre, at Forums on the "Visual Persuaders" and at Monday meetings of the Universities and Left Review Club. No doubt, when some of the novelty wears off, they will take up something else: but I think we can be a little hasty in bestowing them all on the scrap heap of social conformity (as Lindsay Anderson did recently with his audience at a session of the "Visual Persuaders") simply because they look middle class. Those who responded to 1956 understood that what had happened was a social experience. They knew that the fruit of the period would lie in the gradual unfolding of new opportunities and possibilities – in politics, art, communication and living – which many young people had never glimpsed before in the post-war years. They recognized what Arnold Wesker calls "being alive", and turned to it with an act of unashamed reverence.

But now Arnold Wesker is afraid that people will *react* again: that the "new left" will be overtaken by the "new zen buddhism", that the "partisans" will be overthrown by the "beatniks" – and so on, in an unending succession of new crazes, new fads, new faces, none of them achieving anything but a sense of movement. "All around us movements are rising and falling," he writes. "Free Cinema, the ULR Club, the Royal Court. . . ."

I think these are counsels of despair. Because they come from people I love and respect (and also because they are often directed by the "creative" wing at the "politicos", who ought to have all the answers but obviously don't), they are clearly serious fears and reservations. But I am bound to say that when I read *To React – To Respond*, or when I hear Lindsay Anderson mutter "part of the establishment" at a group of people who have given up a week to think through some of the questions *he* was responsible for opening up – e.g. responsibility in criticism – I find more of a *reaction* than a *response* to the difficulties that have opened up for *all of us* in the wake of "1956, ULR, Free Cinema, Vital Theatre and-all-that". I find Arnold Wesker's definition of *response* illuminating but incomplete. I think he has missed the one element which distinguishes a real response from a superficial reaction: a stubbornness, a doggedness, a sense of the continuing struggle called for in the person who responds, a certain stamina and perseverance, and a permanent *openness* which, with the best will in the world, is missing from Wesker's piece. It is easy to respond when everyone else is doing so, when Lindsay Anderson's *Stand Up! Stand Up!* breaks the sound barrier in *Sight and Sound*, and when Jimmy Porter first starts shovelling back into the Dress Circle of the Royal Court some of the stiff soil from the "chalk garden" of the West End stage. But the time we need stamina and the will to survive is not after *Look Back* or *The Entertainer*, but after *Paul Slickey*. That is the real test. For *there* is a "committed" musical which, by and large, fails to torpedo its targets: the music is banal, and the fighting edge of the lyrics altogether too blunt and uninformed. The voices in the production, like every other British musical I have seen for years, are abysmal. The whole shape of the Establishment is drawn too fuzzily to seem true; it is submerged under a welter of quite legitimate but undirected rage: it has to be *criticized* for its own sake. And yet, at the same time, its critics have to defend it against the planned, wilful and conscious attack of Fleet Street and The Critics, who have tried to use it as a weapon with which to overthrow Osborne, *Look Back*, and the whole show. Those are difficult and treacherous waters, occasions when motives are misunderstood or misinterpreted, and they put our responses to the test.

In the same way, long after a sane minority of people have rejected a nuclear-protected future, and denounced the rhetoric of the Great Deterrent, we still have to live with and *through* the fact of the stubborn existence of the bloody Bomb itself. If it is a revolution in our way of living together (politics), and our way of talking together (art) that we are making, then it is just as well to remind ourselves, every now and again, that "the old bitch gone in the teeth, a botched

civilization" is a lively hag: and that the movement of criticism, counter-creation and revolt grows, but at an uneven
and untidy pace. It would be reassuring to think that a
couple of showings of *O Dreamland* would bring the Rank
Organization to a dead stop, that *We are the Lambeth Boys*
would prevent race riots in Notting Hill, and that by now
every new housing estate would have had its open-air performance of *Chicken Soup With Barley*. It simply isn't as easy
as that.

"All around us movements are rising and falling." In fact,
that is far too cynical and simple and detached a way to
describe what is going on. As if, out there, we could see the
lights being extinguished one by one. None of us can stand
that far away from what is happening and pass that kind of
comment. For, if there is anything new which the "new left"
has tried to contribute, it is the sense that the thread of
humanism, feeling and revolt passes through every one of us.
It is a kind of life-line of struggle and commitment which
"connects" us all, whatever our differences of emphasis and
preferences. The sense of life to which Arnold Wesker
responded is not somewhere in the distant future, to be
brought about by the rising and falling of anonymous masses
of people: it is here and now, pushing through the crevices
of our class society and our class culture, breaking fresh
ground where it can, taking root in people's lives, whether
they choose to "live" by producing ULR, writing a play,
making a documentary film, or marching to Aldermaston.
Time and again, it is overcome, superseded: little magazines
go under, good people write bad plays, Free Cinema closes
down, the Establishment arms itself against us, butchering
some, buying some off. What matters is that some who have
tasted "life itself", have lost the appetite for anything cheaper
and shallower: and that those people have the guts to live
out the panic and the isolation which is part of the forms of
life in *this* society and come up again for air.

I think something of the kind *has* been happening over the
past three or four years: and that we should neither over-
estimate the strength of the "response", nor minimize its
achievements. It has been something of a miracle that, with

Odhams and the Amalgamated Press closing their fingers round and about our "free press", one or two voices, independent of the cultural apparatus, have managed to keep going – and to grow: *ULR*, *The New Reasoner*, *Encore*. Nor is that the sum and substance of the voices raised in one place or another during this period: it may be fashionable for the posh papers and weeklies and monthlies to try to capture, and even muzzle, critical voices, but the fact that they feel themselves obliged in some way to cope with this tide of feeling is itself indicative of its strength on the ground. Look at some of the things in *Encounter* or *Twentieth Century* over the past few months: they are not by any means the established voices of the radical or humanist left, but they reveal, in their pages, the pressure upon established journals to take account of (if even to explain away) a current of critical thinking and work which is moving steadily against them. "The Establishment" now has a name and a face: it is in *that* context that we regret the weaknesses in *Paul Slickey* – for it is a failure to define, in words, music and satire, at a time when definition and precision would have been immensely valuable. But for goodness sake let us remember that *Slickey* couldn't have been written, and certainly would not have been either produced or intelligibly criticized in 1953.

The same is true in the theatre, although it may not look so promising. If you think of two plays which have appeared at the beginning and end of the period 1956–9, *Look Back in Anger* and *A Taste of Honey*, you will see what has taken place in the theatre. I don't mean now that we should apply some simple formula of progress – that *A Taste of Honey* is better than *Look Back*: in fact, I think it may probably turn out to be not so good. But the point is that *Look Back in Anger* was painful in its accuracy and immediacy, even for those people who would *not* ever have agreed that "there were no brave causes left". Osborne struck a representative note, he summed up the sense of inverted rage, the bitter raging against the cramped, *pusillanimous* forms of life which stifled Jimmy Porter. If Porter was unbearable, as the stiffer critics said, it was because many of us were on the edge of finding all our relationships unbearable. And what we found in *Look Back* was the language which, at least at that moment, contained something of our sense for life. Constantly critical, it yet called out something more than a reaction in us: it gave us lessons in feeling. In one way at least, *A Taste of Honey* takes us beyond that – I mean, not just as a movement, but as human beings. For in spite of the impossibilities, the misunderstandings between mother and daughter, and between Jo and Geoff in the play, some sort of an image of relationships, built upon love and acceptance comes through. In that sense, the play begins where we are, with this botched civilization; but it takes us out into the unknown country beyond that. It humanizes our frustrations, and our bitter cynicism and anger.

I have taken these examples not because I think they prove that we must, in the end, carry all things before us. But I think we need to take strength from the different things which have happened in the past three years. They have a richness of comradeship and a sense of the shared struggle which cannot be by-passed by fashion, even if it is going to take more of us than there are, longer than we would like, to make the good life.

[SEPTEMBER 1959]

THE HIDDEN FACE OF VIOLENCE
by Tom Milne

"... *of a badness that must be called indescribable.*"
>The Times ON JOHN WHITING'S *Saint's Day*

"*A masterpiece of meaningless significance.*"
>Punch ON HAROLD PINTER'S *The Birthday Party*

"*Another frightful ordeal.*"
>The Sunday Times ON JOHN ARDEN'S
>*Serjeant Musgrave's Dance*

It is surely no accident that on the occasion of the first production of these three plays – *Saint's Day* in 1951, *The Birthday Party* in 1958, and *Serjeant Musgrave's Dance* in 1959 –

the virulence of the critics' attack was matched only by the vehemence of the underground support. Letters to the Press, denunciations of critical imbecility, protest, fury, frustration. The public, by and large, remained baffled and indifferent, and each of the plays closed after a minimum run. Yet, none of them has drifted into limbo. *Saint's Day* is still very much alive and kicking. *The Birthday Party* turns up in production all over the place, and is shortly to be seen on commercial television. It seems certain that the same thing will happen to *Serjeant Musgrave's Dance*.

In the case of John Whiting's play, dropped eight years ago into a theatre which measured its seriousness against a yardstick of Christopher Fry and T. S. Eliot, critical disfavour was to be expected. For the other two plays, appearing in the full flood of a theatre of social protest – where Osborne, Delaney, Behan and Wesker are hailed by all and sundry, and Joan Littlewood, after fourteen years of eye-opening work, is at last noticed – it is a little more surprising. For these three plays *are* social plays; not in the sense that they show working-class lives or cry out for social betterment, but in the sense that they comment, seriously, on the society we live in. Until enough time has passed to set our era in perspective, any such judgement as "*Look Back in Anger* is better than *Serjeant Musgrave's Dance*" (or *Roots* than *The Birthday Party*), is probably a matter of personal preference. What can be said is that all these plays are worthy of serious consideration.

There will probably always be what is so aptly called in France "un théatre maudit" – a theatre which is damned; a theatre where, if produced at all, plays are supported only by a tiny minority of adventurous minds. This condemnation may arise from obtuseness, or from prudery, or simply from expediency. Critical obtuseness is too common to require comment; both Shaw and Ibsen ran up against the prudish spirit when they dared to tackle prostitution and venereal disease in *Mrs Warren's Profession* and *Ghosts*; while expediency is responsible for all the plays which are never seen on the stage, and for those which are never written because the pressure against their inception is too great. Aristophanes, it should be remembered, wrote his great denunciation of war while the Peloponnesian War was actually in progress; an unimaginable theatrical venture for World War Two, when horror of war was inexpedient. So much is not expedient. Attack on Government policy. Attack on the Monarchy. Attack on the Church (not *very*).

Times change, of course, and we laugh at the prim horror revealed by the early Ibsen audiences. We grow more open-minded. We shift our ground about what is expedient, usually as a result of persistent hammering by individuals. But one factor remains constant: people do not like to be disturbed, to be forced to revalue their lives and way of thinking. There are certain subjects – the malaise of the time, if you like – of which people are aware, but which they do not wish to have brought out into the open and squarely faced. Take America, for instance, with the negro on her conscience. With all the mass of cinematic and theatrical material dealing with the negro problem, we have had to wait until the last two years (*A Man is Ten Feet Tall* and *Raisin in the Sun*) for the malaise to be conquered. The old magnanimous condescension has been jettisoned, to be replaced by an acceptance of the simple and obvious fact that, colour of skin apart, white and black are identical members of the human race, sharing the same preoccupations, the same aspirations. The problem remains, but the basic premises have shifted.

All things considered, Shaw and Ibsen, with their attacks on the late-nineteenth-century malaise of sex, were received into favour fairly rapidly. Well-bred audiences got used to the idea that you could hear prostitution and VD mentioned without peeping at your neighbour and reaching for the smelling-salts. But there is a long way from tolerating such references to accepting the implications. Ibsen and Shaw soon became cultural classics. Strindberg, however, had to fight harder for acceptance, and has never achieved the same popular consecration. Ibsen and Shaw treated sex and its appurtenances as a social fact: people *do* contract VD; prostitutes *do* exist; women *do* chafe at the chains of natural functions which bind them. These are facts which, ultimately, could not be denied. To Strindberg, sex, gathering strength from a long era of repression, was a motive force, something which governed behaviour and was all-pervasive. It was an imaginative conception, rather than a marshalling of truths. The result is that Strindberg's plays – *The Father, Dance of Death, Creditors, The Stronger,* for example – retain their theatrical power and excitement, while plays like *The Doll's House, Mrs Warren's Profession* and *Misalliance* have dated, though spasmodically interesting. It was (and is) much easier to admit the validity of the arguments of Shaw and Ibsen than to recognize the truth of Strindberg. Man is, after all, a rational being, so we are told. The refusal to recognize Strindberg was not a refusal to admit the existence of certain sordid facts of life, but a refusal to accept that one was oneself involved in the sordidness.

The difference between the theatre of Shaw and Ibsen on the one hand, and Strindberg on the other, is one of approach. The civilized and the uncivilized. Social criticism or attack is acceptable, even when it kicks you in the belly, so long as you are looking. But Strindberg kicks you in the belly from behind. Which is unfair.

Saint's Day, The Birthday Party and *Serjeant Musgrave's Dance* share a common theme: the nature of violence. We are, as any reader of the daily Press will know, living in an Age of Violence. The cinema, as any observer of C. A. Lejeune's weekly coy burial of her head in the sand will have noted, has placed its finger squarely on this fact: brutality is served in liberal doses, usually for its own sake as a source of entertainment of growing popularity. Many films, however, have made a serious attempt to analyse violence in various contexts, not as something to relish and smack greedy chops over, but as something which is an integral part of our world and shapes our attitudes – notably, the films of Buñuel and Wajda. As far as the theatre is concerned (setting aside Genet as too misrepresented in this country to have truly impinged), one can seize on moments only. The first act curtain of Donald Ogden Stewart's *The Kidders,* when the hero, left alone in his drawing-room cleaning an automatic-rifle (relic of army days), suddenly fires a random burst. "Just kidding, Baby," he explains to his frightened wife. Or, more acutely observed,

the atmosphere of pending explosion in the first half of Ann
Jellicoe's *Sport of My Mad Mother*; the ritual circling of the
American stranger, caught in a blind-alley, by a group of
Teddies; the terror of one of them who thinks he has killed
the stranger, a terror slowly transmuted into exultation –
"A treat . . . a fair treat . . . I feel good . . . I feel bloody good
. . . I feel bloody wonderful." What Pinter, Arden and Whiting
have done is to extend the responsibility for violence beyond
the customary "What can you expect of Teddy-Boys?"
(thugs/Reds/what-you-will) to "What can you expect of
society?" The individual, unable to come to terms with
society, unable or unwilling to place his ideals at its service,
is crushed by society. And society, drained of its life-blood,
slowly dies . . .

"There aren't any good, brave causes left," cried Jimmy
Porter. This, precisely, is the inner dilemma of a world
waiting today for the big bang, in an atmosphere of moral
and social disintegration. The chain reaction of release is one
of violence.

In *Saint's Day*, an elderly poet, Paul Southman, lives in
a small village with his grand-daughter, Stella, and her husband. Twenty-five years ago he had written a bitter satirical
pamphlet which went "straight into my Lady Society's
chamber and lifted the skirts of the old whore". As a result,
Society has ostracized him. Exiled, Southman has directed
his satire against the villagers, so that something like a state
of siege exists between the village and Southman's home. As
the play opens, Southman is to be reinstated by Society at a
dinner given in his honour; the emissary is "The Honourable
Robert Procathren, distinguished young poet and critic,
photographed last week after his marriage . . ." The old man,
both frightened by, and hostile to, all that Procathren stands
for, is suspicious. Stella's husband is a young painter who,
hailed as a prodigy at fifteen, has since refused to show his
paintings, afraid to open his inner self to a hostile world. Into
this situation is thrown the news that the village is being
terrorized by three soldiers who have escaped from a deten-
tion camp. The vicar of the village begs Southman for his aid
against the marauders. Southman refuses, saying that he will

join with the soldiers, to take his revenge on the village and
on society. He taunts Procathren with his weakness and his
intellectual theorizing, and tricks him into taking a gun and
joining them. The direct result is that Procathren accident-
ally kills Stella; accepting, for the first time, responsibility
for his actions, he joins the marauders – he has been pushed
too far. In the third act, it is he who leads the soldiers, he
who precipitates the final holocaust in which the village is
burnt, the villagers become refugees, and both Southman and
the painter are hanged at Procathren's instigation.

The image is clear. It is an image of the disintegration of
society, resulting in chaos. Southman is the visionary cast
out by a society which had no need of him; now, Stella suggests he may be needed – "Perhaps they have asked you to
return because they need you. Perhaps they are in trouble
out there and want your wisdom, your advice." Rejected by
society, Southman now rejects society – "Why should I give
them my advice? They are nothing to me." He refuses to
listen to the vicar, who asks in all humility for his aid. He
refuses Procathren who, in spite of his glossy-magazine overtones, genuinely sympathizes with the older man's prophetic
views. The real battle is between the creative mind (Southman) and Society in two guises (Procathren, the upper-class
/intellectual, and the vicar, speaking for the lower-class/
uneducated). The soldiers are merely the agents of destruction, waiting willingly to carry out any order from anybody
who can, and will, give that order.

The Birthday Party, seven years later, follows a remarkably
similar general plan, though the shifting social distinctions
which this country has undergone are reflected in the play.
The background – a seedy boarding-house in a seaside town
– is even more precise than that of *Saint's Day*, but the agents
of destruction have become anonymous, and are now in complete control. The disintegration has gone one stage further.
In *Saint's Day*, Procathren takes command of the soldiers,
as Southman might have done (and called them to heel), but
in *The Birthday Party*, Goldberg and McCann give their own
orders. Stanley, self-styled a concert pianist, has buried himself in the boarding-house. He never goes out, does not wash,

does not work, is anti-social. The reason he gives for his self-burial is that, after one great concert success, "they" pulled a fast one; when he went down for his second concert, the hall was locked, and no one turned up. Whether Stanley is, or is not, an artist is left in doubt; the evidence (unlike the evidence for Southman) is deliberately contradictory. More direct is the evidence for Stanley's relationship with the elderly Meg, who runs the boarding-house, and Petey, her husband. Both regard him with genuine affection. Typical of Pinter's style is the deliberately ambiguous shifting of ground. In the opening scene, trying to get Stanley out of bed, Meg calls, "Stan! I'm coming up to fetch you if you don't come down! I'm coming up! I'm going to count three! One! Two! Three! I'm coming to get you!" Then, "So he's come down at last, has he? He's come down for his breakfast. But he doesn't deserve any, does he, Petey?" A few minutes later she enters into a grotesque and hilarious seduction scene with him. The mother-son, man-woman relationships are rapidly sketched in one movement by this ambiguity. Stanley, however, does not respond: he is consistently rude, and has one terrifyingly cruel scene in which he brainwashes Meg into believing that "they" have come to cart her away in a wheelbarrow (a reflection, incidentally, of his own fear). Petey's attitude to Stanley is calmer, almost imperceptible, until the final scene when he is "taken away" by Goldberg and McCann, and it is Petey who makes the protest; first, to Goldberg – "We can look after him here" – and then to Stanley himself – "Stan, don't let them tell you what to do!"

Unannounced, and apparently from nowhere, Goldberg and McCann arrive. A Jew and an Irishman, their speeches are full of oblique, shifting references to establishments against which the human being can sin: big business, the church, the IRA, test cricket, morality, and so on. It is Stanley's birthday (Is it? Meg says so. Stanley denies it) and the visitors throw a nightmare party during which Stanley is hounded down, brainwashed, deprived of speech. In the morning he is carted off, clean, shaved, bowler-hatted and anonymous, to an unspecified fate. The image, again, is clear. Stanley has rejected society, both in the shape of his career and in the persons of Meg and Petey. Society, in the shape of Goldberg and McCann, takes its revenge.

In *Serjeant Musgrave's Dance*, four soldiers have deserted from their colonial regiment. They make their way, in mid-winter, to a northern English town in the grip of a strike. Sick of the endless round of killing in which, as soldiers, they have been forced to participate, they plan to canvass recruits for their campaign against war and oppression. The coal-owner and local clergyman try to manipulate them as strike-breakers, "suggesting" possible recruits who would be useful out of the way. They agree to hold a recruiting rally. At the rally, they hoist the skeleton of a former comrade (a native of the town; this is bringing home the facts, with a vengeance). Holding the townspeople at gun-point, they hammer home their story of war. Internal dissensions make the plan break down, and it ends in fiasco with their arrest. The reason for the breakdown lies in the characters of the four soldiers. The leader, Serjeant Musgrave, stands revealed as a religious maniac who believes that he has been divinely appointed by God to administer a logical object lesson which will end all war; on the principle of an eye for an eye, he is to wreak retribution on those "responsible" – here, the coal-owner and the clergyman. The other three soldiers give him their alle-giance for varying reasons. Sparky follows him blindly and in fear, even referring to him as "God", and constantly trying to escape his domination. The night before the rally, he tries to run away with the whore-barmaid, each of them hoping to find some sort of peace in the contact with another human being. He is killed by his comrades, Attercliffe and Hurst, when they try to prevent his escape. At the rally, after Musgrave's plea, the crowd still hesitates. Hurst, closest to Musgrave in outlook, but believing in human revenge rather than divine logic, urges that they open fire on the crowd. Musgrave protests. But it is the weaker-willed Atter-cliffe, sick with Sparky's blood on his hands, who throws him-self on Hurst's gun, with his mouth to the muzzle, to stop him from firing. At once, the crowd is lost. Someone asks where the fourth soldier is. Musgrave explains that he has been killed in an accident, that it makes no difference. "It makes all the difference," cries the barmaid. Again, the image is of destruction. Violence breeds violence. The soldiers are right in their denunciation, and the townspeople are right in their denunciation of the soldiers. But – when "bellies are full", when the town is free of strikes, oppression and hunger, when the atmosphere of violence is dispersed – *then* the message which the soldiers have brought will be remembered.

Each of these plays, over and above the common theme of violence, shares the fact that it creates its own distinctive world, with a mood and logic of urgency, directness and excitement, which makes nonsense of the critical reproach of obscurity and/or dullness. *Saint's Day*'s large, decaying manor, set in an atmosphere of hatred, where a trip to the village becomes a sortie into enemy territory, where the apocalyptic arrival of the marauding soldiers is terrifyingly announced by a Jericho trumpet, and where a crowd of frightened refugees passively watches the final holocaust. *The Birthday Party*, with its nightmare "no-exit" party, in which a game of blind man's buff is transformed into a maniacal witch-hunt, with an attempted murder punctuated in the darkness by the staccato beating of a toy drum. The cold, loveless, frozen wilderness of *Serjeant Musgrave's Dance*, where people live in silent fear and hatred, and where the frightened barmaid can find logical release in sleeping with a different man each night, seeking for contact; where the failure of the soldiers' plan is transformed into a macabre dance of death, with the townsfolk dancing, exulting, round the arrested soldiers.

Each of these plays creates a world before you, the audience, which you must enter, and whose rules you must inevitably follow. With each of them, if you do enter, you are swept along; their truths are hammered home, and you must accept, recognize, revalue. If you withhold your participation, you sit back in disbelief; these worlds become dull, obscure, meaningless.

A play like *Look Back in Anger* creates a world which, in essence, is familiar to us (reality, rather than an imaginative *dislocation* of reality), and it becomes easier for the mind to sidetrack on to an element which may be more pleasing to it than the main theme of the play. Constant reference is made, even by people who liked the play, to Jimmy Porter's *self-pity*, his *neurotic* behaviour, his *cruelty* to his wife. This makes nonsense of the play; Jimmy Porter is devoid of any neurosis or self-pity, and the play is summed up in his cry against a negative world, "Oh heavens, how I long for a little ordinary human enthusiasm. Just enthusiasm – that's all. I want to hear a warm, thrilling voice cry out Hallelujah! Hallelujah! I'm alive." (How Jimmy would have responded to Beatie Bryant in the closing moments of *Roots* . . .) Would *Look Back in Anger* have been the success it was if people had been forced to listen to this damning indictment of themselves as dead souls, instead of being allowed to stray into less dangerous channels (guying of English Sundays, excitingly turbulent sex-life, downtrodden and maltreated wife, etc.)? The same thing, I suspect, may be said of *Roots*. In his preface to the published edition of the play, Arnold Wesker writes in a note, "My people are not caricatures . . . And though the picture I have drawn of them is a harsh one, yet still my tone is not of disgust." Obviously, in writing this note, Wesker felt that his Norfolk labourers might appear to be cruelly or maliciously presented. In fact, the portraits are warm, gentle and moving. In spite of the clarity and force with which Wesker develops his theme, it becomes easy enough to make the wrong response – "Well, they're really alright, fine people, no need to change anything." One can forget that Jimmy Beales, for example, harmlessly happy with his Territorial Jubilee to "Demonstrate and parade wi' arms and such like", driven to angry inarticulacy at Beatie's suggestion that the Hydrogen Bomb makes territorial arms look rather silly, is just the sort of man who answers the first call to serve King and Country without *ever* asking why.

A play which creates its own world, with its own relentless logic, forestalls any such wandering by the audience. Perhaps the price to be paid for such relentlessness is failure, commercial failure at least. A price which *Saint's Day*, *The Birthday Party* and *Serjeant Musgrave's Dance* have already paid.

[JANUARY 1960]

TELLING A TRUE TALE *by John Arden*

"Cruel, cruel was the war when first the rout began
And out of Old England went many a smart young man.
They pressed my Love away from me likewise my brothers three.
They sent them to the war, my love, in the Isle of Germany."

To use the material of the contemporary world and present it
on the public stage is the commonly accepted purpose of playwrights, and there are several ways in which this can be done.
Autobiography treated in the documentary style (Wesker).
Individual strains and collisions seen from a strongly personal standpoint and inflamed like a savage boil (Osborne).
The slantindicular observation of unconsidered speech and
casual action used to illuminate loneliness and lack of communication (Pinter). Tough analysis of a social disease (Ibsen/
Arthur Miller). And so on. What I am deeply concerned with
is the problem of translating the concrete life of today into
terms of poetry that shall at the one time both illustrate that
life and set it within the historical and legendary tradition of
our culture. I am writing in English (British English) and
primarily for an English (British English) audience. Therefore I am concerned to express my themes in terms of
British (English British, but not exclusively) tradition. This
is not chauvinism but a prudent limitation of scope. Art
may be truly international, but there are dangers in being too
wide open to unassimilated influences from north, south, east
and west.

The English public has regrettably lost touch with its own
poetic traditions. There are many reasons for this – one which
is often suggested is the passing of Anglo-Saxon power into
the hands of America. After politics follows culture, and there
is a large deploring of the flood of American Pop that has
clearly caught the imagination of youth to the exclusion of
anything native. In one way, however, this may be not so
bad. The bedrock of English poetry is the ballad. These
ballads have been preserved more vitally in America than
anywhere else and now they are coming back. Let me
sketch a quick line of writers who have always built close to the

bedrock. Chaucer, Skelton, Shakespeare, Jonson, Defoe, Gay, Burns, Dickens, Hardy, Joyce. All these men have known, almost as an unnoticed background to their lives, the enormous stock of traditional poetry, some of it oral, some of it printed and hawked at street-corners, some of it sung from the stages of the music-halls. They are naturally not the only important writers of our history; but they form a line with strongly defined hereditary features, and they wrote from a basic unvarying poetic standpoint. (I have included a Scotsman and an Irishman for the sake of completeness – those nations of course have produced many others as firmly attached to the central thread.) It seems to me that this tradition is the one that will always in the end reach to the heart of the people,[1] even if the people are not entirely aware of what it is that causes their response. Brecht was always alive to this, and, from the German point of view, he consistently worked upon the same principle.

The theatrical poet must be general in his appeal. If he is too private his plays will only be valued for reading, or (like most of Yeats's work) will only be found actable before small private audiences in a drawing-room theatre. England is a country which is at present sick with "tradition". But the truer legends and histories are not those which are acted out by the Beefeaters or the cottage-thatchers for the benefit of the tourist trade. As seen through the eyes of the sort of writers I have mentioned, the English prove to be an extraordinarily passionate people, as violent as they are amorous, and quite astonishingly hostile to good government and order.

"Sally, my dear, shall I come to bed to you.
She laugh and reply I'm afraid you'll undo me.
Sing fal the diddle ido, sing whack fal the diddle day."
Or –
"So young Johnson beat the seven of them,
And the rest he did not mind,
Till this cruel-hearted woman
Took a knife from her side and ripped him up behind."

[1] Not only the English people – other countries have similar traditions, so without deliberately straining for it, the effect of the poetry *becomes* universal.

If the modern idea of a sludgy uninterested nation, married to its telly and its fish and chips, has any truth in it (and I'm afraid it has a little) it is the business of the dramatist to cry out against it even if there seems to be no hope of his ever being heard. That there is no hope, I do not believe.

In the ballads the colours are primary. Black is for death, and for the coalmines. Red is for murder, and for the soldier's coat the collier puts on to escape from his black. Blue is for the sky and for the sea that parts true love. Green fields are speckled with bright flowers. The seasons are clearly defined. White winter, green spring, golden summer, red autumn. The poets see their people at moments of alarming crisis, comic or tragic. The action goes as in Japanese films – from sitting down everyone suddenly springs into furious running, with no faltering intermediate steps.

What does this mean in terms of the theatre? To start with – costumes, movements, verbal patterns, music, must all be strong, and hard at the edges. If verse is used in the dialogue, it must be nakedly verse as opposed to the surrounding prose, and must never be allowed to droop into casual flaccidities. This is the Brechtian technique, more or less. I would suggest a further analogy. The ancient Irish heroic legends were told at dinner as prose tales, of invariable content but, in the manner of their telling, improvised to suit the particular occasion or the poet's mood. When, however, he arrived at one of the emotional climaxes of the story such as the lament of Deirdre for the Sons of Usna or the sleep-song of Grainne over Diarmaid, then he would sing a poem which he had by heart and which was always the same. So in a play, the dialogue can be naturalistic and "plotty" as long as the basic poetic issue has not been crystallized. But when this point is reached, then the language becomes formal (if you like, in verse, or sung), the visual pattern coalesces into a vital image that is one of the nerve-centres of the play. A medieval city, built upon one or two hills, will have in it several tall church towers which stand up proud from the spread of low-roofed houses, which in turn are cramped in by the surrounding walls. Carry the simile further, and we find a river running through the town and looping round to divide the buildings as a play is split up into acts.

The themes of traditional poetry are always the same. Simple basic situations – a pregnant girl is abandoned by her lover – a soldier is recruited for the war –

"I met with Serjeant Atkinson in the market going down
And he said, 'Young man, will you enlist and be a Light
Dragoon?'"

– a sailor returned from the sea finds his wife re-married – the raggle-taggle gipsies at a castle gate carry off the lady and are hunted down and punished –

"O England is a free country, so free beyond a doubt,
That if you have no food to eat, you are free to go without."

– The Turkish Knight kills St George, only to find an interfering doctor who raises him from the dead again. . . . There is no need to be afraid of being corny in choice of a plot. When the stories are as firmly grounded as these, there is scarcely any limit to the amount of meaning and relevance a writer can insert into them. They are themes which can carry any strength of content from tragedy through satire to straightforward comedy, and neither be drowned in it nor seem too portentous. Social criticism, for example, tends in the theatre to be dangerously ephemeral and therefore disappointing after the fall of the curtain. But if it is expressed within the framework of the traditional poetic truths it can have a weight and an impact derived from something more than contemporary documentary facility.

This kind of theatre is easily misunderstood. I have found in my own very tentative experiments that audiences (and particularly critics) find it hard to make the completely simple response to the story that is the necessary preliminary to appreciating the meaning of the play. Other habits of playgoing have led them to expect that they are going to have to begin by forming judgements, by selecting what they think is the author's "social standpoint" and then following it to its conclusion. This does not happen in ballads at their best. There we are given the fable, and we draw our own conclusions. If the poet intends us to make a judgement on his characters, this will be implied by the whole turn of the story, not by intellectualized comments as it proceeds. The tale stands and it exists in its own right. If the poet is a true one, then the tale will be true too. [MAY 1960]

THERE'S MUSIC IN THAT ROOM
by Irving Wardle

Dislodging earlier holders of the title, Harold Pinter now moves into position as playwright currently in favour. In the past four years the success procedure has become standardized. The unknown author's first play is butchered in the dailies and acclaimed at the week-end. Several months elapse during which the buzz of salon conversation rises to a crescendo; then he makes a triumphal entry into the West End and the flattering offers from prestige-hunting television companies start rolling in. *Encore* thereupon comes out with an elegiac note on his blighted career – "Alas for poor X – eaten alive by Harold Hobson and the Society of West End Managers."

I'm not denying the existence of what Mr Alvarez has aptly described as the West End's "negative feedback"; but let's not forget the equal menace inside "vital theatre" itself – the *avant-garde* herd-instinct that yokes the talented, the untalented, and the charlatan together into a chauvinistic group who discredit what they support by smothering it with cant slogans, and emit a howl of protest if a new work that passes their test for intellectual and ideological respectability is not hailed as the equal of *The Wild Duck*.

Harold Pinter, who besides his working-class background is also a Jew, is peculiarly vulnerable to this type of sabotage. The Jewish lobby of the New Left is very active in its drive to preserve the solidarity of the ghetto. Writing in the *Jewish Chronicle*, Arnold Wesker employed this tactic on Pinter:

> Pinter is a Jewish writer and this play (*The Birthday Party*) out of his experience in the Jewish community. . . .

The real weakness is that Pinter has used the right character in the wrong setting. It should all have taken place in a Jewish setting. This was why *Five Finger Exercise* was so weak. It placed a Jewish mentality in Gentile clothing. It is not enough to say Goldberg is universal – people are only universal in their own setting.

In *The Caretaker* (Arts Theatre), thank God, Pinter ignores this advice: the social background that intermittently appeared in his earlier plays has now been cut away, with a resultant refinement of style and increased clarity of dramatic line; I see no point in invoking the name of Beckett or of any other supposed influence – the play is quintessentially the work of a very considerable artist.

On the strength of *The Birthday Party* and the pair of one-acters, I rashly applied the phrase "comedy of menace" to Pinter's writing. I now take it back. *The Caretaker* is certainly comic, but in place of the gangster Eumenides who gave his previous plays their nightmarish overtones, there is an exhaustive scrutiny of three interlocking characters in control of their own destinies. The basic Pinter symbol, the room – the ambivalent image of safety and retreat which is also the place of catharsis – remains dominant; but this time there is no invasion. The newcomer enters by invitation, and he, not the occupants, is the principal victim. Again like the other plays, *The Caretaker* is obsessively concerned with human destructiveness – with what people *do* to each other: but for the first time all the characters are vulnerable and suffer, in varying degrees, at each others' hands.

All are prisoners of private fantasy in pursuit of which they form temporary alliances for as long as their aims seem to correspond: ultimately these prove irreconcilable, and the trio are driven back into solitude. Mick, the landlord, wants to transform his tumbledown property into a palatial penthouse; his brother, mentally destroyed by electric shock treatment, wants to build a shed in the garden; the old layabout wants to be able to pad about in a place of his own. The slight overlap between these three ambitions furnishes the substance of the action and, while methodically focusing its attention on trivia, its significance spreads and expands in a way unheard of in the modern theatre outside Chekhov.

Like Chekhov, too, the writing has the formal quality of music. It is based on Southern working-class speech, but Pinter drains every phrase of denotative association and uses it as pure thematic material, meaningless until he has given it meaning. "If only the weather would break! Then I'd be able to get down to Sidcup!" – the statement is forcefully announced like the entry of a new subject in a sonata movement, subsequently undergoing development and combination with other themes. Each pause, each inflexion is contained in the gesture of the language, and the aesthetic effect is close to that of tautly controlled and continuously evolving counterpoint.

The one passage at which the sense of exploration breaks down is the long speech in which the brother explicitly describes what happened to him in the mental hospital. Pinter, one feels, knew too much about the speech before he began writing it, and its effect is inappropriately naïve – as if a pianist were to interrupt an elaborate improvisation to pick out a nursery rhyme confidently with one finger.

Put another way, my objection to the speech is that it gives a character a biography instead of a style of speaking. Elsewhere the play of language creates its own world, incidentally flowering into biographical detail. It is a world whose limits are bounded by the London bus routes (Pinter is the poet of London Transport), beyond which lies unknown territory – an empty landscape in which a hospital, a monastery, or a transit camp exist in stark isolation like mythological beasts sprawling over unexplored continents in an old map.

Besides its other associations, this view of the world has a distinct smack of the Army. So, incidentally, has the symbol of the room itself – that cushy number in the QM Stores which so many old regulars hug like dear life, always in fear of being rooted out and put back on normal duties. From his way of speaking one knows, long before he informs the audience, that the tramp has done his spell abroad; and is it

an accident, I wonder, that Sidcup, his unattainable El
Dorado, happens to be the headquarters of the Army Pay
Office?

I'm not offering this as a theory of any importance: I
happen to have done my two years and consequently the
play carries those associations for me. Equally valid readings,
no doubt, could be made from many alternative fixed points
of view. In other words the play has universality – attaining
this without any reliance on the localized social framework
currently regarded as indispensable.

The compliments that have been heaped on Donald
McWhinnie's production are well deserved and there is no
point in repeating them at this stage. Donald Pleasence, Alan
Bates and Peter Woodthorpe have made the parts their own
property: no matter how many future productions of *The
Caretaker* there may be, their performances will remain in the
memory as the thing itself.

[JULY 1960]

GOODBYE NOTE FROM JOAN

In 1961, *after several highly successful West End transfers,
Joan Littlewood announced that after the production of
James Goldman's* They Might Be Giants, *she was leaving
England and Theatre Workshop.*

Dear ENCORE

Such a lot of nonsense has been talked about my reasons for
leaving England that I wanted to write to you before I went.
You have always given serious consideration to the problems
facing people working in the English theatre.

It is not unusual for someone to leave a situation in which
they cannot do the work for which they are qualified. That is
my case.

My objective in life has not changed; it is to work with
other artists – actors, writers, designers, composers – and in
collaboration with them, and by means of argument, experi-

ment and research, to help to keep the English theatre alive
and contemporary.

I do not believe in the supremacy of the director, designer,
actor or even of the writer. It is through collaboration that
this knockabout art of theatre survives and kicks. It was
true at The Globe, The Curtain, The Crown, and in the
"illustrious theatre" of Molière and it can work here, today.

No one mind or imagination can foresee what a play will
become until all the physical and intellectual stimuli, which
are crystallized in the poetry of the author, have been understood by a company, and then tried out in terms of mime,
discussion and the precise music of grammar; words and
movement allied and integrated. The smallest contact between characters in a remote corner of the stage must become
objectively true and relevant. The actor must be freed from
the necessity of making effective generalizations.

I could go on but you too know how the theatre must
function if it is to reflect the genius of a people, in a complex
day and age. Only a company of artists can do this. It is no
use the critics proclaiming overnight the genius of the individual writer; these writers must graft in company with other
artists if we are to get what we want and what our people
need, a great theatre.

This does not depend on buildings, nor do we need even a
fraction of the money they are spending on their bomb. Each
community should have a theatre; the West End has plun-
dered our talent and diluted our ideas; cannot each district
afford to support a few artists who will give them back some
entertainment, laughter and love of mankind?

Young actors and actresses, don't be puppets any longer!
The directors and the critics won't help you; in television,
film or theatre they ask for the dregs of the old acting, mere
"expression", exploitation of your "type". In Shaftesbury
Avenue or in the Brecht theatre, it's all the same. The theatre
should be made up of individuals, not pawns. Keep your
wits, develop your talent, take over the theatre which now
belongs to the managers or the landlords. Let's stop this
waste of human ability. I have tried, for nearly twenty-
seven years. I've had my nose to the grindstone and I'm

still, comparatively speaking, alive. I'll be back, I'll be more help.[1]

JOAN LITTLEWOOD
[SEPTEMBER 1961]

[1] Two years later, Joan returned to direct a re-assembled company in *Oh What A Lovely War*, one of her finest productions and the most-decorated production ever staged by Theatre Workshop.

CHAPTER FOUR

CONTINENTAL INFLUENCES

INTRODUCTION

"Brecht is in; Stanislavsky's out!" This is how one observer described the situation in the early 1960s. But apart from sundry workshops and a few drama-school infiltrations, Stanislavsky hadn't ever taken root; never really being in, he could not be said to be out. However, there was no question about the pervasive, all-infecting influence of Bertolt Brecht.

The Method mystique had given way to the Alienation-Effect; the cult of the Group Theatre and the Actors' Studio was supplanted by Weigel-worship and the flying trip to the Berliner Ensemble.

Emulations and imitations abounded. Osborne's disastrous musical, *The World of Paul Slickey*, tried to cram acid political comment into a conventional musical-comedy format. Although the tone was unmistakably Osborne, the attitude behind the show had clear affinities with Brecht. Robert Bolt's *A Man for All Seasons* made use of Brecht's sequential structure and anti-illusionist devices. Christopher Logue's *Trials by Logue* was a satirical application of the Brechtian method; and Logue's later songs were conspicuously patterned on Brecht's lyrics. Osborne's *Luther*, essentially a chronicle play, also bore superficial resemblances to the Epic Theatre in its use of set-pieces, sermons, first-person narrations and short episodic structure.

In Brecht, the English dramatist found a writer who combined commitment with poetry; aesthetic discipline with dialectical rigour. To be "Brechtian", then, was to be politically concerned, theatrically bold and artistically disciplined. It is little wonder he became the national paragon.

For the past few years, British drama had taken a long,

hard, disenchanted look at the contemporary scene, and now almost every playwright one cared to name was rumoured to be writing an historical play. Distantiation was setting in; horizons were opening out. At the same time, the visionary Beckett began to outstrip Ionesco as an influence. *Rhinoceros* set the final seal on the sad fact that Ionesco was trying to go on shattering the same conventions he had attacked years ago. And then, in 1961, three plays came to London of an intellectual scope and power which demonstrated how far the British theatre still had to go: Sartre's *The Condemned of Altona*, Genet's *The Blacks* and Frisch's *The Fire Raisers*.

THE REAL BRECHT *by Ernest Bornemann*

I first met Bert Brecht towards the end of the 1920s in an apartment on the Hardenbergstrasse in Berlin. I cannot remember now whether it was his own apartment or someone else's, but I recall (and this made an even greater impression on me than the extraordinary clothes he wore) that one of the other men present was the German heavyweight boxing champion.

Brecht had asked me and a number of other Berlin school children to act as guinea pigs in the performance of a "school opera" he had just written, "Der Jasager", *The Yes Sayer*, based on Arthur Waley's adaptation of the Japanese play "Taniko". The story, briefly, was that of a Japanese schoolboy who fell ill during an expedition and was asked whether, to save the lives of the others, he was willing to be killed. He answered "Yes", sacrificing himself for the common weal.

This was one of Brecht's first attempts to write purely functional drama for a specialized audience. It was meant – so Brecht told us – to be "instructive rather than entertaining". We were asked to say (*a*) whether we agreed with the message; (*b*) whether it coincided with our experience; (*c*) whether we thought it suitable for performance at our school.

A year later, when he first published the play, he printed

our comments at the end of it and said that they had been most useful and had caused him to make major changes in the play. Since our comments had been almost unanimously negative, this would indeed have been an act of individual submission to collective demand – an act of the sort which the play itself advocated.

In practice, of course, he did no such thing. What he really did was as characteristic of the man as it was indicative of his working method: he finished the play exactly as he had proposed to write it in the first instance, and then wrote a second play, "Der Neinsager", *The No Sayer*, in which the opposite view was being advocated. Then he published the two of them together, appended our comments on the first one, and introduced the pair by saying: "These two little pieces should, if possible, not be performed one without the other."

This is what Brecht did all his life: he went to his audience for guidance, convinced himself thoroughly that he was not doing things for *his* pleasure but for *their* enlightenment, and then wrote something which conformed nominally with their ideas and practically with no one else's but Brecht's own. In essence he stuck to this recipe all his life. In his later years his Western critics have often accused him of kowtowing to his "Communist masters". This, of course, is positively comic to those who have observed Brecht's lifelong battle of wits with the Party.

True, he turned from vaguely anarchist, nihilist and pacifist views to professed Stalinism, but it was not Communist insistence which caused him to seek out and consult his audience: it was his own desire. From childhood on he had made it his business to try art on the dog and to ignore the dog when it barked at him.

The secret of his first verses, which burst upon the German public with an effect that no other twentieth-century poet has had on his audience, was that they had been composed *in* public and *for* a public rather than in private and for the author's own pleasure. They were sung rather than written. He had made them up at gatherings of his friends during his school and university years and had sung them a hundred times in country inns around the Black Forest before he ever published them.[1] Thus they had more in common with the kind of songs Villon had sung to the *coquillards* than with the delicately composed verse of Rilke, George and Hofmannsthal who ruled German lyric poetry at that time.

To understand how very great, how altogether unprecedented, the effect of Brecht's verses proved upon his first German readers, one has to remind oneself of the fact that there has never been such a thing as colloquial writing of true value in German literature. In the early years of the Weimar Republic, when Brecht's first verses were published, the bulk of his readers still thought of Germany as the Country of Poets and Thinkers. And in the public mind, the two were indissolubly linked.

Goethe, the philosopher-poet, was the ideal for which to strive. The "naturalist" playwrights – Gerhart Hauptmann, Hermann Sudermann and their followers – had temporarily opened a road to realistic dialogue, but the gulf between stage realism and works of "art" was so great as to be considered unbridgeable. In fact, when Hauptmann decided that he was going to become a modern Goethe, he dropped realism like a hot brick and began to devote himself to the mysticism of "Die versunkene Glocke" and the turgid versification of "Hanneles Himmelfahrt".

In the public mind, as in Hauptmann's own, poetry remained rhymed thought, and prose remained narrated thought. There was no precedent (*a*) for colloquial poetry; (*b*) for plain storytelling. There was no German equivalent to writers like Kipling, Mark Twain or Hemingway.

The language itself militated against it: you either wrote *hochdeutsch* or you wrote dialect. And if you wrote dialect, like Anzengruber, Rosegger and Reuter, you remained a

---

[1] Brecht's first verses were set to German folk tunes or popular ditties. Later he made up his own melodies. Fourteen of the poems in his first and second collection carry his own notes. Thus a great deal of the music of *Mahagonny*, *Dreigroschenoper* and other plays of his, though rewritten by, and formally credited to, Weill, Eisler and Dessau is at least partly Brecht's own. The astonishing unity of feeling that runs through all the music of all his plays, regardless of who signed his name as composer, thus goes back to Brecht himself.

parochial figure and were automatically barred from succession to Goethe's crown.

Brecht was the first writer of his generation who broke out of this vice of language and made up a tongue of his own, based on a juxtaposition of four utterly alien worlds: (1) South German colloquialisms; (2) an antimetaphorical poetry of colours, textures and other concrete images; (3) officialese; (4) anglicisms and exoticisms.

This, of course, was a wildly artificial language: no one really ever talked like a Brecht character – except Brecht himself. And this is where the ultimate key to his genius lies. He had, from his school years on, a manner of speech so very personal as to amount to total idiosyncrasy. None of this was affectation: it was a genuine oddity of outlook – and it gave his work, from his first verses and his first plays on, a quality so utterly unlike that of any other German writer as to make him seem, to most of his readers, like a man whose mind and thought moved in channels unlike their own.

Not that there was ever anything "difficult" about his work in the sense that Joyce or Eliot or Pound might be considered difficult; on the contrary, Brecht used language which was baffling mainly because of its simplicity. The words were everyday words, slang, colloquialisms, and the greyest of grey officialese spiked with occasional foreign words. But these anglicisms or exoticisms were germanified in a peculiar manner – germanified as a child or a man utterly ignorant of foreign languages might modify them. The total impression was hauntingly elusive – something that sounded vaguely familiar, like the speech of a poetic tramp or the local idiom of a region which none of us had ever visited. It was maddeningly reminiscent of *something* – but what the something was no one but Brecht could ever have described.

All this is untranslatable because it derives its effect not so much from its poetic imagery, nor from the thought behind it, but from the manner in which it deflects and contradicts the expected rise and fall of German speech.

When Brecht published his second collection of poems, he called them *A Household Book of Homilies* and introduced them with a mock-serious "Instruction for the Employment of the Individual Lessons", which constitutes one of the strangest and least translatable parodies of office jargon that he has ever used anywhere. Yet the total impact of the instructions, for reasons almost impossible to pin down, was essentially a lyrical one.

For example:

"Chapter 6 (*Ballad of the Sea Robbers*) is to be read primarily in the white nights of June. But it is permissible for the second part of the ballad, in so far as it relates to the ship wreck, to be sung as late as October. The melody is that of L'Etendard de la Pitié. Chapter 8 (*Ballad of the Hanna Cash*) is meant for times of unprecedented persecution (in times of unprecedented persecution the devotion of a good woman will become apparent)."

The overtones of this sort of prose are, of course, elusive. What sounds like easy persiflage in English has an underlying element of earnestness which indicates unmistakably to the German reader that Brecht means at least part of what he says. He cultivates the same tone when he instructs his actors. All his essays on theatrical theory are written in the same prose. All of them are blocked out with footnotes, annotations, explanations, discussions of the reviews which the plays received, dissections of the actors and their performances, revised endings, alternative versions printed side by side, and so on.

This, of course, is more than a mannerism: it is part of a lyrical approach to red tape. From a Western artist's point of view this may sound preposterous. But Brecht was first of all a German; secondly a professing and professed Communist; thirdly a theatrical administrator as well as a playwright. To him there was great poetic attraction in the grey world of officialdom, in the finicky detail of administration. As unconventional as he made himself out to be, he was fascinated with all forms of convention, etiquette and formalism. Grey was his favourite colour.

At first glance his solemnity, his deliberately stilted prose passages, his madly involuted essay style give the impression of parody. But after a while one becomes aware that there is an oblique beauty to this starchy office prose, a lopsided attraction like that of an old telephone or a Victorian railway bridge. What, then, is Brecht really after?

The answer is that he, the most vocal advocate of the lucid statement, is after nothing less than ambiguity.

Ambiguity is the formal principle of his work, the key to its charm, the secret of its success. Form and content walk along different paths. Content itself is divided into advocacy and negation of advocacy by means of persiflage. Form is divided into lyricism and the negation of lyricism by means of the excessively prosaic.

And, in fact, when one got to know Brecht well, one became aware of the same ambiguity in his own character – an ambiguity which he deliberately cultivated. His obsession with the neatness of his working papers, for instance, was so excessively typical of all the German office virtues and all the German office vices that it became positively comic for the onlooker; and Brecht deliberately overplayed the part so as to stress the effect of self-parody.

He was by temperament a lyric poet, endowed with a most exceptional sensitivity towards mood, climate, landscape, season and human relationship. His conversation was governed by his awareness of the most delicate shades of emotion. But he discourages all forms of "private emotion" in himself and others with a violence bordering upon shame. The only emotion worth communication was a social emotion, and there were few poets who could serve him as guides in that small realm. He despised rhymed philosophy: he believed that in literature, as in mathematics, the concise statement was the beautiful statement. If a complex statement could be made in an unusually small number of words, then it was poetry.

That, at any rate, was what he professed when you argued with him. But the masters who governed his own education as a poet were Villon, Baudelaire, Verlaine, Rimbaud, Kipling and Büchner. To those who are new to Brecht's work this must, of course, seem a singularly queer assortment. Villon, Baudelaire, Verlaine, Rimbaud – very well. But what is Kipling doing in this company?

The answer is that he provided the colloquial element, the same element that attracted Brecht to Villon. Kipling wrote songs about men of action, and they were the only men that Brecht was interested in. Kipling wrote in an aggressive, popular verse form with a pulse like drum beats, and that was precisely what Brecht, at least professedly, was after. Kipling was an empire builder, and Brecht was concerned with building a socialist empire. In other words, switch the values around and you have a workable form of working-class poetry.

There is only one German writer from whom Brecht might have acquired some of this miraculous balance between extreme poetic sophistication and deceptive simplicity of expression – the young revolutionary Georg Büchner who wrote *Woyzeck*, *Leonce und Lena* and *Dantons Tod* some hundred years before Brecht and died in 1837 at the age of twenty-three.

Büchner influenced Brecht in more ways than one. Brecht's boundless admiration for the older dramatist, his conviction that Büchner was the *sole* German playwright who (*a*) understood Shakespeare and (*b*) understood what a *German* play should be all about, caused him to take Büchner as his model in life as well as in art.

Büchner was a doctor, and Brecht became one. Büchner turned from medicine to natural science, and so did Brecht. Büchner became a man of action, and Brecht had to turn himself into one. Büchner was an active revolutionary, and so Brecht became one.

After the First World War, when the Spartakisten, the predecessors of the German Communist Party, formed their first Soldiers' and Peasants' Soviets, he helped to organize his local Augsburg cell. But even at that time he was far from Communist orthodoxy. He was so wholly and so incurably an eccentric that no political party, least of all the KPD, the singularly orthodox German Communist Party, could conceivably absorb him: he was refused Party membership time and time again. And it should perhaps be said here, in advance of chronological order, that he never became a Communist in his later years either – though he flattered himself into thinking, and loved telling his friends, that he was a far better Marxist than Pieck or Grotewohl.

He was an eccentric in behaviour, speech and dress as well as in politics. He wore clothes that kept a neat balance between those of a soldier, a workman and a tramp. His glasses, through many years of his life, were iron-rimmed and made him look like a village schoolteacher. He discouraged any sign of comfort in his rooms. Carpets and paintings were frowned upon, though he loved to pin roughly scissored news clippings to his walls. Occasional Chinese scrolls were permissible, but only as long as they remained unframed. And he liked to associate with athletes, engineers, explorers and misfits – in fact, with anybody except artists.

There was a time in Berlin when every one of the Brechtians looked exactly like every other one. And those who, for reasons of sex, could not model themselves on Brecht, were married to the Brechtians. Thus Lotte Lenya, Brecht's first leading lady, was married to Kurt Weill, his composer. Carola Neher, his other leading lady, was married to Klabund, the poet whose "Chalk Circle" Brecht later turned into his *Caucasian Chalk Circle*. Brecht, Klabund, Dudow, Caspar Neher and Paul Samson Koerner, the German heavyweight boxing champion, all sported exactly identical haircuts – something between a crew-cut and a poodle-cut. The hair was sliced off abruptly after two or three inches' growth, all around the head, and hung down vaguely like the coiffure you see on busts of Roman emperors.

Brecht wore "knickerbockers" made out of a material known in German as "Kord", an indestructible greyish fabric usually worn by chauffeurs, over black leather puttees. He also sported a brown leather jacket, again modelled pretty much on the type of garment worn by chauffeurs, motor cyclists or unemployed ex-officers.

When I asked him why he wore his hair that way, he said: "It saves combing." I should, of course, have asked him why, in that case, he didn't wear a beard, but he probably would have said: "Oh, aren't I wearing one?" For he certainly looked forever unshaven, and his thin, ironic mouth was forever stained with brown tobacco juice dribbling down from the ghastly stogies he smoked – the cheapest cigars he could find and certainly the vilest smelling ones obtainable for love or money.

Although he made it his practice to discuss every aspect of his work with every member of his Kollektiv and was willing to tolerate any amount of criticism from them, he would lose his temper and become violently abusive if you cornered him on his own and compared his work with anybody else's – even when the comparison was in his favour.

One day I thus compared a passage in one of his plays with a passage in a Hemingway story, and Brecht, who professed to despise Hemingway as a bourgeois romantic, became so angry that he got up and said in a tortured voice: "No more! Get out, get out, get out!" And then, in perfect Brechtian officialese, "No, show me your identification first! Show me your passport so I know where you belong! Then take your exit permit and *go*!"

At the sound of the last *go*, his wife, Helene Weigel, now the head of the Berliner Ensemble and one of the most perfectly controlled actresses of our day, came out of the kitchen, a frying pan in her hand; and without having the vaguest desire to know what the argument was all about, she joined her husband in shouting loyally, "Yes, go, go, go," swinging her frying pan like a sword.

All of Brecht's women were loyal to him – and he had a vast consumption. He was a singularly ugly man, and he certainly was anything but a charmer, but his very contempt for all the traditional rules of conduct between the sexes made him peculiarly attractive to women. Strangely enough, for one who positively prided himself on his ugliness and ill manners, he had the rare gift, too, of retaining not only the love but also the respect of the women he had known.

In 1933, the day after Goering set fire to the Reichstag, he packed up his family and went abroad – first to Austria, then to Denmark, Sweden, Finland, Russia, France, England, USA and Switzerland. Almost throughout his fifteen years of exile he lived in unbelievable poverty – frequently eating only one meal a day, and sometimes none. But he always managed to get hold of his vile cigars, and he was rarely without a drink. Completely oblivious to the ugliness of the boarding houses, hotel rooms and lodgings in which he lived, he continued, as always, to collect a fantastic mountain of news clippings from all around the world, to keep up a fabulous reading schedule on all aspects of politics, science, history, verse and crime fiction, and to go to the movies as often as he could.

He loathed the film which Pabst had made of his *Dreigroschenoper*, but he loved the cheapest kind of Hollywood musical, and when he was asked to write a shooting script for a screen version of *Pagliacci*, featuring Richard Tauber, of all people, he accepted with alacrity. It was, perhaps, the most incongruous job of writing he ever did, and the film certainly was almost catastrophically bad, but it still showed the touch of the master in such unlikely scenes as the epilogue in which Tauber suddenly turned to address the audience like a commissar in a *Lehrstuck*.

Yet it was in exile that Brecht wrote much of his best work. The playfulness, the scurrility, the idiosyncrasies vanished and a new, sparse, pointed style broke through in his superb *Svendborg Poems*; his deeply felt *Furcht und Elend des dritten Reiches*, a sequence of brief scenes of life under the Hitler régime; his *Puntila*, written in Finland in 1940; and the poignant life story of *Galileo Galilei*.

In Denmark, England, France and America his old and new plays were performed: none made any major impact in translation. While in Hollywood, Brecht wrote a number of films, and one of them, *Hangmen Also Die*, was directed by Fritz Lang for United Artists release. It was a mess. On July 30, 1947, Joseph Losey staged his *Galileo* at the Coronet Theatre in Hollywood, with Charles Laughton in the lead. *Variety* commented: "There is a symbolic bit of business in the final scene of Bertolt Brecht's new play. Galileo, investigating the laws of motion, rolls a small metal ball down an incline and measures its ability to roll up the other side of the u-shaped chute. The ball doesn't quite make the grade. Neither, unfortunately, does the script."

Wrong: it wasn't the script that failed, it was the performance. Although Brecht himself had worked with Laughton and Losey for nearly a year on the production, it was scrappy. It had a single set, slides projected from the flies, exposed stage lights, a ballad singer, a group of three boys acting as a "Sprechchor", music by Hanns Eisler, all the paraphernalia of Brecht's technique. But the very element on which he prided himself – the cool, unemotional presentation of a case offered for contemplation rather than for identification with the characters – failed disastrously with the public, as it had failed with one public after another throughout his long, busy life.

As early as 1931, when *Mann ist Mann* was presented at the Staatstheater in Berlin, the theatre critics of the Börsen-kurier, a Berlin newspaper of some distinction, had complained that it was impossible to sympathise with any of Brecht's plays, to identify oneself with one of his characters, or to recognize any verisimilitude in the style of acting. Brecht replied at length in a letter to the editor, pointing out patiently that those three so-called shortcomings were precisely the goals he had set himself. The Ibsen theatre with its evocation of conflict between the protagonists, its invitation to the audience to identify itself with the characters and laugh or cry with them, its attempt to direct the actors as if they *were* the figures they portrayed – all this, Brecht said, was dead and could never be revived. The time now had come for a theatre in which exactly the opposite had to be attempted.

And indeed for the next sixteen years Brecht had worked with phenomenal ingenuity at devising an infinitely complex and most thoroughly integrated stage technique, which broke with almost every theatre tradition from Ibsen to Stanislavsky. The only trouble was that his critics, capitalist and Communist alike, kept making the same point over and over again: that Brecht's break with the three elements of (1) dramatic confrontation, (2) verisimilitude and (3) audience identification, might well be deliberate but still wasn't right.

Variety said in its review of *Galileo*: "In the seventeenth century scientist's battle with the church there is material for forceful drama." ("Forceful drama", of course, was exactly what Brecht did *not* want to write.) "But *Galileo* in

its present form is ponderous rather than powerful." (Had
the critic said "epic" instead of "ponderous", Brecht would
have felt this as praise.) "There are fleeting moments that
are exciting" ("excite" was the one thing Brecht didn't want
to do). "But the peak level is not sustained" ("peaks" was
precisely what Brecht tried to *avoid*, and every conceivable
form of interruption was introduced so as to *prevent* any
sustained continuity) "and the overall impression is one of
dullness."

"Dullness" – this, at last, was what hurt Brecht; and this,
of course, is the achilles heel of the Brechtian theatre. For
how can you inform, instruct or guide your audience to action
if you bore them? The truth, of course, is that Brecht never
bores those who are at all susceptible to his lyricism: but he
bores almost everybody else, and he bores them precisely in
ratio to his success at carrying out his proclaimed aims.

Thus he succeeds where he does not wish to succeed and
fails where he is most afraid to fail. Technically, his theatre
avails itself of a number of simple devices. The stage, on the
whole, is bare. Props, sets and utensils are either implied or
announced with posters. But to counteract the danger of
stylization (and Brecht considers style a form of bourgeois
formalism), an occasional object of complete realism is introduced, such as the armoured carrier in *The Private Life of the
Master Race*.

The stage is brightly lit, and the stage lights are exposed
so that the public at all times is being made aware of the fact
that "this is not life, this is not a room with the fourth wall
cut away, this is a *stage*".

At the beginning of the play, or at appropriate intervals,
slides are projected or posters held up which carry messages
either to elucidate points or to destroy any possible impression of reality, of looking at real events rather than at a play.
The same "alienation effect" can, of course, be obtained by
sending speakers out on to the stage who interrupt the flow
of action by addressing themselves directly to the audience,
sometimes with the text of the play visibly in their hands,
so as to read out stage instructions and author's comments.

Similarly, so as to prevent the audience from being steeped

into a sort of emotional warm bath by the accompanying music which Brecht favours, he will project the *titles* of the individual songs on to the stage while they are being sung. Or to prevent the audience from being caught up in a sense of expectation, suspense or tension, he will read out or project a *synopsis* of the scene to follow. This, he says, should allow the audience to *contemplate* the scene and receive its full impact as a *guide to action*.

Having worked as a producer and director under Reinhardt, Piscator and at the Munich Kammerspiele, Brecht knew exactly what he wanted from his actors when he started producing his own plays. He wanted them to *present a case* rather than to identify themselves with a character. He asked them to recall in their performance the uncertainty they had felt in their first rehearsal. He asked them to think of their lines as if they were not in dialogue but in descriptive language: in fact, he re-wrote whole scenes from his plays in descriptive form and rehearsed them that way before he allowed the actors to speak actual dialogue. That is to say, instead of allowing character Jones to say "Yes", he made him say: "Jones answered in the affirmative".

Instead of allowing them to present decisively one aspect of any given character, and that aspect alone, he encouraged them to think of all the alternative actions which the character might have taken at any given moment and to imply those alternatives in their acting – either by hesitation or by starting the action in one way and then finishing it in another.

To remind his actors that they were *actors* rather than embodiments of characters in a play, he made them read out the stage directions as well as their lines. And to prevent them from trying to "melt their audience together into a single emotional lump", he asked them to think of their audience as a divided group of friends and enemies, rich and poor, and to *divide* their audience accordingly by addressing themselves to one part of the audience now, to another part the next moment.

Small wonder that a technique so alien to the Actors' Studio should have bewildered his American audience, whose *avant-garde* had just barely caught up with the Stanislavsky tradition which Brecht had disowned twenty years ago. Small wonder, too, that Brecht began to feel by 1947 that it was almost hopeless for him to make his case before the public unless he had continuity of production. So when the East German government offered him the Theater am Schiffbauerdamm in the Soviet Sector of Berlin, he accepted the offer. Since then he has had what probably amounted to the most generous financial support that any modern playwright or producer has had in any country of the world.

By 1955, towards the end of his life, he had some 240 actors, 60 technicians, and the best designers, musicians and choreographers in the country working for him. Nominally, his wife, Helli, was head of the "Berliner Ensemble". Practically, as in every Kollektiv that Brecht ever participated in, he ran it.

During the last five years of his life, he was the undisputed Old Master: he, who had begun as a *Bankelsanger*, an idiomatic versemaker with a pronounced bias against the literary tradition of German poetry, a crusader against the professorial tradition of German literature; he, of all people, had now inherited the mantle of Goethe: he had become a poet-philosopher of the accepted German pattern.

His political allegiance, of course, went contrary to everything that the bulk of West Germans believed in: but they acknowledged him nevertheless as a master in the great tradition. What he had to say might be wrong, even dangerous, almost certainly seditious, but he said it with the true professorial air of the Herr Geheimrat from Weimar.

He dressed, as he always had, in an odd military-styled grey jacket (though the cut and collar now strangely resembled Stalin's) and a cloth cap. He lived as humbly as he always had, in the back part of an unfashionable house in an unfashionable district. He smoked the same old cigars and he frequently wore the same old stubble beard as in the 'twenties.

But he was given complete freedom to carry out his ideas. He was given the means to experiment. And he was rarely attacked in public. The argument over *The Trial of Lucullus* has been wildly exaggerated in the West: there was no disagreement over the ending. Brecht had written the first version in 1939, at the outbreak of the Second World War, when the Party line had been essentially one of "after Hitler our turn". So the tone was pacifist, and the Party accepted it.

In 1951, he re-staged it, and by then the political situation, and the Party line with it, had changed: it called now for condemnation not so much of war as of imperialist war; not for pacifism, but for a re-assertion of the class struggle.

There were long discussions between Brecht, his audience, his collaborators and the Party, before any changes were made. Brecht took to the discussions like a duck to water. This was what he had done all his life, and this was what he could do best. He made his changes, published a new version, and had the old one printed side by side, explaining exactly why he had made the change. It was, he said, not only a political but also an artistic improvement.

But behind the scenes the battle went on. Again and again the cultural representatives of the Party argued the case of socialist realism with him. Again and again he was charged with formalism. Again and again he was told that his audience simply could not follow his logic, his style of presentation, his theatrical objectives.

All this happened – and it might have broken a lesser man. But the Western critics who have sighed for poor Brecht's ordeal completely misunderstand the man's character. He never felt himself restricted in his freedom of expression. He felt, on the contrary, that it was not only the right but the *duty* of the Party to correct him. And he felt that he was constantly improving the political effectiveness and the artistic clarity of his work.

But, of course, the more changes he made, the more Brechtian became his prose, his logic, his dramatic technique. And however often he re-wrote a play, he never changed the one aspect on which his whole theory of drama was based – the deliberate alienation of his public – and so it goes without saying that he lost his working-class audience in the end. He lost them and he lost the Party, but he gained something else in their place.

Towards the close of his life, his theatre probably had more visitors from the West than from East Berlin. The ratio of intelligentsia to working class must have been higher than in any other theatre in Germany, East or West. And what did they come to see?

They came to see an intellectual freak show – the spectacle of a man of genius proclaiming a *credo quia absurdum*. It was as if a circus strongman, perhaps the strongest man in the world, were to give an act wholly devoted to proving the kind of things which no human strength can do: for everything Brecht did went to demonstrate the paradox of his own life; everything was a public exhibition of immense talent pitted against a self-defeating theory.

Every play that was successful with his audience succeeded for the wrong reasons: only those passages that did not conform to his theories, that were unextruded remnants of conventional theatre, really moved his audience, while those passages on which he had worked hardest and which most lucidly demonstrated his theories of the epic stage pleased no one except his fellow-artists.

Thus his theatre became ultimately something that Brecht himself, had he allowed himself to acknowledge it, would have been the first to reject: a *l'art pour l'art* studio – a theatre for theatre people – a workshop where theatrical theories were being put to a breaking test. And just as it is the task of a testing lab to ascertain at what point a steel girder might snap, so it became the historic task of the Brechtian theatre to demonstrate night after night at what point Brecht's techniques would break under the strain of audience reaction.

The ultimate paradox was this: Brecht's theatre remained, to the last, a delight for those who were susceptible to his lyricism. Every device which he had contrived to destroy the "magic" of theatre became magic in his hands. The exposed stage lights, far from alienating us, communicated all of Brecht's love of the stage: the stage itself, thus deified, became a place of poetry.

His posters, lantern slides and announcements – ostensibly conceived to destroy the magic of the play – were worded with such supreme poetic diction that we forgot their content and surrendered to their form.

The songs, curtains, choirs and other deliberate interruptions, far from breaking our bond of empathy fortified it, because it was impossible for Brecht to write a line or conceive an image without communicating a sense of poetry and wonder. The very rhythm of interruptions became a poetic pattern and destroyed the purpose for which they had ostensibly been conceived.

And his insistence that his actors should retain the wonder and bewilderment they had felt when they had first discovered the implications of their part, far from de-romanticizing the play, made it more miraculous than Ibsen's theatre had ever been. Instead of preventing the audience from "melting together into a single emotional lump", it fused them into a new unity by communicating the wonder of discovery.

Thus every aspect of Brecht's stage technique militated against the purpose for which it had been conceived. His theatre became a place of utter magic – but only for those who loved Brecht as a lyric poet and were sensitive to that inexplicable gift in him which transformed everything he touched. The bulk of his audience – even those who were sensitive to dramatic values – missed all that he had to give and were bored with his lack of "drama", of "conflict", "characterization", "climax", and even – most humiliating to Brecht who canonized lucidity – his lack of intelligibility: more than half of his working-class audience simply could not understand what in hell the whole thing was all about.

The tragedy of Brecht's life then boils down to this simple fact: he gained the admiration and respect of those whom he professed to despise – the poets, the intellectuals, the West; and he failed to gain the one audience in the world for whom he claimed to write: the working class, the Party, the East.

[JULY 1958]

THE NEW SARTRE *by Ian Dallas*

It was after midnight when we left the Théâtre de la Renaissance and set out for supper at the Brasserie Lipp. We did not get far, however, before a large battered saloon car forced our own to the edge of the pavement. Six heavy, vicious-looking men leapt out. I thought they were gangsters, but wisely my friend made no attempt to evade them for then I might not have lived to write this article. Rudely and aggressively our identification papers were demanded and with equally disinterested savagery the car door was slammed shut and we drove on our way. The feeling, even though it was so brief, of suddenly being at the mercy of police power and all that that means, was disturbing. What made it significant was that it was a reflection of the troubles that still assail France under de Gaulle's not yet secure dictatorship. For, in France where the Revolution was born, democracy has failed, hopelessly, humiliatingly. In despair, a whole nation had turned to one man, had surrendered its rights, its freedoms to his authority. Ironically, while under the fourth Republic there was spirited Leftist criticism of the régime and frank unmasking of Fascist. policies – under the new régime to criticize the army or the police or any aspect of the establishment is to criticize de Gaulle, and this is not tolerated. People DID read *La Question*, only a handful of people ever got their hands on *La Gangrène*.

My preamble is vital to my subject because it is against this fascinating background of the death of a democracy and the founding of a neo-monarchist state that the new play by Europe's greatest living thinker has been created. With the open disapproval of France's new Minister of Culture, the hysterical André Malraux, Jean-Paul Sartre's play opened last year. *Figaro's* critic, normally a coherent man, lost himself in a whirl of vicious invective, spluttering out that he could not understand a word of the play's meaning. So unjust was the "official" attack on the play that Nobel prizewinner and Academician François Mauriac, a man once harshly criticized by Sartre, openly rebuked the critic, and insisted on a more careful and considered approach to the work of a man of Sartre's intellectual status. The battle was on. The play in some deep yet not unfathomable way was an affront to de Gaulle's soi-disant Republic. The play also happened to be a masterpiece.

Les Séquestrés d'Altona is a modern tragedy. It is the most important play to be written in Europe since the war. I have read two English reviews. Harold Hobson clearly did not understand what the play was about, and Alan Pryce-Jones, while respectful, failed to see beyond the faults of the production and mistook the piece for a play "about" Germany.

The play tells the story of Frantz von Gerlach who for thirteen years has lived in voluntary isolation, sequestered in a room with bricked-up windows, seeing no one except his sister who jealously guards over him and feeds him. Four people revolve around Frantz: Léni, his sister, who would keep him as he is, bound forever by their incestuous liaison; Johanna, his brother's wife, who begins by wanting to discover the secret of Frantz's seclusion and ends by wanting to free him from his torment; then Werner, the brother, weak and without confidence in his own authority, longing to return to his vocation as an advocate but forced to inherit the vast industrial set-up ruled by his father who only puts up with him because he is a Gerlach. The father is dying of cancer, and faced with his death has to prepare Werner for a role he would wholeheartedly like to have seen Frantz assume. But on the walls the vast photographs of Frantz bear a black mourning ribbon across the right-hand corner. To the world Frantz is dead. Why?

Early in the war the Nazi Government chiefs had visited Hamburg and asked Frantz's father to sell them a plot of ground. It was to be turned into a concentration camp. He had acquiesced, saying that to refuse would be to alienate the Nazis, and furthermore they would simply have gone to another landowner and built the camp elsewhere. He explains that he has lost his conscience "out of modesty. It is a prince's luxury." To his son he says: "Do you want to carry the world on your shoulders? The world is heavy . . ." With the morally weak wisdom of the liberal that was so soon to crumble to cynicism before the force of Nazi power, the father Frantz worships had made his first gesture of betrayal. A Polish rabbi escapes the Camp, and Frantz, in an attempt to be responsible to those for whom he feels concern, tries to help him escape. To save Frantz's life his father intercedes on his behalf to Goebbels. The Nazis spare his life but slaughter the rabbi before his eyes. Frantz then goes off to the war, wins many decorations, and finally returns from the Eastern Front after a hazardous retreat through Poland.

On his return to Altona, Frantz at first shuts himself in the house and drinks, and then in his room. He chooses an isolated existence without newspapers or a watch to mark the passage of history. All the above is revealed in a series of brief, fierce flashbacks, while the family wait below looking up to the room where Frantz lives his lonely life, and where he in turn looks up beyond space to another century, another race that will judge modern man. "Man is dead," says Frantz, "and I am his witness." On to his tape recorder Frantz records and re-records what he considers to be a true defence of the German people who in his imagination still live in the desolation of 1945, a dying race, scrabbling among the ruins of cathedrals, and over the stone deserts of their raised cities, starving, devouring each other, under sentence for their crimes. The judgement is both false and unbearable and Frantz searches to find the argument that will acquit them in the eyes of another century and even another race, the Crabs, who, Frantz declares, will take over after the failure of men on the earth. Thus, he seeks not only to expiate the guilt of his people but of his species. He is alone, despite Léni, for she, even in incest, is no more than an object. Then Johanna tries to break through his isolation. She sees that the only way to get to him is to enter his fantasy and she is even prepared to do that. She plays the game and a cold chaste love grows between them. She has broken the chains of his solitary existence. He again wears his watch and waits impatiently like a lover for Johanna's return. Now she stands before him as a more vital and living judge than the Tribunal of the Crabs. In vain he tries to construct an acceptable version of his behaviour with the Russian prisoners he encountered on his retreat from the East. Léni, desperate at the invasion of Johanna, faces him with a newspaper. Frantz is forced back to the present. Germany is the richest power in Europe and his father is an industrial giant, richer than before. Léni forces out the final, horrible truth. Frantz not only killed the

Russian partisans but he had them tortured as well. He, too, has shared in the Nazi crime, he, the witness of man before the centuries.

His isolation is useless. He agrees to see his father. They face each other at last, they speak together, confess, but cannot judge. They are both responsible, both guilty, and both unable to bear their self-knowledge. Only one thing is left for them. They decide to die together by driving their Porsche car into the sea. The empire passes into the hands of the mediocre couple and Léni mounts the stairs to continue the lonely existence that was once Frantz's, in expiation of her incestuous bond. On the empty stage the voice of Frantz's final and definitive defence of men and of himself is heard unwinding on the tape machine. Frantz at his death has accepted the total responsibility for his existence and his era. He is free. The curtain falls.

It is hard to précis a tragic situation without in some degree suggesting melodramatic tensions. Sartre has scrupulously avoided the sensational, and presents the irresistible movements of his characters to their final choices in a formal, classical manner at once sombre and ferocious. Written in his most muscular prose, the dialogue is capable of lithe sinewy movement and when necessary flexes into powerful dramatic stance. Frantz's great speeches on the play's central theme have a force and dignity utterly devoid of the rhetoric that mars so many excellent French plays. The last speech has a philosophic weight and a poetic vision that renders it unforgettable. The sheer intellectual virtuosity of the writing cannot easily be overestimated. Not only are the great aphoristic statements buoyed up by the turbulent, twisting movement of the play's dialogue, but continually Sartre flings the action against some rock-like paradox before it is allowed to flow freely again. "You would be invulnerable if you dared to say: I did what I wanted, and I want what I have done." Or, after explaining the power he had as a Nazi soldier Frantz declares: "I was the wife of Hitler!"

In this play Sartre has combined the dramatic intensity of *Huis Clos* with the philosophic density that has informed his two great works, *L'Etre et le Néant* and *Saint Genet*. The last sentence of *L'Etre et le Néant* was "Man is a useless passion." This statement can only be grasped after examining the intricate, often tortured, but always dedicated attempt to define the human condition in terms of freedom. In that work he stated: "Man can not be sometimes slave and sometimes free; he is wholly and forever free or he is not free at all." Or again: "The most terrible situations of war, the worst tortures do not create a non-human situation. . . . Thus there are no *accidents* in life; a community event which suddenly bursts forth and involves me in it does not come from the outside. If I am mobilized in a war, this war is MY war; it is in my image and I deserve it. . . . For lack of getting out of it I have chosen it." He goes on to say, "Thus, totally free, indistinguishable from the period for which I have chosen to be the meaning, as profoundly responsible for the war as if I had myself declared it, unable to live without integrating it in MY situation, engaging myself in it, wholly and stamping it with my seal, I must be without remorse or regrets as I am without excuse; for from the instant of my upsurge into being, I carry the weight of the world by myself, alone, without any thing or any person being able to lighten it."

I have quoted at length because this is the intellectual centre of the play and its releasing climax. Frantz in his last speech says: "O tribunal de la nuit, toi qui fus, qui seras, qui es, j'ai été! j'ai été! Moi, Frantz von Gerlach, ici dans cette chambre, j'ai pris mon siècle sur mes épaules et j'ai dit: j'en répondrai. En ce jour et pour toujours." There is a victory but it is a tragic victory. It is not a romantic victory or perhaps M. Malraux would have given the play his Imprimatur. No, it is an anguished and realistic exploration of our condition that faces us with what we have DONE as well as what we are. There is a gulf between the stoical dignity of the last sentence of *L'Etre et le Néant* and the tragic, agonized cry from the depths: "Man is dead" that rings throughout *Les Séquestrés d'Altona.* With this terrible sentence we enter a new philosophical era as surely as the modern world was born when Zarathustra declared that God was dead in 1891.

One of the most thrilling things about Sartre's new play is the way the drama of the Gerlach family is acted out at the

personal and at the social level. Frantz's search for a defence
of the Fatherland is also inextricably bound to his attempt
to find a justification for his father's actions under the Nazi
régime. The whole body politic of Germany was corrupted by
Nazism, Frantz's father is dying of a fatal cancer. The actual
wasteland of the Germany of 1945 is perpetuated in Frantz's
interior life and jealously guarded against the movement of
history which goes on, building on ruins, renewing without
discrimination the good and the evil men. Germany, however,
despite Frantz's nightmare, has *not* paid for its crimes, and
an historic justice (and therefore, meaning) is not discernible.
It is by virtue of this outrageous Absurd that Frantz is
forced into the anguish that yields to him his final choice. A
final choice that can only destroy him. In other words, Sartre
has chosen a hero at the limit of an unbearable situation in
order to force us to consider more critically and more urgently
our own situation. In an interview with *L'Express* Sartre
stated that by making Frantz address a tribunal of superior
beings, while what he said was not really the truth of our
times, he hoped that the audience would in some way sense
the presence of the Judges, "or, more simply, the centuries
to come". "Our century will be judged in the future with the
same objectivity that we in our turn judge the nineteenth or
the eighteenth century." Sartre has clearly tried in this play
to introduce an element of Alienation by his attitude to time.
He "distances" the present by letting his central character
address a future Tribunal and he further distances the recent
past by presenting it in flashbacks of past events that still
insinuate themselves into present actions.

And here reference must be made to the Paris production.
It is not good. The play is produced in the style of a late
Ibsen play. It has not been written like one. A naturalistic
production in a solid, built set can only present the play as a
"crise de famille". There is no social aspect permitted in this
structure. Also it makes the flashback scenes, so vital to the
play's purpose, seem examples of bad construction. Sartre
has had to bear the blame for this. Actually the play is as
sound as a drum in its structure. The play demands a more
Brechtian approach. The play is NOT too long as some critics

said. What happens in Paris is that one's ears do all the work and one's eyes are allowed to go to sleep. A more imaginative and poetic style of *mise en scène* would seem necessary to this play. The audience should never for a moment be allowed to forget that outside the Altona house the new, shining city of Hamburg stands, symbol of the resurrected Reich. If a cloth or cyclorama depicting the new Hamburg had dominated the stage throughout the action, and the sets of the house had been fitted in front of it, the irony of Frantz's situation would have been visually expressed. The flashback scenes, which in Paris were played apologetically upstage in an ineffectual spotlight, should be played centre front, preferably on a specially projected apron. The past of the characters must assault the audience if we are to get the full impact of the Gerlachs' extreme condition. It would be unfair however not to praise the proud, affectionate performance of Fernand Ledoux as the father, and the electrifying, tormented portrayal of Frantz by Serge Reggiani. Reggiani harrows our souls with the ruthless examination of his conscience that bit by bit becomes our own during the play.

Why did the right-wing critics attack the play? It is not overtly political, although Sartre has insisted that its political dimension has reference to France's Fascism in Algeria as well as Germany's in Europe. The key to the attack is probably contained in Servan-Schreiber's review of de Gaulle's new volume of memoirs, *Le Salut*. He quotes some lines of a frightful poem that Claudel wrote in the form of a dialogue between de Gaulle and France. The General says: " 'Femme, tais-toi! et ne me demande pas autre chose que ce que je suis capable de t'apporter.' 'Que m'apportes-tu donc, ô mon fils?' Et le général, levant le bras, répond: 'La volonté.' " Servan-Schreiber rightly is horrified by the implications of this sexual image of France in submission to one man, who puffed up with the conviction that he incarnates all Frenchmen, then turns to God and says "When I look at the stars I am aware of the insignificance of things." Bitterly, Servan-Schreiber adds, "Les choses – c'est nous!" The parallel with this remark and Frantz's admission, "I was the wife of Hitler", cannot be overlooked. France is a dictatorship, not a democracy. Men

have been robbed of any sense of being responsible for their
country's destiny. Eternal France, Glory, all the empty
slogans of a totalitarian rule are the order of the day. Small
wonder that de Gaulle's supporters have opposed a play that
examines the philosophical basis of a politique that allows
men to shed their responsibility to history.

Sartre's play RELATES to the world we live in. And for
his hero Sartre has chosen neither a revolutionary nor a saint.
He has chosen a torturer. Not simply a thug, but a man who
knows what he has done and who sees himself under judgement. He chooses a hero on the verge of insanity, split from
top to bottom with the contradictions of his century. He
chooses a man whose long dark night of the soul has been
shot through with equally unbearable seconds of illumination.
"Voilà vingt ans qu'il est minuit dans le siècle: ça n'est pas
très commode de garder les yeux ouverts à minuit." All his
life Sartre has rejected the bourgeois concept of something
called "human nature". Man is what he does, he defines himself by his actions. And here he presents us to ourselves. Man
is dead and his hero is no more than a witness to what was
once known as man. The witness himself acquiesced before
the absolute assault of evil that assailed Europe under
Nazism. Alternatively throughout the play Frantz salutes
and reviles the photograph of Hitler pasted on his wall. But
before Frantz drives the Porsche into the depths of the sea
his last act in the Gerlach house is to remove the black
mourning band from his own photograph. At his death
Frantz has said yes to his life. The tragic victory which
Arthur Miller once noted eludes the modern playwright has
been recaptured at last in this magnificent play. Sartre cannot
be ignored any longer. "Attention must be paid to this man!"

[JANUARY 1960]

ANTI-IONESCO THEATRE
by Charles Marowitz

There is a moment in *The Bald Prima Donna* which has
always unnerved me. It is when the maid, explaining the

confusion of the married couple who have just recognized each other, announces: "My real name is Sherlock Holmes." It disturbed me because this line had the ring of the simple buffoon about it. It was the kind of "joke" which would never have escaped from the pen of a genuine humorist, and the sort of easy comic interpolation which cheapened the real comedy of the play's idea and form. It was an intrusion which suggested that, in addition to having a scopic theatre-sense and a feeling for universalities, Ionesco also had a niggling little lightweight mind. A mind prone to puns and playful exuberance; a mind which equated levity with comedy and was distracted by the one at the expense of the other.

In *Rhinoceros*, that small disturbing trait has overwhelmed everything else. The mind which delighted at comic trifles is now employing trifles as an approach to dramatic art. The little unfunny buffoon who inhabited the body of the comic artist has now taken control of that body and from this new vantage point, all the subversions of the past loom larger than ever.

The great fault of *Rhinoceros* is that it is a simplification only a minor writer could make. It is a two-act ramification of the kind of joke that people usually associate with college professors. It is just as cerebral; just as contrived, and just as spiritless.

The new play unfolds like one great dramatized metaphor; a metaphor unconnected to any real body of work, and a metaphor so simplex that in the intellectual realm it is the equivalent of the June-moon rhymes or the sledgehammer symbolism of talentless undergraduates.

It mitigates nothing to admit that Ionesco is dealing with an important theme. In the theatre a theme is as important as its treatment. Individuality and Conformity are merely two enormous labels unless a writer delineates a dramatic conception of one and an equally dramatic conception of the other. Although Ionesco's hero Berenger is put forward as capital M-Man, he is barely lower-case m-man. He is just an elaborately stitched piece of gauze. Conformity is a herd of rhinos; a diverting expedient which makes a simple theme even simpler to handle. Argument: the plague of uniformity is transforming men into rhinoceri; Berenger, for no dynamic reason, resists the transformation. (Here is a cartoon-enlargement of Kafka's cockroach and a vulgar expansion of the theme in "Metamorphosis".) The play has all the large windy spaces of the unqualified generalization, and a lot of dramatic trellis-work to persuade us that what we are feeling is not wind but the creative heat of the true artist.

In director Orson Welles, Ionesco has found his intellectual equal. The production at the Royal Court is as broad, bold and humourless as the writer's conception. (Welles – *Men From Mars*, *Citizen Kane* – is a sucker for the massive abstraction; his speciality has always been the symbol which is so stunning no one questions its relevance.) The *specific* performance of Laurence Olivier is a long, sharp hyphenated stroke underlining the vacuity of the play. It is ridiculous to speak of a brilliant performance in a vacuum. A climber, no matter how adept, cannot gain a summit without a mountain!

The polyphonic conversations that stud the first act of *Rhinoceros* are a deft piece of playwriting, but they are not, as intended, a significant complex in which one idea illustrates another. They are a hit-or-miss spray of words and ideas (or words sans ideas) in which practically anything which is suggested is appropriate. Appropriate in that it does not violate any particular contention. (At this point in the play, there isn't any.) We understand that Ionesco is excused from weaving credible dramatic relationships, but licence cannot extend so far that characters merely bump together like the prongs and pellets of a pin-ball machine. If they illustrate neither action nor idea then what in hell is their function? Or is this too conventional a question for the unconventional Mr Ionesco?

The ennui which gradually overcomes the audience at *Rhinoceros* is the inevitable result of aimless gallimaufry. Anti-Theatre is a healthy impulse if it rescues us from the familiar and the drab, but a fool's paradise if it tries to pretend a series of cadenzi is a feasible substitute for symphonic form.

Ionesco's trouble (and it is fast becoming N. F. Simpson's as well) is that he believes a play can be made by drawing a strand from a wad of bubble-gum and stretching it out for two and a half hours. This strand is inevitably a light-hearted ramification of logic and language, but we have seen that trick too often; it no longer delights us. Once a man has shown us he can stand on his head, we also like to feel he can walk with his two legs. Ionesco has made the ridicule of logic his running-gag. It is a simple gag; almost anyone can do it. It demands the same kind of mental resources required for punning. It is an insight into the great theme of human non-communication, but it is not in itself a powerful illustration of that theme. Ionesco has been doodling around the margins of great ideas for ten years, but he has not yet demonstrated his ability to mould them into something dramatically positive.

His greatest achievements have been the compact treatises of *The Chairs*, *The Bald Prima Donna*, *The Lesson* and *The New Tenant*. These were small works in small frameworks, but they were vast miniatures – in the same sense that a tele-scope lens is a small thing in which a man can see a great deal. But an image glimpsed from a distance is not the same thing as a landscape which is set squarely in front of your eyes. Ionesco has proven himself the master of the wide implica-tion, the striking suggestion, the broad impression, but he has not once created a full-fledged work of art whose impact produced specific reverberations which like a boomerang, returned to its original centre of energy. And, perhaps, he *has* not because he *cannot*; because his mind is big enough to recognize the great themes, but his talent not subtle enough to grapple with them.

He is constantly being distracted by his own digressions; he takes more delight in his fancy footwork than he does in his overall strategy. He is as light as his lightest moment, but not as strong as his strongest thought. Like the bad comic who will incite laughter at any price, he mugs to help drive home a weak punch-line and does not realize that one's own restraint is what provokes laughter in others. With Beckett, we feel, here is an artist whose very nature is the conditioning-factor in his work. The nature of his plays is as troubled, diffuse and wracked as the man himself. Ionesco has contemplated an-guish in tranquillity and then gone about simulating it. He handles his tools with more skill than Beckett, but Beckett (the greater artist if not the better craftsman) succeeds by dint of the intensity of his experience, and it is this which ultimately determines the character of the material. While Ionesco arranges wood-blocks, Beckett hews into marble.

Rhinoceros is the kind of play a shallow writer scrapes out of the bottom of a drained ingenuity; its presumption to depth is precisely what reveals it to be the crust it is. Ionesco may be an inspired pastrycook, but he's not a major playwright.

[JULY 1960]

HAPPY DAYS AND MARIENBAD
by Peter Brook

I had originally volunteered to write about the new Beckett play *Happy Days*. I'm not a critic, but I wanted to write about this play because I had just seen it, was full of excitement and enthusiasm and shocked to find New York so indifferent. (In fact it has already come off.) In the meantime, after beginning to write the review I went to see Alain Resnais' film *L'Année Dernière à Marienbad*. Then I read Robbe-Grillet's statements in defence of his script and found that the more I thought about Beckett the more I wanted to talk about *Marienbad*. I know *Encore* is a theatre magazine: for me the theatre and the cinema have always intertwined – and so, I think, for us all: God knows, what with television in the middle, it is largely the same people and the same influences that pass to and fro. So I hope to be forgiven for trying to extend the scope of this piece and make sense of these confusingly overlapping thoughts – particularly if, in the process of writing, I can find the links to the questions about the abstract in the concrete theatre left open at the end of my *Encore* article a few months ago and which are the questions that bother me most at the moment. Some people seem surprised that – in that piece – I did not reach "solutions". I can only say that I believe less in the answers than in the process of searching: with a long perspective of film work ahead of me, it is by churning over theatre theory that I can edge towards a dimly sighted goal: if I am churning publicly it is in the hope of catching the interest of anyone else who happens to be on the same road. The link between Beckett and *Marienbad* seems to me that both are attempting to express in concrete terms what would at first sight appear to be intellectual abstractions. My interest is in the possibility of arriving, in the theatre, at a ritual expression of the true driving forces of our time, none of which, I believe, is truly revealed in anecdote or characterization.

The marvel of the Beckett play was its objectivity. In that last article, I described a Vera Cruz statue that was an attitude and a state of feeling turned into object and about how an actor's gesture could similarly exist in its own right. Beckett at his finest seems to have the power of casting a stage picture, a stage relationship, a stage machine from his most intense experiences that in a flash, inspired, *exists*, stands there complete in itself, not *telling*, not *dictating*, symbolic without symbolism. For Beckett's symbols are powerful just because we cannot quite grasp them: they are not signposts, they are not textbooks nor blue-prints – they are literally creations.

Years ago I directed a production of Sartre's *Huis Clos*. Today I cannot remember one word of the dialogue, not one detail of the philosophy. But the central picture of this play – the hell made up of three people locked in an eternal hotel room – is still with me: it was cast not from Sartre's intelligence – like his other acute journalistic plays have been – but from somewhere else – in a creative flash, the author found a stage situation which I think has actually entered into the terms of reference of our whole generation. I think that to anyone who saw the play the word hell is more likely to evoke that closed room than fire and pitch-forks.

Before Oedipus and Hamlet were born in their authors' minds all the qualities these characters reflect must have been in existence as nebulous formless currents of experience. Then came a powerful generative act – and characters appeared giving shape and substance to these abstractions.

Hamlet is there: we can refer to him. Suddenly Jimmy Porter was there – we can't throw him off. At a given moment Van Gogh's Provence came into existence – inescapably – as did Dali's desert. Can we define a work of art as something that brings a new "thing" into the world – something we may like or reject, but which annoyingly continues to be and so for better or for worse becomes part of our field of reference? If so, this brings us back to Beckett. He did just this with those two tramps under a tree. The whole world found something vague made tangible in that absurd and awful picture. And those parents in the dustbin. Now he's done it again. A woman is alone in the middle of the stage. She is up to her (ample) bosom in a mound of earth. Beside her is a large handbag, out of which she produces all the little things she might ever need, including a gun. The sun shines. She is where – in a sort of No Man's Land? After the Bomb? We cannot tell. Somewhere at the back in a dubious anal region, her husband ekes out some sort of existence. Occasionally, on all fours – and once in top hat and tails – he emerges: for the most part he is a grunt, a mutter, or just a thin squeak. A bell chimes: it is morning. Bell chimes: it is night. The lady smiles. Time, she fancies, does not pass. Every day is a happy day. By the last act the mound has risen to her neck, her arms are imprisoned but her head is free, and it remains as plump and cheery as before. Does she have intimations that all may not be for the best? Yes, fleetingly – in tiny seconds wonderfully caught. There was a beautiful performance by Ruth White and a quite perfect production by Alan Schneider. Her husband crawls out for the last time. He reaches up longingly – towards her face? Towards the gun a few inches away? We never know.

What's it all mean? If I attempt any sort of explanation, let me hasten to say that it will not be *the* explanation, my admiration for the play is that it is not a treatise – and so any explanation is a partial view of the whole. Certainly this is a play about man throwing his life away: it is a play about possibilities lost: comically, tragically, it shows us man atrophied, paralysed, three-quarters useless, three-quarters dead – but grotesquely it shows he is only aware of how lucky he

is to be alive. This is a picture of us ourselves endlessly grinning – not as Pagliacci once grinned, to conceal a broken
heart – but grinning because no one has told us our heart
stopped beating long ago.

This is a disturbing enough theme, real and vital to any
audience today – more than anywhere in New York, which
has rejected it. I do not see how this subject matter can be
expressed by any more "Realistic" means. It is a desperate
cry, but at the same time it is implying something very
positive, perhaps more positive than any other Beckett work.
It is a paradise lost that is about man, only man, not about
any other state, and in showing man bereft of most of his
organs it is implying that the possibilities were there, are
there still buried, ignored. Unlike the other Beckett plays
this is not only a vision of our fallen condition, it is an assault
on our fatal blindness.

It contains its own answer to the obvious reproach that it
is just another piece of pessimism and gloom. For the lady
looking at us ensconced in her mound as comfortably as ourselves in our stalls is the very picture of facile optimism. Here
is the audience (and the critics) at any play (or film) which
after two hours finds the answers, which glibly asserts that
life is good, that there is always hope and that all will be well.
Here is Walter Kerr, and the audience of *The Miracle Worker*,
and Ike and most of our politicians grinning from ear to ear
and buried up to their necks.

It is a long jump and a short step to *L'Année Dernière à
Marienbad*. For those who haven't seen it, this film is an
attempt to split open the pure convention that time is consecutive. The authors of the film, speaking from a mid-
twentieth-century sensibility and experience, refute the
notion that the past is the past and that events in the present
follow one another in chronological order. This is how time
passes in films, they would claim, and this is a very arbitrary,
shallow and unreal convention of film-makers. Time for man
can be an overlapping of fugitive experiences and in no way
resembles the time of objects, for these remain untouched by
the passage of events: time in the cinema is the moment of
watching a shot – and there can be no difference between a

shot taking place in the past or the future. The act of watching a film is a chain of "nows". A film is a passionate assembly of "nows" – montage is not order, but relationships.

In *Marienbad* in a wildly over-ornate Bavarian castle – ostensibly a hotel – a man and a woman exchange broken fragments of pure relationships; the sequence is not one of time or sense, but of the growth from attitude to attitude. The past and the present exist side by side, at once playing with one another, against one another, in endless repetitions and modulations.

The film is a time experiment – and attempts things I have been longing to see. I wish I could say I liked the result. But curiously, between a (in my view) totally right starting point and unquestionably superb execution (direction, photography and cutting are magnificent) it falls completely flat. I found it empty and pretentious, arty and imitative.

The trouble is that the authors were moved by the fascination of their experiment, nothing more. The set of images they present to us – and here I would compare them unfavourably to Beckett – are meaningless – this is the abstract/abstract as against the abstract/real. It may be said that my reaction is completely subjective, that what are meaningless pictures to me may be very disturbing to someone else. I'd dispute this, because the very point I am trying to establish is this giant difference – which we are very well equipped to judge – between the real and the phoney, between the Picasso and the brush tied to the donkey's tail.

I feel that the world of *Marienbad* – in which the deadly monotony of riches is symbolized by po-faced figures in dinner jackets and Chanel dresses sitting in elegantly frozen groups or playing endless silent games – is an intellectual illustration using visual material that we've grown used to over the years in the ballet, in Cocteau's films and so on. This is a very different cup of tea to the haunting, worrying, challenging images struck by Beckett. (I think quite simply that the film-makers here had – in the real sense – nothing much to say. They made a film for a congress of directors and cutters, but they did not make a film arising from a true creative need.)

Yet, though the film does not succeed in itself, a radical experiment has been made and its interest to me is its relation to the theatre.

It convinces me again that in the theatre, even more than in the cinema, we need no longer be bound *at all* by time, character or plot. We need not use any of these traditional crutches – and yet we can still be real, dramatic and meaningful. In *Marienbad* the characters are called Mr A. and Miss B. – but alas they then converse in an equally bloodless cerebral way. I cannot believe that this is a necessary consequence. I believe that an intellectual writer will obviously make ciphers speak like ciphers. But I also believe that a true writer – like Beckett – one whose stomach is full of his own experiences, whose wit and whose passions speak together, if faced with Mr A. and Miss B., will find another sort of language and this in turn will engender in us another sort of response. The art of serial music is that of taking a series of notes – like a discipline – and then confronting this discipline with the sensibility and the wish of the composer. The burning shapelessness meets a rigid shape – and a new chain of order is forged. Take a stage – four characters – in this atom there is already an infinity of possibilities. (In one sense, this is *Beyond the Fringe* and look what brilliant variations it spins.) Four characters – four actors, rather – for an actor can be old and young, consistent and inconsistent – one person or many – and here is already a set of relationships out of which like chinese boxes, other relationships, tender, farcical and dramatic, can grow. Here the value of the work – like an abstract painting, like in serial music – would be directly a reflection of the nature of the dramatist himself: his nature in the deepest sense, his imagination, his experience and the endless interplay in him between society and his temperament.

Perhaps I could develop this subject some other time. There is a serial theatre to be found like serial music which would stem directly from experience and which could lead to a new language and a new reality.

[JANUARY 1962]

THE REVENGE OF JEAN GENET
by Charles Marowitz

"We've reached the point at which we can no longer be actuated by human feelings. Our function will be to support, establish and justify metaphors." *The Balcony*

Genet creates characters the way witch-doctors create effigies, and for the same reason: to torture them, to humiliate them, to revenge himself on them.

For Genet, it is not enough merely to rail against authority. He is not an agitator; he is an activist; not a character-assassin, but an assassin. Therefore he creates living symbols of his enemies – the pillars of society, the queens, the bishops, the generals – and methodically destroys them. This is Genet's recurring "ritual"; a Rite of Human Sacrifice.

As Genet quells his personal needs, he simultaneously unearths terrible truths about the world common to us all. We see through Genet that the "pillars of society" have always been pillars of salt; that beyond our bitterest satires and harshest criticism, there was a worse truth; a more damnable state of affairs. Genet, to whom the underside of life is home, sees all of this with the clarity of a native. We have seen reasonable facsimiles of this world before, but contrived with that difficulty which always accompanies the attempt to create with only intellectual understanding. With Genet we feel the true heat; we can almost smell the real fire.

It is preposterous to claim, as many have, that Genet's theme is merely the struggle for power. This is the kind of categorical brummagem critics are always hatching out of academic incubators. They try to dispense with Beckett, Ionesco and all the rest of the new dramatists by repeating that *their* theme is "the impossibility of human communication". As if the proclamation of an incontestable half-truth ended matters once and for all.

The power-element in Genet is strong but marginal. Genet's overriding preoccupation is with the indeterminate mutability of life. The traditional concepts of Yin and Yang, Illusion and Reality, Mask and Face pushed to their furthest extreme. With Pirandello (as Bernard Dort pointed out – *Encore* 31), Illusion was a transparent skein under which we could easily trace reality. With Genet, beneath the illusion of reality lies the illusion that one sees beyond illusion to a genuine reality. In Genet, the tangible universe – the non-illusionary world – is continually being unmasked so that, in the end, the only real truth is the semblance of it. It is not so much a denial of reality as a contention that the elaborately-untrue is the only reality we are going to get, and so we had better start re-evaluating it. (In an otherwise level-headed piece, Bernard Dort deludes himself when he suggests that Genet's theatre "is now ready to face reality – our reality". This is an optimism dear to the liberal temperament but alien to Genet's philosophy and insupportable in the light of his work.)

I have no doubt that a man who follows Genet far enough will arrive at madness, for he forbids even those few shreds of illusion which are absolutely necessary to sanity and to life. After Genet has drilled down to the heart of the matter, he keeps drilling and so the heart bursts. The excitement of his pursuit is comparable to that of the scientist who refuses to concede he has arrived at the primal source; whose every discovery is only a hatchway into a deeper truth.

Like the first play of any writer who subsequently reveals artistic consistency, *Deathwatch* is full of hints, germs and suggestions which the later works develop. In itself it is neither successful nor important.

Deathwatch has the garbled prolixity of an overly-subjective modern painting. It throws out a number of dramatic ideas, but is devoid of particular emphasis so that one is never certain what is surface and what is splinter. Set in a French prison and concerning homosexuality, one assumes it is based on personal experience. (Its structure is conspicuously influenced by *Huis Clos*.) Throughout the whole of the short play, it seems to be straining towards a higher plain; towards the rhetoric and ceremony of the later plays. But a tendency towards personal observation holds it back.

Genet, unlike biographical playwrights, must transcend his personal framework in order to fully express his experience.

(Even *The Maids*, his most realistic play, wriggles to escape the arrondissement. Here, the maids' ceremony is realistically contrived and subject to credible interpretation. In the later plays, Genet dispenses with realistic justifications and moves directly into ritual for its own sake.) Despite what appears to be a naturalistic surface, Genet envisaged even *Deathwatch* as a *ceremonial*. In his direction to the players, he states "the whole of the play unfolds as if in a dream" – and in its performance, he called for harsh colours, excessive make-up and stylized gesture. The recent Sunday night production at the Arts seemed to approach the play as a prison melodrama, and in stumping for realistic effects it violated the spirit of the play at those very places where it was being best (realistically) acted.

Already in *Deathwatch*, we are beginning to see the idea of *pretence* tentatively explored. Lefranc's murder of Maurice is little more than the assumption of a magnitude the character does not possess. Lefranc murders in order to enter the world of Green Eyes and Snowball, characters who have achieved a kind of purity and stature from instinctive violence. Lefranc learns, what is perhaps the only lesson in the play, that violence must have something divine or diabolical about it if it is to escape being a mere show of egotism.

Genet's mania for the multi-layered pretence was exemplified in *The Maids* which was commissioned by Louis Jouvet. Here, the initial pretence is that the sister servant girls take turns playing the role of Madame, their mundane employer. But this relatively simple deception wasn't enough for Genet and he insisted that the girls' parts be played by male actors impersonating maids impersonating mistresses. It was with the greatest difficulty that Jouvet dissuaded the playwright from this tack which could well have blurred the play's point.

In *Deathwatch*, the closest Genet comes to satisfying his spleen is by destroying an artifice in a fellow convict. In *The Maids*, he still hasn't the courage to strike down the true enemy (Madame) and contents himself with poisoning her by proxy. With *The Balcony*, he dispenses with all pawns and underlings and goes directly for the leaders.

In *The Balcony*, Genet has not really mastered the fusions

of form and content. In one act, he posits his characters; in another, he complicates them with a theme. The play takes a giant step forward and then drags a second leg across to meet it. And yet, despite the piecemeal dramaturgy, *The Balcony* is perhaps the clearest expression of Genet's philosophy, and the closest he has yet come to successfully dramatizing it.

The highest ideal in *The Balcony* is for characters to attain that point of social definition at which others desire to impersonate them. Reality corresponds to the density of one's artifice. When a man achieves his highest reality he can serve as a fantasy for another man; and in a frightening Genetic turnabout, both then become equal.

In perhaps one of the most shocking hypotheses ever put forward in the drama, Genet suggests that the only thing that distinguishes the sexual pervert who masquerades as priest, king, or hero from his legitimate social counterpart, is a certain timidity. The sexual pervert lives his fantasies in private and is therefore harmless; whereas the social personages play out their roles in public which, on the one hand makes them hypocritical and on the other, dangerous. It is a contention the Establishment Mind must abhor, but one which is delectable to contemplate. For psychiatrists have been telling us for years that we all carry around Idealized Images of ourselves which direct us, feed us, motivate us. Are the zones of erotic sex fantasy and the desperately-maintained myths of public life so unquestionably disparate? To be under the sway of M. Genet is to be tortured by outrageous doubts.

There is a crude boldness in *The Balcony*, as if our most private thoughts were being publicly dramatized. It is one thing to chalk "The Queen is a whore" on a lavatory wall and another to demonstrate through dramatic sequence the way by which a brothel-keeper becomes enthroned. Just as it is one thing to confide to your neighbour that the Chief of Police is a prick and another to show this official adopting an enormous phallus as public symbol for himself. Here, as everywhere, Genet lovingly elaborates the humiliation of his enemies. And again, the satisfaction of his personal hates reveals certain hypocrisies we can all believe in and share.

In the poetic suppositions of *The Balcony*, I discern a number of stark truths about our world today. Because Genet's insights are fundamental rather than partial, it is difficult to weed them out or glibly paraphrase. But in its sparks and flickers, *The Balcony* momentarily illuminates the elaborate deceptions by which we all live. Maybe it's a good thing they only last a matter of seconds.

As a craftsman, Genet still gets tangled in the web of his own metaphysics. He overwrites because he overthinks. His thoughts are not confined by any dramatic necessity and because his form is loose, it encourages rather than checks his tendency to ricochet ideas. In *The Blacks*, he begins by asking quite rightly; what is black? What is its colour? While he seeks his answer in his own imagination, we get some dazzling insights into the black mind and temperament, but the cliché of what, in the classic cliché, is called "The Negro Problem" trips him up, and he disappears in a swamp of high-sounding rhetoric. At times, we get a tame French version of the New Paternalism. (This is the liberal antonym of the "Uncle Tom" syndrome where the Negro is revered as A Natural Man, Instinctive Musician, Ideal Hipster, etc.) This is uncharacteristic of Genet and what's more, I don't believe he feels it. But his material gets tangled up in it because he lacks control. The planning-sense is as alien to Genet as it is intrinsic to Sartre and, of course, the conscious mind intervenes only when inspiration begins to flag. In Genet, one can almost pinpoint the line at which instinct freezes and ingenuity comes to the rescue.

Before one accepts *The Blacks* as evidence of Genet's budding social conscience, one would do well to remember that the germ of the play can be traced as far back as *Deathwatch*. There, the Negro character Snowball is the subject of an almost maudlin idolatry. The hymns to his spiritual magnificence are accompanied by a steady train of homosexual adoration. "He shines. He beams. He's black but he lights up the whole two thousand cells."

Snowball is a kind of Black Titan. Although an inmate, he is the recognized master of the prison ("The Number One Big Shot") feared by the warders; respected by the convicts.

"He's got the luck to be a savage," says Green Eyes. "He's got the right to kill people and even eat them. He lives in the jungle. That's his advantage over me . . . I'm alone, all alone. And too white. Too wilted by the cell. Too pale."

Genet champions the blacks not because they are socially downtrodden but because they personify two of his favourite types: The Rebellious Outcast and The Splendid Primitive. Lorraine Hansberry is quite right when she argues (in a recent *Village Voice*) that Genet's black-man remains the traditional Exotic, and that "despite its sophistication [*The Blacks*] is itself an expression of the more quaint notions of white men".

Of course Genet immediately responded to a request for "a play for an all-black cast". Here was a hero who, for Genet, represented all the savagery and vengeance that he admired in whites. Here was a pure Genetic prototype; a natural outlet for his own social spleen. Genet uses the blacks, the way a man who has just emptied his revolver reaches for the knife at his side.

But because Genet is something of a genius, *The Blacks* is much more than a convenient weapon in a personal crusade. The play depicts the Negro ambivalence in a way which has never before been seen in the drama. The Negroes' suspicion that there was an element of love in Village's murder of the white girl, suggests that the real combat between the races cuts much deeper than political issues: that the blacks not only resent the white man's power, but secretly long for white treasure – either in the form of assimilated material comfort or sexual conquest.

The ultimate massacre of the white Establishment-figures satisfies Genet more than it would the blacks. To Genet, the highest victory the blacks can attain is the annihilation of the whites. I doubt that the blacks would support Genet's thesis. I would imagine a practicable integration which guaranteed their rights as individuals would satisfy them. It is the white man's mammoth guilt that believes the only just revenge for centuries of exploitation must be death. And Genet, of course, is a white man. On a social-realistic basis, *The Blacks* is preposterous, but as a projection of Genet's ubiquitous conflict with authority, it becomes a fascinating psychological confession and, for the same reason, a fascinating piece of theatre.

The great incongruity is that *The Blacks* is written for actors who are incapable of performing it. The subtleties of thought, complexities of speech and changes in rhythm require actors of wide range and enormous sophistication. Of all minority groups, I would wager Negro actors get the least work. A Negro theatre which, on the face of it seems the most logical thing in the world, has not been created in London, and Negro actors mill around waiting for the next race-problem melodrama or possibly, a new Blackbirds revue. Consequently, when a Negro actor obtains a few weeks' work, he uses it as an outlet for years of pent-up frustration and the result is (as it was at the Royal Court production of *The Blacks*) an effusion of feeling which overwhelms in the worst possible sense. More serious than the incoherence of speech, was the absence of the pseudo-formal ceremony. A ritual loses all solemnity when the High Priests themselves seem nervous and ill at ease, and the absence of the self-mocking facetiousness which underlies the ceremony never established the essential reality of blacks *pretending* for the sake of their white spectators.

In my definition, a social dramatist is anyone who sheds light on the nature of the struggle which people have been waging with people since the beginning of time. On this basis, Genet is a thorough-going social dramatist. And in a play like *The Maids*, although he shows us "the monstrous soul of servantdom", he is depicting a conflict more profound than the traditional bickerings of management and labour. With *The Blacks*, it is easy for left-wing factions to assume Genet has slithered into their camp, but as I have tried to suggest, Genet would look powerfully incongruous as a guest speaker at a Labour Party Conference. Genet will never be Sartre because Sartre reveres justice and aspires towards a moral weal. Genet respects nothing and sees morality as simply another mask to be torn aside.

Or perhaps, Genet is the *supreme* moralist in that he teaches that good and evil are equally shallow disguises, and that before we can profess a genuine morality, we have to determine the difference – not between right and wrong, but between real and unreal.

If Jean Genet had not come along, the manifestos of Antonin Artaud might have seemed like so much metaphysical bosh; the rantings of the maniac he was. But now, Artaud's concept of a Theatre of Cruelty exists as a blueprint which the works of Genet are gradually realizing. They might be taken for the same man, this shillelagh-brandishing theoretician and the thieving ex-con, so alike are their visions of theatre. One can select almost at random from the pages of *The Theatre and Its Double* and find Artaud trying to summon up Genet. "We intend to base the theatre upon spectacle before everything else" . . . "the theatre must give us everything that is in crime, love, war or madness if it wants to recover its necessity" . . . "a violent and concentrated action is a kind of lyricism; it summons up supernatural images, a bloodstream of images, a bleeding spurt of images in the poet's head and in the spectator's as well" . . . "the image of a crime presented in requisite theatrical conditions is something infinitely more terrible for the spirit than that same crime when actually committed" . . . "a drama which, without resorting to the defunct images of the old Myths, shows us that it can extract the forces which struggle within them" . . . "a theatre that induces trance, as the dances of the Dervishes induce trance" . . . "a passionate and convulsive conception of life" . . . "the reality of imagination and dreams will appear on equal footing with life" . . . "great social upheavals, conflicts between peoples and races" . . . etc., etc., etc.

The whole of Artaud's work exists as a dynamic corollary to what Genet has done on the stage. And perhaps in the last analysis, the greatness of Genet will be that he was the first to penetrate the interior of that unknown land spiritually charted by Artaud. The first twentieth-century playwright to reach that realm of psychic myth and instinctual poetry which is the only alternative to a debilitating, mind-dwarfing, sense-dulling, repulsively-predictable naturalistic theatre.

Despite a generally obtuse London reception, Genet has arrived. I fear for him, now in the distinguished company of

M. Sartre, Cocteau and the other lustrous littérateurs. I can
almost visualize the ceremony at which Genet is ushered into
the French Academy – quietly poisoning the goblets of his
fellow-members in one last annihilating gesture of social
defiance. I can imagine Cocteau (miraculously saved by a
fortuitous stomach-pump) elegizing the act as Genet's last
stab at salvation.

The rebel catered to and approved of, soon becomes conscious of the traits which distinguish him. Genet, like his
character Lefranc, stands in danger of "willing" his defiance
rather than letting it leap out of him. Still, the Artaud-Genet
Theatre is young; *Les Paravents*, Genet's newest play, though
banned, is published; the "taste" is slowly being acquired.
We shall see.

[SEPTEMBER 1961]

NO GRAVEN IMAGE
Some notes on Max Frisch by Michael Kustow

First, the barest necessary facts about Frisch's life. Born in
1911 in Zurich, the town in which Georg Büchner died.
Studied German literature at Zurich University, travelled in
the Balkans and to the Black Sea. Was forced, for money
reasons, to leave the University without his doctorate (a
degree carries a much greater social cachet in Switzerland
than here). Took up journalism, published his first essays.
Renewed his studies, and became a trained architect. He constructed his first ambitious building and his first novel in the
same year, 1943. It was followed by a travel book, his *Journal
1946–49*, and his two major novels, *I'm Not Stiller* and *Homo
Faber*. He has written nine stage plays: *Now You Can Sing*
(1946); *Santa Cruz* (1947); *When The War Was Over* (1949);
The Chinese Wall (1946–55); *Count Oederland* (1951–61); *Don
Juan, or The Love of Geometry* (1953); *Biedermann and The
Fire-Raisers* and *The Fury of Philip Hotz* (1958); and *Andorra*
(1961).

He gave up practising architecture some years ago, and
now lives in Rome as a writer, having travelled extensively,

especially in the United States and Mexico. I should like to stress the fact that during his formative period he was simultaneously writer and architect, for it bears on the singularity of his art and its concerns. The narrator of *Homo Faber*, a technologist, says of another character, an artist, "He got on my nerves, like all artists who think themselves loftier or more profound beings simply because they don't know what electricity is."

Much of the first part of these notes will be concerned with his novels, and I should like to justify this method of presentation. Frisch's plays occupy a very definite and significant place in his work. One of the qualities which for me sets him above so much of what is being produced today is his faculty of probing the spectator, of opening wounds in the sides of his experience, of creating works which are like barbs. They stick into us, stirring up our unresolved contradictions, which we had blithely thought healed over.

"I would consider my task as a dramatist fully accomplished," he writes in his journal, "if one of my plays managed to put a question in such a way that the spectators would henceforth be unable to live without finding an answer for it – their answer, their own answer, which can only be found in life itself."

He wants to drive the spectator to the very limits of his experience, make him question and re-question the habits and impulses that make up his life. Art, as such, is an unstable enterprise, it is deferential upon living. This need which Frisch feels expresses itself formally in the novels by the use of the journal form, in which the chief character talks to the reader. Two-thirds of *Stiller*, and the last part of *Homo Faber* are just such notebooks kept by the protagonists. Both the notebooks end up by bringing us down to the here-and-now instant in which the narrator is writing: "8.45 *a.m.*: They're coming," and "I have just heard Julika coming along the corridor. My angel, keep me on the alert."

The domain of the theatre is this here-and-now. It seems to me that the very shape of Frisch's development as an artist testifies to this straining towards the quick of the instant moment, and that, having worked through his living contradictions in the novel form, Frisch is virtually obliged, by the living logic of his art, to move from the novel into the theatre in order to actualize and realize these painfully reached conclusions. Putting this another way: we know that there are moments when we feel we have grasped the meaning of our experience in a useful way. But we also know that this grasp is fragile and ephemeral. Frisch needs the theatre in order to re-create these gestures and moments of realization in a manner that is almost as fragile and unstable as in life itself.

The sub-title of *The Fire-Raisers* describes it as "A Didactic Play Without A Doctrine". This is obviously a very important description, for the German word *Lehrstuck* ("didactic play") refers back to the agit-prop plays Brecht wrote in the 'thirties. By using this Brechtian term in such a paradoxical way, Frisch is taking up an attitude to Brecht's work, acknowledging his debt, and at the same time proclaiming that he is living and writing in a different time and situation. This continuation of Brecht is something I shall refer to later. It is not exactly a doctrine which we gain by going back to the novels, it is more the time and situation in which Frisch sees himself placed. Once we have grasped Frisch's vision as it is laid out in the novels, we shall be in a better position to explain and appreciate the searing incisiveness of the plays, and perhaps to realize how works which are apparently so simple on the surface can have such a complex and disturbing action upon us. With the aid of extracts from the novels, I should like to draw a map of Frisch's landscape of our modern situation in the civilized Western world.

"We live in an age of reproduction. Most of what makes up our personal picture of the world we have never seen with our own eyes – or rather, we've seen it with our own eyes, but not on the spot: our knowledge comes to us from a distance, we are televiewers, telehearers, teleknowers. One need never have left this little town to have Hitler's voice ringing in one's ears, to have seen the Shah of Persia from a distance of three yards, and to know how the monsoon howls over the Himalayas, or what it looks like three hundred fathoms beneath the sea. Anyone can know these things nowadays. Does it mean I have ever been to the bottom of the sea?"

So Stiller. It may sound like the familiar back-to-earth argument that all these new-fangled gadgets are taking us away from the eternal verities and direct truths of existence. But remember that Frisch, architect, is also a technologist. There can be no question of discarding the devices of modern technology. The problem, and one of the basic movements of Frisch's work, is to come to terms with their effects, to pose the questions which are *adequate* to the material conditions of our lives now, and then to see what blame, if any, is to be attributed to the world of television, detergent and dentifrice.

The artist of today must know what electricity is, and still remain an artist. Frisch devotes one whole novel to a story in which the incapacity of his hero to give any value to his life, *and the deeper failure to admit this incapacity*, is explicitly linked with the technological frame of mind, the mind of Homo Faber, Man The Maker. Walter Faber, on a boat-trip from America to Europe, meets and falls in love with a girl half his age. He finds out that she is his own daughter, child by the woman he didn't marry in Zurich twenty years ago. He has made his own daughter his mistress. She dies, and he is left to patch up some kind of common life with the woman he never married. All the decisions which he thought shelved are undone and start to ache again.

It is the texture of the book that makes it almost the legend of a paradoxical Oedipus of the consumer commodity world. Frisch is concerned to show how far the very patterns of perception and response to experience have become moulded in this man's mind by the processes and suggestiveness of the machines and instruments he is used to handle: "Her lips were remarkably light and at the same time strong, gripping them was like gripping the steering wheel of my Studebaker.'

So far, so good. This awareness of our subjugation to the machine is something which he uses for fruitful comic effect in his plays as well, but it can hardly be called new after Chaplin's *Modern Times* and Tati's *Mon Oncle*. Frisch is engaged at a much deeper level. It is not just the sensible perception of his hero that has been turned a certain way, there is a deeper disjunction, affecting the very motive-springs of choice in his life:

"Hanna [the woman Faber never married] doesn't find the way I behaved with Sabeth [the girl] incomprehensible; in Hanna's opinion I experienced a kind of relationship with which I was unfamiliar and therefore misinterpreted, persuading myself that I was in love. It was no chance mistake, but a mistake that is part of me (?), like my profession, like the rest of my life. My mistake lay in the fact that we technologists try to live without death. Her own words: 'You don't treat life as a form, but merely as an additional sum, hence you have no relationship with time, because you have no relationship with death.' Life is form in time. Hanna admits that she can't explain what she means. Life is not matter and cannot be mastered by technology. My mistake with Sabeth lay in repetition. I behaved as though age did not exist, and hence contrary to nature. We cannot do away with age by continuing to add up, by marrying our own children."

In *I'm Not Stiller*, Frisch plunges deep into the area of this deeper disjunction. It is in this book that we realize why Hanna could not have explained what she means. And when we realize that there are human situations in which reality as one human being lives it can never be *told* to other human beings, simply because its existence is in the living rather than the telling; when we appreciate that this reality is constantly threatened every time another human being fails to recognize it, then we realize that Frisch is dealing in finer distinctions than words alone can provide, and we know how much he needs the theatre. For Frisch sees man as a creature who may be split apart and reduced to nothing more than a chasm – what Stiller calls "the black hole" – from one instant to the next. And the business of theatre is the instant.

"Thou shalt make no graven image." This void, this gulf, comes upon us when those who surround us imprison us in *their* fixed image of what we are, project upon us, if only for a second, by some chance remark, by an expression that moves across their features, their graven image of what we are, really. And our anguish, our discomfort, lies in our utter inability to recapture that second, to erase it and reconstitute ourselves as *we* know we are. Words are no tools for this craft, they cannot recapture the time that has just passed, they are forced into the role of excuses, exculpations, and rationalizations after the event.

"You can put anything into words except your own life. It is this impossibility that condemns us to remain as our companions see and mirror us, those who claim to know me, those who call themselves my friends, and never allow me to change, and discredit every miracle (which I cannot put into words, the inexpressible, which I cannot prove) – simply so they can say:
    'I KNOW YOU'."

. . . Plonk! the graven image settles over us, and the moment in which it was formed is irretrievable. Frisch believes that the central human experience, that which defines a man who is living his life in any significant way, is by nature quivering and unstable. The "miracle (which I cannot put into words, the inexpressible, which I cannot prove)" is the sense of a fully human freedom which is the only thing we really, dumbly, and of necessity inarticulately, live for. It is at this centre that change and growth and any mastery we may gain over our life occur.

But he is also aware how hard it is to attain, how many people give up before they get there, how many delude themselves they have reached it when they are not even started on the journey, and how fragile it is once attained. In *Stiller*, he charts this "black hole", which is both the chasm into which our makeshift lives may at any moment tumble, and the only well in which any human attainment takes place. This perilous centre of potentiality is always at the mercy of graven images, fixed, ossified outlooks that men accept, almost without knowing, and in so doing, give up whatever free play and spontaneity their lives may have been capable of.

The fruitfulness of this view of experience is that it enables Frisch to deal with the extremely personal and the extremely social on the same plane. For the graven images which threaten whatever is unfixed and exploratory in a man's life are both private and public ones. The wife who harbours a fixed image of the man society calls her husband, thinking she has circumscribed and exhausted all his potentialities for change, and the John Birchite who harbours an image of all Russians as sado-masochistic Stalinists: both of these people are nurturing graven images of the same order.

Once again, in this area of his work, it is as if Frisch had stepped off from a point Brecht had reached, moving forward and extending Brecht's achievement in accordance with the development and change of the world. For Brecht above all men cherished this centre of change and growth in men. One of the most telling of his Mr Keuner anecdotes is this:

> "A man who had not seen Mr Keuner for a long time greeted him with the words:
> 'You haven't changed at all!'
> 'Oh!' said Mr Keuner, and turned pale."

Mr Keuner's pallor leads us into Frisch's world, a world in which the influences that blunt and impinge on the centre of change have multiplied, and more and more men are deterred more and more subtly from seeking and groping for the fragile point of their humanity. In his novels, Frisch details agonizingly the precarious route to the centre. In his plays, he lays before us with disturbing clarity the normal piecemeal void that has come to replace this human exploration. But it is not a mysterious fertile void like "the black hole". It is a bloated surface, swelled out with hollow affirmations of good intention, and hearty hailfellowing to all humans, a surface not blank and intense, but constantly pricked by the little niggling attentions and anxieties demanded by the rituals of our advanced industrial civilization. To depict this sell-out, Frisch deploys the most devasting humour. But he does not just snigger in contempt, he is not just concerned to place men in a ridiculous light. Behind the deftest deflation of our self-important surfaces lies a real anguish that knows how easily and swiftly it may fall into the same delusions, and how hard it is to keep to the true route:

> "I see their faces: are they free? And their gait, their ugly gait: is that the gait of free people? And their fear, their

fear of the future, their fear of one day being poor, their fear of life, their fear of dying without life insurance, and finally their fear that the world might change, their absolute panic fear of spiritual audacity – no, they are no freer than I am, as I sit here on my prison bed, knowing that the step forward into freedom (of which no ancestor can relieve us) is always a tremendous step, a step with which we leave behind us everything that has previously seemed like solid ground, and a step that no one can hinder once I have decided to take it. For it is the step into faith, everything else is not freedom, but empty chatter."

The depth of Frisch's preoccupations as revealed in the novels, his awareness of the difficulties of making any meaningful life, mean that he approaches the theatre with a sense of urgency, with his back to the wall. Edna O'Brien, in a review of *Biedermann* in the last issue of *Encore*, called him "a European mind", and this label has a precise sense beyond its value as a cocktail party compliment. Examining his plays, one comes to admire a characteristic deftness and cleanness of effect, a scalpel-like probing, a cutting sense of the contrapuntal. But these are not merely effects, the stock-in-trade of a playwright who "knows what he's doing". The precision and sureness with which plays like *Biedermann* and *Philip Hotz* pick their way to our centre are not just devices in the armoury of an "effective" writer. Their point and poignancy are the qualities of a writer who is so comprehensively involved that he brings to bear on the segment he has isolated for his play the weight of his total preoccupations. In this sense, it is useful to say that Frisch is European (i.e. metaphysical) rather than English (i.e. empirical); for the distinguishing formal features of the kind of theatre he creates are governed by the fully human situation he is living, and which he outlines in the novels. In other words, he comes to the theatre because it is necessary for him to do so, and because he has the kind of mind that can appreciate that it is necessary.

In true European non-empirical style, this involves Frisch in a number of considerations which we would label "theoretical". We remember that his existential explorations in

the novels led him to the Dilemma Of The Graven Image, the
problems of identity and continuity which could not be communicated or sustained in words, but only in behaviour, in
living from instant to instant. In *Stiller*, he tentatively reaches
towards the possibility of a superior reality or authority or
god as a pledge to a purely human reality. This possibility,
whether it is a delusion or a tangible support, is anyway a
deeply individual concern, a man's angel is what he keeps
closest to him, and it does not enter into the sphere of the
plays. In his theatre, Frisch is concerned with the behaviour,
the mechanisms of living, which the novel only permits him
to grasp partially. Thus, when he considers the theatre
"theoretically", he tries to pin down the *essentially theatrical*
tools and gestures which will enable him to cut deeper on the
level of living than he could do in prose narration:

"Hamlet with the skull of Yorick:
When this scene is narrated, one must conceive of both
things, must imagine them both, the skull in the living
hands of Hamlet and the jokes of the dead Yorick, of
which Hamlet reminds himself. The narration, in opposition to the theatre, rests wholly and completely in language, and everything which the narrator has to impart
reaches me on a single plane: namely that of the imagination. The theatre performs in an essentially different way:
the skull, which is only an object, the grave, the spade, all
these things I already possess through sensible perception,
involuntarily, in front of me, inevitably at every moment,
while my imagination, wholly reserved for the words of
Hamlet, has only to call up the vanished life, which it is
capable of doing all the more intelligibly, since I use it for
no other purpose. The past and the present, the once and
the now: divided between imagination and sensible perception. . . . The poet of the theatre uses two antennas in
playing with me, and it is evident that the one, a skull, and
the other, the jokes of a jester, are of little significance in
and of themselves; the complete statement of this scene,
everything about it which moves us, rests in the relationship between these two images, and only therein." (*Journal*)

Armed with this tool, we may now begin to answer our original question: how can a work as apparently simple as *Biedermann* exert such a strange and disturbing hold upon us? It is possible to show that the complexity of this play is a truly theatrical complexity, that Frisch has built a theatrical structure in which the tension between sensible perception and imagination calls out our more fragile capacity for living, and holds it entranced through an hour and a half of what, considered purely verbally, is inexorable and agonizing repetition, a snake slowly swallowing its own tail until it vanishes, literally, in a puff of smoke.

Biedermann is A Bourgeois, that is a man who has accepted a graven image of himself, and is incapable of seeing that he has done so. Thus he offers us the surface of which I have spoken; a puffed out surface, bloated with protestations of good faith and well-meaning to all men.

Such a man is the total antithesis of the anxious heroes of Frisch's novels. There is simply no point in talking to him about change and growth and the ability to learn as you go along. He is Graven Image Incarnate. In the Epilogue to the play, which was not performed in London, it is manifestly clear that this man is stiff as stone. After the conflagration, Biedermann and his wife find themselves in Hell. He cannot profit from his experience of the disaster for which he knows himself responsible; all he can do is reiterate:

"I'm not guilty! You know I honoured my father and my mother, especially mother, I honoured her so much it used to drive you crazy sometimes. All my life, darling, I've respected the ten commandments. I've never made unto myself a graven image of God, but never. I've never stolen a thing: we've never been hard up. Never killed anyone. Never coveted my neighbour's house, or if I have coveted it, I've gone and bought it. Buying things is allowed, I presume! I've never committed adultery, darling really . . . compared with other people! . . . You're my witness, darling, if an angel comes: I only had one crime on earth, I was too good perhaps, too good."

It is Frisch's achievement to have found purely theatrical

means that bore in relentlessly to the hollow centre of this bolstered vapidity, that rub our noses round and round in its blank emptiness. We are not merely presented with a parody of a human being, a man without a centre, but with a parody of this parody, a centreless man who attempts to construct the simulacrum of humanity with the only tool he has – ingratiation. There are many actions in the play which show, through the tension between perception and imagination, how Biedermann is manipulating the instruments of his own destruction. The most farcical – such as his holding the fuse for the fire-raisers, or handing them the box of matches as proof of his good faith – are also the most terrifying, since they lay bare the absolute void in this man which forbids him to act otherwise. There are grimmer techniques in the way Frisch handles his plot. Biedermann has just sacked the man who invented the hair lotion by which he lives. The man kills himself. His widow comes to see Biedermann, and we see her below in the living room, waiting to see him, while he is above, performing fantastic social gymnastics in order to keep the men who might be fire-raisers happy. We see her; a widow in black, waiting throughout this scene. Biedermann comes down, throws her out, and sets his maid to lay the table for the fire-raisers who are coming to dinner. In order to make them feel at home, he says, she is not to lay the fingerbowls or the knife-stands or the candelabra or the serviettes, but to serve the meal out of the oven casserole on to a good, simple, bare, wooden table, "like at Mass". And she is not to serve in her starched white apron, but in a sweater. So that they should feel at home. "Something human, brotherhood!" The falsity of all this is underscored by the black widow *whom we have just seen.*

It is by palpable hits like this that Frisch creates before us the enormity of this man's central absence, justifying the accusation of the chorus: "When you fear change more than disaster, how do you avoid disaster?" In stage terms, Frisch renders this man's lack of core an almost palpable thing. He lays it before us, and asks: is not this also *your* absence? Biedermann comes to the footlights and asks us, "Well, what in hell would you have done in my shoes, gentlemen? And when?"

Frisch has succeeded in the task he set himself; to put a question to which we must find our answer, our own answer, which can only be found in life itself. *Biedermann* is not a political play about the rise of totalitarianism: Brecht wrote that in *The Resistible Rise of Arturo Ui*. It is not a play about a man searching for his human identity: Ibsen wrote that in *Peer Gynt*. By using his faculty for what is essentially theatrical, Frisch makes it a play about a terrifying flabbiness which is both personal and social. And so acute is his feel for the stark nature of what is the prerogative of the theatre that Frisch makes this flabbiness into an object and a gesture that satisfy as art, as comic and terrifying art.

We could pick out examples of a similar acuity in many of the other plays. In *The Fury of Philip Hotz*, there is the same kind of contrapuntal use of objects as in *Biedermann*: here, however, Frisch makes much more use of direct address to the spectators. Once more he does not allow himself the luxury of mere indulgence in a new theatrical trick. The device in the theatre must be related to the situation in life; and so the direct address carries its own self-criticism, for Hotz is a man who still half-believes that once you can put a solution to a problem into words, you have solved that problem.

This Frisch will never allow. One last extract from his journal will illustrate his rigorous exigency:

"This general demand for an answer in general terms, this demand which so often seems a pathetic reproach, is not perhaps as sincere as the questioner would like to think. Any human answer which transcends the personal plane and aims at a more general application is arguable, we know this. The feel of satisfaction, of tranquillity which we find in refuting the answer given to us comes from the fact that it allows us to forget for a moment the question which is tormenting us. To put it another way, it's not so much an answer we want to hear as a question we want to forget. All this just so as not to be responsible."

In *Biedermann*, there is no lack of these general answers. Biedermann speaks of "brotherhood", "goodwill", "a little trust", "an end to suspicion". What finally makes us shift uneasily in our seats is the fact that the real emptiness Frisch lays before us is not just the bad faith of a specific social class; it is also, by extension, a political perplexity, a moral puzzlement in face of the action of post-war history.

Biedermann, having driven his employee to suicide, hasn't got a leg to stand on when he tries to challenge the fire-raisers. At Nuremberg, some of the accused put the question, "What right have you got to condemn us?" After Hiroshima, we hadn't a leg to stand on. Certainly, the general answers which we invoked – "the rights of free men", "the defence of the free world" – were not reliable moral strongholds. Note the way our politicians try to work up the semblance of passion when they wish to rouse the indignation of the Free world against the crimes of the Enemy. It is a model example of bad acting, of over-emoting. You can see this bad acting in newsreels of Nuremberg and post-war political speeches; you can still see it today, when our leaders make pronouncements from the heart. Could it be that deep down they suspect that their words refer to nothing, refer merely to the furbelayed emptiness of Biedermann?

"In the name of what do you condemn us?" And we have no leg to stand on.

It is the awareness and description of this void that above all separates Frisch from Brecht. For Brecht, in his published texts, exposed the contradictions of the civilized Western world with the same deftness. But he had a positive he could move on to, though admittedly it became more and more oblique. In the 'thirties, with the *Lehrstucke* and up to *Die Mutter*, his positive was mass revolutionary socialism. But neither the German nor the Russian working classes lived up to this exhortation, and the "capitalist" Second World War took place. When Brecht puts Schweik into the Second World War, he speaks, not of a mass movement of revolution, or even resistance, but simply of the canny shrewdness of individual people, a kind of inspired hustling. With Azdak and Shen-Te, he retreats further into a celebration of the hardheaded common-sense of the will to survive, and the wiles it must use.

In Frisch, there is not even this refined and filed-down ideal. His subject is the void that is left, and his job is to strip away the deceptive dressings with which we try to patch it up. In this respect, Frisch may be called a socialist writer, for he performs the vital task of demystification, of drawing men's attention to their alienations, and asking them to reject them. But he is not socialist in the "visionary" sense, for he suspects men who breed false hope in visions that do not work in the world. There must be no false hope.

"In the United States," announced a recent *Guardian* editorial, "and to a lesser extent in Western Europe, the visionary side of democratic socialism has faded. In practice, though not in theory, most democratic socialist parties are closer to the liberal wing of the Democratic Party in the United States than to their predecessors of fifty years ago. But although the ideas of Jaurès or Hardie have little practical relevance to present-day French or British politics, they have a great deal of relevance to Asia and Africa. One cannot imagine Mr Gaitskell saying that 'Socialism is life for a dying people': and one cannot imagine his audiences understanding him if he did. But Keir Hardie's audience understood— and Mr Nehru's audience would understand today."

This details the Western-European process which has continued since Brecht's death, and which is one of the crucial differences between his situation in the 'thirties and Frisch's in the 'sixties. Yet it also points to the roots of what might be another intellectual escape-route myth: salvation for the maimed conscience of Europe through the under-developed countries. Such salvation may indeed happen: but it is not something we can imagine in detail. In the meantime, Frisch, in *Andorra*, his latest play, focuses on the only problem that can usefully occupy our immediate attention: how do we alter the status of the Colonized, the Inferior Races? In fact, he doesn't offer any solution; this is not the theatre's business. He contents himself with detailing, with all its ironic involutions, the mess of prejudice and attitude we have got ourselves into, and which we have to work out of if we really wish to drop the graven images, Colonized and

Inferior Race, if we really wish to speak, not of Jews or Blacks, but simply of other men.

Max Frisch must be nearly as old as my father. How is it that a man of that generation, which we post-war kids regard as the most ham-handed of all time, still strikes a note and presents an attitude to life which I respond to, find sympathetic and adequate? I think it is because, unlike so many others of that generation, Max Frisch has faced up to his experience of the first half of this century in a useful and valuable way, that he has neither fallen into scepticism and science, nor mysticism, nor the Cold War posture, nor crept back to the ivory warrens of little magazines and literary cliques (affix appropriate names to appropriate sins).

Here it is interesting to note that in both the key novels, he almost suggests that the personal trials which the antagonists undergo are intimately linked with two political events which could only have occurred in our century through the inadequate idealism of our elders: Hitler's rise to power, and The Great Crusade Of The Spanish Civil War.

Both Faber and Stiller, horrified by the public terror they have allowed to happen, attempt to preserve their self-esteem in the face of these public catastrophes, to redeem the helplessness they now feel as the events they might have controlled, had they known in time, burst forth on the front pages of their newspapers in all the historical fixity of Great Events reproduced in headlines and agency photographs. They "fail" to redeem themselves, and the "repercussions of their failure" spread through the rest of their personal lives.

Walter Faber: "She shook her head and wept. I was only marrying her to prove I wasn't an anti-semite, she said, and there was just nothing to be done."

Anton Stiller: "Stiller, as we know, took part in the Spanish Civil War, while still a very young man, as a volunteer in the International Brigade. It is not clear what impelled him to this militant gesture. Probably many factors were combined – a rather romantic Communism such as was common among bourgeois intellectuals at the time, also an understandable desire to see the world, a desire to subordinate his personal interests to some higher historical force, a desire for action: perhaps too, at least in part, it was flight from himself. He passed his ordeal by fire (or rather, he failed to pass it) outside Toledo, where the Fascists had entrenched themselves in the Alcazar."

Frisch has gone through these defining historical experiences of our century. He has examined them, and has come out with an attitude that is guarded, open, and fiercely sceptical of any false engagements, private or public. Perhaps this is why he is so much to our taste. For we, too, cling to these qualities. We know in our bones that there is now so much power in our hands that we can no longer afford false engagements, self-deceiving actions buttressed with the reassuring phraseology of good intention.

The pilgrimage to Republican Spain or the sell-outs throughout Germany cannot happen again; for the world has grown more clenched, more anxious, as it becomes aware of the possible price for such errors. Frisch has created a theatre that lays bare the convolutions and contradictions of this clenched anxiety, and asks men instead to respect their centre of change and growth and learning. It offers no solutions: it is a theatre of presentation and waiting. Waiting until men realize and then start living their realization. Never before has there been such a need for this realization. The pressures which forge our graven images, and the need to cast them off and step out into a precarious area of flexibility and possible freedom are greater than ever. Frisch's full response to these pressures shows itself in the peculiar, unmistakable intensity of any of his plays. His imperturbable working-toward a truth that shall be both human and liveable still allows his gift as an artist full scope to be unfixed and exploratory, to write farce (*Philip Hotz*), high comedy (*Biedermann*), or epic drama (*Andorra*), which are all adequate to the situation in which we live.

"The process which led us to Bikini is not completed. The Flood has once more become a possible event. This is the crucial point. We can do whatever we want. All we need is to know what we want . . . At the end of our journey through history, we find ourselves back where Adam and Eve started. The moral problem still remains to be solved." (*Journal, 1946–49*).

[MAY 1962]

A MAN FOR ALL SEASONS
Review by Tom Milne

Brecht, it seems, is the thing. First Rattigan, now Robert Bolt and *A Man for All Seasons* (Globe). One must applaud the cool thought and detachment from emotionalism that the influence has brought, and the freedom from dying techniques. But it would appear, alas, that it takes a Brecht to be Brechtian.

"The 'Life' of a man like Thomas More," says Robert Bolt in a programme note, "proffers a number of caps which, in this or any other century, we may try on for size." True. But we may also feel that none of them fit very well. Although the caps are similar to those which Miller, in *The Crucible*, and Brecht, in *Galileo*, made into perfect fits, Bolt merely leaves them lying about hopefully.

We are shown a *cas de conscience*. Sir Thomas More, refusing to take the Succession Oath, stands between Church and State, between King Henry and his urgent desire for a divorce, and he holds out until martyrdom. Why does he refuse? We are not told. What effect will this refusal have on the growing Tudor state and its people? It is never discussed. In *Galileo*, Brecht very firmly ties the issues involved in Galileo's denial of his own discoveries to the state of society; the play shows how his compliance with the Inquisition retards the progress of science, and how a refusal to comply might have started the world off with a bang on a new era. *A Man for All Seasons*, as the author himself has claimed, "shows the frightful price which may have to be paid for that refusal to comply – the end of life on any terms at all". Sir Thomas dies, and so? Vivat the next conscience, presumably, whether it is worrying about the world or its ivory tower.

The progress of More's problem is unfolded in a succession of brief episodes, the scene-changes being indicated by banners and signs dropped from the flies. There is an interlocutor in symbolical black tights, called "The Common Man", who introduces each scene and takes part in it, adding appropriate costume (juror, servant, executioner, etc.). All very Brechtian. The result, however, is more like Anouilh. The Anouilh, on the one hand, who drained the protest of Sophocles' Antigone from its social context, leaving a woman who protested just because. And the Anouilh, on the other hand, who, in *L'Alouette* and *Becket*, reduced history to cosy fireside chats. For *A Man for All Seasons*, despite its serious intent, is a simplification – and not only in its examination of conscience. More becomes the standard loyal dissenter. King Henry is the Merry Monarch. Cromwell, the Hollywood villain. More's wife, the Suffering Wife. The Duke of Norfolk, the nobleman from any modern comedy. Worst of all, that graceless insult to actor and audience, the "Common Man" interlocutor (through no fault of Leo McKern). The only excuse for this character would be if he acted as an irritant between the audience and More's ideas; given nothing to do or say, he is reduced to a mannerism.

As a result of this simplification, what might have been a fine play becomes simply a collection of mannerisms. Even Paul Scofield's brilliant performance (suggesting a man who might have had a lot to say had the author ever got round to it) becomes, through lack of sustenance, merely a Variation on a Whisky Priest. And we, the audience, are left wondering why More – and the author – bothered.

[SEPTEMBER 1960]

THE INDIVIDUAL EYE *by Joseph Losey*

PROLOGUE

For nearly twenty-five years Bertolt Brecht has been part of my life and work, but only very recently have I consciously examined him, his work, our work together, and his "influence" on me. It was not because the work or influence was unimportant to me, but more because they had always been like the very air I breathed – there, practical and in progress.

In recent years, much guff and nonsense has been written about Brecht the man and his theories of theatre. In his own early processes of work he contributed a certain amount to the now "unending highways" of his band-wagons, laden with the concealing, smothering manure of the hangers-on, the discoverers, the enshriners, the entourages, and the entombers – all those who are there for the ride and not because they are going anywhere.

Who is going Brecht's road? Who really belongs in this company of explorers? Two things identify them for me: first, the doers and among them chiefly those with what I call "the eye"; and secondly, those who *know* – in their guts, their bones, their hearts, by whatever antennae it may be that the human race communicates at its highest level. When Brecht's works are played right, the audience *knows* – the great mass of it does. The inheritors and successors of Brecht *know* – the other "eyes". Some of those who worked alongside of Brecht, or elsewhere in other parts of the world, at the same time, but lonely like him and separately – some of them though perhaps lesser talents, less obstinate, less lucky – know. For Brecht, while great, was also lucky.

To write about Brecht is for me a prodigious task of selection. It is also highly personal because of the accidents that brought us together, sometimes tangentially and sometimes closely, until that last year of 1946–7 which we spent in almost continuous work together. I have no wish to add to the cartloads of obfuscation which have been written and spoken, nor have I any desire to join the faithful. (By these remarks, I do not mean to condemn serious works such as John Willett's *The Theatre of Bertolt Brecht*, incomplete, inaccurate and mistaken as I believe it to be in part.)

THE MAN

In *Galileo Galilei* there is one of the great scenes of theatrical conception and writing of all time – the investiture of the scientist-cardinal, Barberini, as Pope. This scene will serve admirably as a touchstone for nearly everything I wish to say about Brecht.[1] It is a perfect example of how Brecht's theatre relates to cinema; it demonstrates the high visual theatricality of the man (above all he was a man of the living theatre); it presents his own posthumous comment on the idolaters and all those who would attempt to "fix" him in some permanent niche, define him, enshrine him, establish him. Brecht won't remain fixed or embalmed. He will resist all efforts to make him a sacred cow or even a profane divinity snugly justifying a *status quo*. Willett says (p. 164) that Brecht cannot be imitated without the risk of seeming "dated" and "affected". How true this is and hence how absurd the canonization of him and his theories. Helene Weigel, his actress-manageress-widow, above all others knows this and tries to combat it. Brecht needs to be "devestured" a little. Take off the robes: who and what was there? Brecht ...

> His sardonic death mask looks down at me from above my desk. He is the most undead dead man I know. The mask is exactly as he was in life.
> He was the most theatrical theatre man I ever knew.
> He was the most professional "pro".
> He saw everything – he saw you and through you – though there was never any "personal" talk.
> He was uncompromising, but flexible and open.
> He had the drive of a puritan without the self-penalizing guilt. (How he escaped the latter I will never know.)
> He was an individual among organized and organizational men.
> He recognized the necessity for organization but he never abdicated his individual vision and responsibility.

[1] To those not familiar with the play *Galileo*: this is a scene in which Barberini, layer by layer, is ceremonially invested in the robes of the office of Pope, with the Cardinal Inquisitor attending and slowly, persistently exacting the right to torture Galileo. As the scientist and man Barberini disappear beneath the robes, his "no's" become weaker and weaker until he finally concedes all that the Inquisition needs. The scene is almost entirely visual. It would be quite clear without any words.

Brecht's humour was enormous. The twinkle and often malice never left his eyes. He giggled like a girl and his laughter was a great, high-pitched bawdy hacking laugh that emerged around his chewed foul cigar. The cigar was always there, sometimes fleetingly removed from his mouth because he would have choked with the laughter, or sometimes because he wanted to emphasize a point with it in the jagged jabs that were his gestures when he was not still.

Stillness was another aspect of Brecht and his work. He could listen. He could sit still, though sometimes his impatience to clarify or correct or supplement led to an agitated, frenetic walk, words starting and then deferring. Disciplined as few other artists I have known. The combination of boundless energy and the ability to relax. Rigid hours of work, régimes to be broken and extended, when necessary, limitlessly. And then the nap; flat out on his back, the cap which was part of the uniform, pulled over his eyes.

Objective in all his visions, but never passionless. He was the most passionate of men: full of anger and sudden rages, quick to take delight, utterly enthusiastic, but opinionated and intolerant of the unseeing, unfeeling or tasteless.

Compassionate he was, perhaps more of people than persons. In his life he was a man-eater; every person, every thing served his art.

What he looked like has been described often enough now and the photographs are now familiar and always strikingly like him: small, electric, balanced like a dancer, eyes jabbing like his hands, quick in all things. The linen and fabric of his clothes just right and always the same denim: simple, working-class derived but upper-class fashioned (all part of the eye).

Brecht happened. As sometimes happens, something was in the air the world over; a little later in the USA, perhaps a little sooner in the USSR, slightly different in each place – but of the same stuff. Brecht well knew as he wrote in *Galileo* that "there is no such thing as a book only one man can write". Or play or theatre: And yet he knew quite as well (also clear in *Galileo*) of the critical difference one man of genius can make to the tempo of development and the particular character of one time and place in space.

Brecht was absolutely certain of his own special role, his destiny, his "job" I think he would have put it. He was not arrogant, he was quite simply certain of his way, and his "eye". The individual eye. It never had to be discussed between him and me. We knew and we saw together. In all of my times with Brecht he never once mentioned "theory".

Once, when I was nervously preparing for the first readings with the cast of *Galileo* I made an attempt to read some of Brecht's writings on theory and some of the expositions of the academicians of the Brecht school of that time (1946–7) in order to "indoctrinate" the Company. In the middle of my carefully prepared introductory talk to the cast, I suddenly became horribly aware of the irrelevance and pomposity of my effort. In work we used every theory and every previous experience of acting and theatre which was useful, but we didn't talk.

THE EYE AND STYLE

To get even a part of my personal experience and awareness of Brecht down on paper would take months of work and might not be nearly so useful as this more or less random remembrance. Perhaps because I always took Brecht and my work with him for granted, I never analysed it or ever sought his approbation. Nor did he give it. He accepted. Brecht's life is full of suppliers whose work he absorbed and used – some didn't exist without him – others went their own merry ways. None I think suffered. Some were unconscionably aggrandized, the "entourage".

Others never got the credit which was certainly theirs.

For instance, John Hubley, the artist who drew the now world familiar sketches for my production of *Galileo*, exactly set down Brecht's precise image as much as any man who worked with him. And yet I have never seen a credit to Hubley. Not one of the *Galileo* productions from our first in Hollywood to the last of The Berliner Ensemble would have been quite the same, quite so right without Hubley, and yet no credits for him.

The second American production of *Galileo* in New York City, which is referred to in both Willett and Esslin as "the same" as the Hollywood production, certainly was not. Same in general shape, yes. Impossible without the first which was in active collaboration with Brecht, yes. But different cast, different performances (especially from Laughton). Different words, thanks in part to the collaboration of George Tabori in rewriting with Laughton and me from notes left behind in New York by Brecht. Different and much better. The many who fed, nurtured, protected the man-eating Brecht . . . Weigel, the housewife and co-worker through all those long years of exile; Hanns Eisler, the friend and companion, slave and colleague. All those who helped on the long road of emigration: Hella Woulijoki, and the countless others I don't know. Those who worked for nothing to raise the essentials for a first production in Hollywood: John Houseman and T. Edward Hambleton – the managers and patrons – all the actors, all the builders.

And these are only a few along the road.

But I believe that none of these, nor I, felt any awe or any sense of making history in our work with him. Because not only was Brecht as certainly (as *he* was certain) entitled to his position of maestro, but because he in a very real sense *was* the times. All or much of it channelled and funnelled through him, the individual eye of the times – whether it was observation of the elegance of the line of an arch, the rightness of a colour or the poetic, cutting-edge of an observation of character or society. This is what elicited the unconscious devotion and this too is what encourages idolatry in lesser men now. Though Brecht expressed his time and ours, it was his personal eye that saw, his ear that heard. The reason he can't be imitated or set-down academically is because to do it, you've got to have it yourself.

Brecht's plays are frameworks for live theatre, for acting,

for high theatricality. They observe nature but do not reproduce it. His is a process of stripping reality and then rebuilding it. To do this, what is replaced must in every instance be perfect:

Acting: perfectly observed and perfectly performed. Once he said of an actor who could not sustain a simple business of getting a coin from his purse and giving it grudgingly to a beggar (in *Galileo*), "He should have observed a thousand instances of people giving in different ways and different circumstances, and stored them for use now."

This did not mean naturalism. Art is larger than life. None of your English squeamish fear of over-acting or exaggeration, or "showing feelings". When your son is shot you feel it, *umph*, directly, in the belly, like Weigel in *Mother Courage*. But the *Actress* is not feeling it at that moment; she is thinking.

When an actor, playing in a scene in the Vatican where monks mock the waiting Galileo and his theories of the roundness of the earth – when this actor queried: "What is my motivation?" as he mimed a ballet designed to demonstrate that one cannot stand on a moving ball, Brecht sitting beside me whispered, "Does the tightrope walker need a motive for not falling off the wire?" And then he burst into roars of laughter.

And yet when Laughton (seeking to master "the pelican scene"[1] in which Galileo rips open his own breast and exposes his own perfidy to his one-time pupil now suddenly an idolator) went to mass at St Patrick's Cathedral on Fifth Avenue (his first attendance at mass in twenty years) – Brecht would have applauded because it produced results. For the first time after months of playing and rehearsal Laughton used something in himself and exposed the raw quick of it to achieve the scene. No method. Any method. Style and content.

The selected reality-symbol must be perfect. I shall never forget a grotesque midnight scene in the office of Mike

---

[1] The pelican is fabled to feed his young with his own blood by wounding his breast with his beak. So Galileo exposed his very guts to his pupil in order to give him a final demonstration in thinking.

Todd who once was supposed to present *Galileo*. We all met in his executive suite at Universal Pictures in Hollywood: Todd, Brecht, Howard Bay (then to be the designer), Jack Moss (associate of Todd) and I. Todd talked of how he would "dress" the production in "Renaissance furniture" from the Hollywood warehouses . . . Brecht only listened and giggled nervously. But from that time forth there was never any chance that Todd would do the play. The single chair which ultimately took the place of the "Renaissance furniture" in our production was a perfectly made so-called "director's" chair of canvas and wood. Why this to stand for Renaissance? Because it resembled one of the chairs of the period in structure, because it was *beautiful*, because the *textures* were right, because it worked. I remember another occasion at 4 a.m. after a dress rehearsal of *Galileo* when a coat of shellac given the wood structure of the bare, beautiful, functional set we had devised sent Brecht into roaring, tearing tantrums because it "destroyed the grain of the wood". And it did, he was right; we were all too tired to care, but he was not. And the wood was stripped of its lacquer and restored before the first performance that evening.

The examples can be multiplied a thousandfold. The single important point remains: perfection, style, the eye, the line, the texture, the colour. I think I could always see (and this was perhaps the chief reason Brecht and I got along together) – could see not just the rightness of the line of a curving stairway but the line of the content and intention. We saw together. But Brecht taught me scrupulous attention to detail in everything; the visual, the word, the gesture, the composition in movement, the sound, the music.

PERSONAL HISTORY IN BRIEF

In 1935 I was a wandering disillusioned student-professional. I had already directed on Broadway. With the 1929 crash I had entered the Broadway theatre from University. In University we had already tried the expressionism of Denis Johnston's *Bride for the Unicorn* and O'Neill's *Great God*

Brown. Disconsolately I wandered toward Europe – via Britain, Scandinavia, to Leningrad and Moscow. That year, Moscow was to theatre and film intellectuals what Florence had been in the 'twenties when Gordon Craig held forth there. In fact, Craig that year was himself in Moscow with unlimited facilities for a production of *Macbeth* at the Mali Theatre (it never saw an audience of more than Craig, so far as I know). Piscator was there; Brecht; Eisler; Vassar "students of theatre"; Norris Houghton, the theatre designer and historian; Leyda, the chronicler of Eisenstein; Paul Strand, the greatest of stills photographers; and various exponents of the Group Theatre including Clurman and Cheryl Crawford. Howard Lindsey I remember. Of course, Muriel Draper; and always our art-patron American Ambassador, William Bullitt. It was the year of hobohemia and the locusts. I met Brecht and Eisler. I laboriously translated Piscator's *Political Theatre*. But I didn't really know who any of them were or what they represented. I knew of the devastations of Hitler, but not really much of the Berlin which had preceded Hitler.

Theatre in Moscow that year was great. Okhlopkov was breaking down the proscenium and presenting theatre in the round and the rectangle and the hexagonal as it had never been dreamed of before or approached since. Long hours of forgotten talk with this wonderful actor-director-manager and man – forgotten the words, but the image and effect, never. . . . And then the already slightly decadent brilliance of Meyerhold, etc., etc.

I returned to New York to help create "The Living Newspaper" – a real breaking down and rebuilding.[1] This was

---

[1] "The Living Newspaper" was a form created in work by me its first director, Arthur Arent its chief writer, and Morris Watson a newspaper man, its administrative head. It was a popular theatre, popularly priced, subsidized by the Federal Government, and giving us extraordinary freedom of content, and enabling us to experiment in form. We used circus, variety, ballet, projection, music, but somehow achieved an artistic whole unified in each instance by a subject (for instance, the Roosevelt agricultural programme in *Triple- A Plowed Under*, the use of court injunctions historically against trade unionism in *Injunction Granted*). Unfortunately, the Federal Theatre and its subsidy came to an end before we had completely achieved a style, but the highly filmic

Brechtian theatre but I didn't know it. Brecht saw it and loved it. And in spite of his "austerity" about colour and propensity for white bright light and neutral shades, he saw and laughed with appreciation when I dressed my proletarian mob in fuchsias and pinks. I was in revolt against the idea that the proletarian mass is visually drab or working-class dress necessarily colourless.

I remember Brecht cross-legged on the floor of the drawing-room, cap and cigar and denims against the satins and Japanese mats and Noguchis and the Calders, Mirós, Lurçats, etc., that were the background of my then wife, couturière Elizabeth Hawes, expounding his enthusiasms, articulating his "eye" which was our eye too. But none of us conscious then of the parallels.

devices and impact of "The Living Newspaper" had an incalculable influence on the American theatre.

Later, a number of us, including myself, Nicholas Ray, Kazan and others – whose names are now known in films – tried to continue the form in a private theatre enterprise which I called "Social Circus". I still have the blue-prints for this theatre plan, but unfortunately it never got beyond the idea stage.

There were many parallel experiments which I and others were participating in in the middle 'thirties in the United States, can one ever say how directly or indirectly influenced by Brecht? Kenneth Tynan in *The Observer*, October 23, 1960, wrote a brilliant piece about the influence in the late 'twenties of the pre-Hitlerian Berlin of cabaret on the development of Brechtian theatre, and relates this to the present renaissance in the American theatre as it is being influenced by people like Mort Sahl, Mike Nichols and Elaine May and other cabaret satirists. That this kind of influence was equally true of the New York middle 'thirties is generally not known: for several years every Sunday afternoon in a long deserted church in the East Fifties a wide assortment of theatre people produced a political cabaret out of which came the first genuine anti-Fascist theatre, the first real attempts at central staging (or "theatre in the round" as it is now called) and from which directly came a very exciting play titled *Who Fights this Battle?* Staged in the centre of the stalls of an old ballroom, about the Spanish Civil War, it was written and produced in the fury and passion of the first few months after the outbreak of civil war in Spain in '36, script by Kenneth White, music by Paul Bowles, direction by Joseph Losey.

It is interesting to note that one of Brecht's first attempts to translate the songs of *Galileo* into English was with Abe Burrows, now well known as the writer of *Guys and Dolls*. It was the right idea but did not quite work

I also remember Brecht rising up in the middle of a Theatre Union rehearsal of *Die Mutter* to exclaim "Drecht!" and make a furious exit. And he was right. The production had no style. It had no passion. It was just the shell and it was heavily sentimental.

After that Brecht vanished from my life, until much later when I came to cinema and Hollywood. And there we came together in work on *Galileo*.

There I found him again in his little box of a frame house in Santa Monica, all the familiar stamps of his personality and Weigel's, the scrubbed wood floors, the Chinese prints, and battered upright piano, the chest of manuscripts, the beautiful iron-stone china which "Helle" had collected from the flea markets. Nothing was wasted in exile. The work went on. He accepted the consequences of his convictions and would be ready, whenever the time came, for a production or to make his theatre. I never heard any complaints.

When he went as one of "the ten" to testify in Washington I went with him and all night long we walked the empty streets of that mausoleum city talking of the fearful ordeal confronting him the next day before that "bauern" court headed by Congressman Parnell Thomas, later to become a convicted misappropriator of funds and to share jail with many of his victims. The calm, wit, finesse, and showmanship with which Brecht conducted himself on that occasion is now history. I saw him off on his plane to Switzerland and eventual return to Germany. We corresponded sparsely. I never saw him again.

After that Laughton and I did the New York production of *Galileo*. And after that too, Laughton cleared his heels of Brecht and me with as little regard to accuracy as is usual in these cases. But Brecht would not have been surprised at Laughton's monstrous mis-statements in his "authorized biography" or his failure to answer any communication either from me or Weigel upon Brecht's death. Brecht was a great romantic about talent, a "sucker" for it. But he never made the mistake of equating talent with character. It's fine when it happens together, even though it seldom does. Brecht was a pragmatist. Does it work? Can I use it?

Brecht was merciless but no sadist. He was full of wonder and passion for the content and form and shape of dynamic, dialectic life – out of which his personal eye shaped his art. The inscription from Galileo's *Discorsi* which he quoted on the title page of the play, would do well for Brecht himself:

"It is my opinion that the earth is very noble and admirable by reason of so many and so different alterations and generations which are incessantly made therein."

Galileo Galilei

DIE WAHRHEIT IST KONKRET

This Hegelian legend was tacked in bold letters to the bare wall above the draftsman's bench which constituted Brecht's desk in his New York apartment on 57th Street, where I lived for six months in 1946. I took it to mean to Brecht not that the truth was absolute, but that it was precise – there is a right and a wrong way, no more and no less than necessary, exactness of observation, economy of means of communication.

This economy and precision is taken by many to be coldness or meagreness. Brecht in theatre is said to be dull, cold, boring, pedantic. Yes, it can indeed be dull, if the actors and director are dull. Boring, if they do not use the opportunity which Brecht affords to enrich and soar in the theatre. Meagre if it is not exactly right of line, of gesture, of timing, of composition, of texture. Pedantic, if all that is understood is the didactic aspects of Brecht. Brecht taught through poetry, beauty of form and word and thought. Brecht was a true dialectical Marxist. He understood the constant change, interchange, the interaction of all life and living. Brecht understood that living is "becoming".

The Brechtian theatre and eye is cold only to the unseeing or those who mistake bareness for selection. His flat in New York was bare white plaster, the bookcase was hand-fashioned of piled bricks and unfinished planks. The couch and curtains were of burlap (hessian). The light was high, white, and exposed. The decoration, a single, perfect Chinese scroll. The selection and placement were right, the eye never tired in that flat. It didn't roam, it wasn't irritated, neither was it without focus. The visual aspect of Brecht's theatre is comparable to the best of Lloyd Wright or Mies van de Rohe in architecture. Brecht taught by juxtaposing contrasts, by the demonstration of dialectics, by the undeniable internal truth of his observation. His own style, of person and of work, demands to be met by equal style in his director and actor. Brecht the man, himself, as well as his work was the essence of style – i.e. of rightness. This may all sound highly mystical, it isn't. Is it not clear that Churchill, like Brecht, has style of person, of dress, of manner, of speech, of thought? Is it not equally clear that this is not true of, let us say, Nixon?

Like all truly individual art, Brecht's is untransmittable to disciples and yet his influence is unending and vast – because it is of its time – but the image and the word are unique, insidious, inescapable and continuing.

Brecht has often been abused with a quotation from himself to the effect that one must not only know what one wants to say, but have "the guile" with which to say it – substitute for guile – craft, wit, art, "eye".

Did it matter that the costume of The Prince in *Galileo* was taken from a painting of a tailor of the period?[1] It was right. Did it matter that many of the people were dressed from Breughel, although this was the Florence of the Medicis? No, because it was right.

BRECHT AND CINEMA

What are the particular aspects of Brechtian theatre and Brecht the man as I knew him that might directly relate to film and which have influenced my work in cinema?

The stripping of reality and its precise reconstruction through selection of reality-symbols.

The importance of precision in gesture, and texture and line in objects.

The economy of movement, of actors, of camera – never to move excepting with purpose. The difference between stillness and the static.

[1] *The Tailor* by Morani. (National Gallery, London.)

The focusing of the eye through exact use of the camera, lens and movement.

The fluidity of composition.

The juxtaposing of contrasts and contradiction through editing and in text – this is the simplest way to accomplish the much misunderstood "alienation effect".

The importance of the exact word, sound, music.

The heightening of reality to ennoble.

The extension of the vision of the individual *eye*.

CONCLUSION

Like Galileo, Brecht enjoyed thinking as much as any man I ever knew. Unlike Galileo he was moderate in his eating and drinking, but like Galileo intemperate in work and love. I am told by the magazine *Encore* that whenever they publish a piece on Brecht they lose readers: perhaps they publish the wrong commentators. Brecht is not to be produced or acted by the wrong people, no more than to be written about by them. In case this piece lends itself to any of the morass of "emmerdement" which has come to surround Brecht, I should like to conclude with a list of the things which he was not:

He was *not* just a theoretician – he was a man of the living theatre, always changing.

Not a politician, but aware of the definitive role of politics in organized contemporary life.

Not cold, or austere – but no bleeding heart.

Germanic he was, but *never* lacking in humour.

Selfish he was, but never unaware.

Not a dogmatist, but obstinate as hell he was. He held out, he stuck for the original rightness and truth of his eye in all things; and for this, above all things, I value and honour him in theatre and cinema: that is to say, he was not a "hedger" when it came to the individual vision by which each true artist must stand or fall.

He was not divorced from life, but always of it. His life and art were inseparable but in a sense art came before life: that is, it took precedence where individuals were concerned. And what of the ethics of that: well, life lived and grew on his art, as on the art of every pure and purifying practitioner of it. People got sacrificed sometimes. If not Brecht, then another, he himself would have said.

And yet how much the world lost when his heart cracked. He had only just begun and when will there be such another! He was on the side of life and beauty and the wonder of change and growth. He was a profoundly moral artist.

> *May you now guard Science's light*
> *Kindle it and use it right*
> *Lest it be a flame to fall*
> *Downward to consume us all.*

> (The curtain boy, *Galileo Galilei*)

[MARCH 1961]

CHAPTER FIVE

HARBINGERS OF THE FUTURE

INTRODUCTION

By 1963, the term "New Wave" sounded odd and anachronistic. Osborne had produced two slim one-acters under the title *Plays for England*, both of which had disappointed; although new plays were promised, he seemed more and more preoccupied with films. N. F. Simpson had virtually stopped writing. Ann Jellicoe, after *The Knack*, busied herself with Ibsen adaptations rather than original work. Arnold Wesker had reached some kind of apogee with *Chips With Everything*, and spent most of his time lobbying Labour MPs and trying to construct Centre 42, a massive culture-dispensary for the working classes. Robert Bolt was turning out elaborate trivialities like *Gentle Jack*. And Alun Owen, author of *The Rough and Ready Lot* and *Progress to the Park*, was the willing captive of the TV studios.

Without the Littlewood impetus, both Shelagh Delaney and Brendan Behan seemed to have come to a dead halt. Pinter had taken to adapting television plays like *The Collection* and *The Lover*, or patching up undergraduate novels like *The Dwarfs*. He too seemed to be gravitating towards the cinema. The National Theatre, finally in existence – in name at least – after a 115-year campaign, had wooed away Kenneth Tynan, and without his weekly column in *The Observer* it felt as if no one was guarding the fort.

John Arden, of course, went on writing boldly, disgruntling his stationary critics, and a few new writers of promise had appeared: most notably Henry Livings, David Rudkin and Charles Wood. Livings, an alumnus of Joan Littlewood's Theatre Workshop, turned out proletarian slices-of-life which frequently had charm, always had wit, and felt forward insistently to new structures. Rudkin and Wood, despite realist trappings, bore the stamp of Genet; the work of both writers drew impressively upon ritual, and sparked off disturbing ambiguities.

But the subsidence of the New Wave wasn't the only concern. Something else seemed to be happening. Something radical and destructive was in the wind. One caught glimpses of it in American plays like Jack Gelber's *The Connection* and Kenneth H. Brown's *The Brig*; in the anarchic experiments of the Happenings-men of New York and San Francisco; in the attitude behind improvisational satire, and in the dae-monic, brooding person of Lenny Bruce; in an increasing preoccupation with the work and theories of Antonin Artaud and in the Theatre of Cruelty season launched at the LAMDA studio-theatre in London.

It is too early to even attempt a definition, but there is certainly something brewing. It was ominously alluded to at the 1963 Edinburgh Drama Conference as "the death of the word". Just as the Brechtian resurgence is rooted in the political output of the 'twenties, so this trend is connected to the Dadaist and surrealist experiments of that same decade. It is preoccupied with form, but shuns formalism. It admires the experiments in discontinuity conducted by the French *nouvelle vague* film directors; learns from the techniques of action painting and the found-object school of art; is at home with collage, with William Burroughs' literary splice-ups and the American existentialism of Norman Mailer and Jack Kerouac.

It is the sworn enemy of psychology and psychological realism, runs from the premises of the New York Actors' Studio, and finds Ibsen, and the writers who followed his example, particular anathema. It is impatient with narrative and stylistic consistency, and inclines towards fragmentary structure and the juggling of antithetical elements. It finds story-telling inadequate, and fixed characters a restriction.

Its attitude to Shakespeare and the classics can be gleaned – slightly – from Peter Brook's *King Lear*, Jerzy Grotowski's adaptation of *Dr Faustus* in Opole, Poland, and the Marowitz *Hamlet* experiment at the Theatre of Cruelty. It is concerned with reconstruction and rethinking rather than clever inter-pretation. It approaches writers like Shakespeare and Mar-lowe as providers of source-material rather than creators of static masterworks. Essentially, it has an irreverent attitude to the arts, and provokes the kind of outburst Kenneth Tynan made at Edinburgh when he defined Happenings as "totalitarian" and "apocalyptic".

Like all new trends in art, it will probably claim to be more realistic, resorting to prefixes like *hyper, super* or *ultra* to distinguish it from nineteenth-century naturalism and twentieth-century realism. At the time of writing, it is impossible to say whether it will be a flash in the pan or the touchstone for an entirely new direction in theatrical endeavour. But the portents are unmistakably there.

BEYOND NATURALISM PURE
The First Five Years by Stuart Hall

No Brecht: no Arthur Miller: no Sartre. It is worthwhile beginning there. Things have been accomplished on the British stage in the last six years which were never dreamt of in the philosophy of H. M. Tennent and Co, but it is neces-sary to say what has *not* happened. Certainly, the gains have been immense. Not simply the number of plays and play-wrights of quality, liberated from the ethos of the West End stage, recognizably of our age and times: but in addition, the special achievements of Theatre Workshop and the Royal Court, the spread of new plays outwards from the metropolis, the rescue operation via the theatre in progress in the cinema – even *Encore* itself and its growing band of readers. Still, neither Wesker nor Osborne, who have come closest to it, have managed anything with the peculiar social centrality of *Death of a Salesman*. More disturbing is our utter inability to engage at the level of ideas with anything approaching the seriousness and power of *Altona*. In spite of the windy reaches of Logue's *Antigone*, Bolt's rather flat intellectualism and Nigel Dennis's perverse academic card-trumping, British hostility to ideas has carried the day.

Brecht is the most intriguing comparison. Like Crusoe's Friday he has left his footsteps all over the bloody shop, but of the man himself – or any talent comparable for sheer originality – not a sign. A very skilful critic, reconstructing the dramatic history of the decade from the charred fragments of a nuclear war, might deduce that a composite dramatist lived and worked in Britain in the 'fifties whose name was probably Bertolt Brecht – he has been so omnipresent. The visit of the Berliner Ensemble was surely a turning point. His influence runs straight through into the Theatre Workshop method, which is the most exciting theatrical development of all, not only directly in plays like *The Hostage*, *Fings*, *Taste of Honey*, but further away, *Lily White Boys* and *Paul Slickey*. His shadow lengthens over *Altona*, Bolt's *Man For All Seasons* and Osborne's *Luther*. His influence has been modulated through the writing of Ken Tynan, who has been more than critic – midwife, almost – to the movement. But no British *Good Woman of Setzuan* survives to tell the tale.

The crude thesis is that what we have managed to do best is either a kind of *pastiche* (e.g. *The Hostage*) or a specially British brand of naturalism. And this, it is argued, is only natural since the mood and feeling which informed the movement had deep roots already in naturalism: the desire to recreate working-class life, the preoccupation with humanist values and an interest in the attack upon Establishment values through social criticism. Certain things have been done which fit this description – the low-lying working-class comedies of manners of the Willis Hall-Keith Waterhouse variety, of which *Billy Liar* and *Sparrers Can't Sing* are prime examples: at a higher level, Wesker's four and Delaney's two. On the other hand, the pattern was never so clear-cut as the "kitchen sink" school of critics would have had us imagine: and the break-up is now advanced. Arden never belonged. Osborne has moved steadily from *George Dillon* through the heroic exercises of *Look Back In Anger* towards (in *The Entertainer*) a blend of naturalism and expressionism and (in *Luther*) an almost cinematic version of the historical chronicle. The pull towards historical drama is much stronger than we might have estimated. In addition, thrusting Beckett before them and dragging Ionesco behind, Pinter and Simpson have advanced towards the centre in the mode of the naturalistic-absurd. Looking back, naturalism in any pure sense has never been an adequate form: but the attempt to capture the rhythms and situations of real life has always been there as a main-stream.

Naturalism in its purest form is certainly to be seen in *The Lion In Love*. Although the play dealt with the adult relationship between husband and wife in a remarkably mature way, it came as close as any play of substance in the period to reproducing the naturalism of everyday life. It was almost as if *The Lion In Love* could be seen going on outside the window any time you chose to look. It had no climax to speak of – extending and returning on itself with a circular movement surprisingly like life. If you left at the end of the second act, you could be sure it would be there when you returned. But when you turn to *Taste Of Honey* – a better play in every way – the naturalistic form is already under pressure. Shelagh Delaney is not at all self-conscious about her ability to portray Salford life, but she accepts this as a framework for what she is really interested in communicating – her extraordinarily fine and subtle feel for personal relationships. No themes or ideas external to the play disturb its inner form: her values are all intensive. In Jo she achieves something stubborn and calm, a composition in tough idealism and mature despair. But her real forte is the interplay between relationships. When Jo's idealism tends to take off, Geoff or Helen are on hand to puncture her reveries with a biting realism. What there is between Jo and Helen – compounded of love and bitterness – contrasts with what there is between Jo and Geoff – the tender explorations of all the levels which lie between love and need. A spirit of acceptance – larger, more embracing than all the tribulations through which Jo lives – infuses the play: but Helen herself is a decisive break with naturalism, drawn direct from the good-time working-class woman of the music hall, with, somehow, flesh and blood as well as "heart".

Wesker, on the other hand, has had to do battle with his

impulse to shift the naturalistic form, with which he is most comfortable, in the direction of "themes" and "ideas", with which he is less at home. In his hands, then, the form tends to fragment from internal pressure – "life" here, "words" there. As the poet of the everyday, his settings are true to life – his Norfolk and his East End especially. In *The Kitchen* he manages to transpose the rhythm of physical work into the substructure of his play most successfully. But neither *Chicken Soup* nor *Jerusalem* achieve a proper organic relationship between setting and theme.

I argued in a review of *The Kitchen* in the last *Encore* that this is certainly because, in Ronnie, he fails to create dramatically the conscience and sensibility of his generation. Ronnie really does not spring from life at all – he is Wesker's artificial creation: a rather verbose, priggish and insensitive abstraction. Through him the words are loosed from the action, with Ronnie endlessly verbalizing the theme. Perhaps this is exactly why, by contrast, *Roots* is so successful. The verbalizing, which in other plays is a distraction at the margin of the play has been brought into the centre of *Roots*. "Talking" is not just something irritating which Ronnie is always doing – it is exactly what Beatie is constantly trying to do: she is trying to be able to "talk", to "do it for herself" – and speech, words, actually, at the end, constitute the very form of her liberation. Nor is the Norfolk family merely the naturalistic background to a monologue of comment – they are part of Beatie herself. What she challenges in them – conservatism, stubbornness, inertia, gossip and triviality – she is herself an instance of. Thus she embodies and dramatizes her theme, as Peter does in *The Kitchen*, where elsewhere Ronnie merely reflects on his. Thus at the end of both the second and third acts of *Roots*, the theme of the play dances and speaks through her, it moves under its own steam, it is *performed* for us as a play must be. All of Wesker's plays seem to me to move towards some such very special moment of high dramatic revelation – an "epiphany" as James Joyce called it. It is striven for in *Jerusalem* too, in the naming game which the child plays with his parents, but with embarrassing results. When, however, as in *Roots*, the plays gather themselves around some such moment on the stage, naturalistic reportage ends and drama begins.

If *Roots* is open to question, then, it is at the level of theme rather than of drama. The point of the play is the conflict, instanced in Beatie but more generally true, between two images of "community": the stubborn, rooted way of life of the rural community for which the Bryants stand, and the larger, more liberated but individualized world of which Ronnie is the symbol. The problem is that these never properly confront one another in the play. The Bryants are so substantially *there*, whereas Ronnie is present only through the exaggerated parodies of Beatie herself, and, more questionably, in that embarrassing letter which Mrs Bryant reads at the end. The play, then, is not a drama of conflict as it appears to have been planned, but rather a celebration – quite overwhelming at times – of the rich solidity of the rural tradition, and, of course, the final liberation of Beatie. The question which Wesker poses to himself at the beginning – is the best in the Bryant tradition *enough* for working people in a modern world? – never gets answered. Beatie grows into herself, but it is something richer and finer and more complex than that which Ronnie appears to offer us through her words. It is, in itself, a remarkable releasing dramatic experience to watch her grow, but the question of the fate of the "community" out of which she grows and to which she so clearly still belongs is postponed to another time and place. And the failure of the return to the rural crafts in *Jerusalem* suggests that the impasse which Wesker now faces, if his art is to develop, is not only dramatic but intellectual as well.

Wesker's failure in Ronnie to create the "conscience of his race" contrasts with Osborne's unquestioned success in adding to the representative galaxy of heroes of our time. If Jimmy Porter heads the list, Dillon, Archie Rice, Slickey and even Luther cannot be far behind. Already, in *Epitaph For George Dillon* – the story of a failed-artist who sells out (a theme with real compulsive attractions for Osborne) – he could be seen moving towards the dominant hero. In *Look Back* a sheer explosive pressure of feeling and language propels Jimmy Porter into our consciousness. Osborne is bad at the kind of personal relationships which Delaney manages so well in *Taste Of Honey*: he hasn't the objectivity to divide his affections so evenly among his characters as she has. His mind is far too partisan, identifying with his hero even when recognizing his limitations. Nor does he have his dramatic senses attuned, as Wesker does, for the reverberations of his themes at the level of social and community life (except in *The Entertainer*, which is a different affair). It is the corrosive drive of the central protagonist, fired by a distinctively puritan, protestant imagination of a secular kind, which powers his plays.

Where Wesker is trying to find a way of linking dramatically Beatie with the community she grows from, Osborne is trying to burn his way back into that tangled subliminal area where the issues of politics and the issues of love and sex merge, mingle and collide. The answer to the prolonged critical debate about whether *Look Back* was really about politics or about sex is, of course, that it is about *both*. Jimmy Porter is like a destructive element, blasting away at some indistinct target, trying to shift layer after layer of cant and cynicism, until he reaches that inner core where people either "feel" or are irretrievably "dead". The dead thing which drives Jimmy to distraction within Alison, and the "death" which looks out from Archie Rice's eyes, is also the dead heart of England, the bloody unfeeling core. It is useless to point out that Osborne scatters his blows too wide, that he is not sufficiently selective, as if he were merely some kind of exalted social critic. What the critics call his "targets" are merely the surface symptoms of a deeper sickness, which Jimmy, for all his bitter words, never penetrates to, but which he is sure is in there, somewhere, quietly rotting away the England he loves. His very excoriations spring from a nostalgia, deep and true, for England which, protestant that he is, will not let him rest. *Luther*, for all the transpositions of time and place setting, is a logical development: the man driven from within, with the secret cause literally working away in his bowels. Osborne himself has called his plays "lessons in feeling": and whereas, when Wesker makes the mother shout "if you don't care you die" it is a public utterance, Osborne is constantly seeking for the moment when the audience will identify so closely with what is going on on the stage that they will rise up and lift their voices and make "a great big beautiful fuss".

Where these different themes come together in the most satisfying dramatic form is in *The Entertainer*, where Osborne finds both the properly seedy hero and the representatively public symbol in the failed artist and the declining art of the music hall. It is also, of course, the point at which he is furthest from naturalism (much further than in *Luther* for instance), as he says in his prefatory note:

> "In writing this play I have not used some of the techniques of the music hall in order to exploit an effective trick, but because I believe that these can solve some of the eternal problems of time and space that face the dramatist, and, also, it has been relevant to the story and setting. Not only has this technique its own traditions, its own conventions and symbols, its own mystique, it cuts right across the restrictions of the so-called naturalistic stage. Its contact is immediate, vital, and direct."

Osborne makes his own case. The music hall is not only a real dramatic symbol, sufficient in itself, yet representative of the whole society: but its traditions are useful to the dramatist in assisting him to surpass the limited connections which can be made between different levels of meaning within the naturalistic conventions. The song-and-dance traditions of the boards enable him to employ song and parody in an emblematic representation of his theme ("Why Should I Care?"): the two level conventions of the stage-within-a-stage enable him to make expressionist connections between the two levels, at least, on which the plot moves, and the many levels at which Archie Rice exists. The ironic, anti-heroic posture of Archie Rice, confronted with his own failure, suits Osborne better than the heroics of Jimmy Porter. Whereas Jimmy stands outside us, battering us into sensitivity (and sometimes, one suspects, *in*-sensitivity) by his verbal pyrotechnics, Archie identifies us with "the secret cause" in him. So that where audiences at *Look Back* were tempted just to stand back and leave Jimmy there threshing about on the stage, in the final moment of *The Entertainer* the whole burden of Archie's "Why Should I Care?" is shifted directly to *us*. Our contact with the play, as Osborne says of its method, is "immediate, vital and direct".

To be properly complete, this article should go on to account for the quite different achievements of John Arden and the poets of absurd naturalism, Pinter and Simpson. But both these deserve full treatment on their own. The point, however, is that both these developments stand at the outer limits of what, I have been arguing, is the line of development within what we have always taken to be the mainstream of the new drama – the stream of naturalism. Arden plunged straight past this line, into a highly concentrated kind of poetic realism, powered by a depth of perception of an intellectual force (I don't mean that his plays are at all intellectual) which make both Osborne and Wesker seem minor. Only perhaps an imagination which is so much at home with the kind of concentration of dramatic effect which is necessary to write *Serjeant Musgrave's Dance* could draw together, without the devices of shifting conventions employed in *The Entertainer*, the complex anarchist and humanist themes of that play. Arden's purpose everywhere in his work (as Tom Milne has pointed out in a recent issue of *NLR*) is never to satisfy the confident liberal expectations which his themes rouse in his audience: in that way he has an intellectual stubbornness of fibre which Wesker could well do with. If he is to take us into the heart of war and violence, it is in a way (in *Musgrave*) in which the theme will, in all probability, rebound so astonishingly on the audience as to leave it irritable and dissatisfied. The ironic movement in *Musgrave* is the complex way in which the man, driven by his hatred of war, becomes the instrument of violence. Thus he touches not only the outer edge of pacifism, where we are all comfortably distant from the violence of others, but the secret core of violence in human nature itself. Musgrave's final scene is neither a celebration, like Beatie's, nor the touch of despair of Archie Rice, nor the tender sadness of Jo – it is a terrible, physical contortion of the spirit, a writhing.

There is something hard and stark about this imagination which finds a natural place in the historical which is less successful in *Luther*. And it is difficult to separate this now in one's memory from the beautifully controlled rendering which Ian Bannen gave of Musgrave, and Lindsay Anderson's production.

We are, I feel, beyond naturalism pure – and that means, inevitably, at another turning point in the development of the new dramatic movement. Something of the same kind is true in the cinema too (not the British cinema which would be glad of naturalism, or symbolism, or expressionism or *anything* – but the continental and Japanese cinema). The search for form adequate and organic to theme and temperament could end, either in a bewildering hodge-podge, or a really new mutation. The mood which sustained the early developments has certainly broken up, and, once again, it could be the dramatists who are capable of telling us, while it is happening, what it is we are thinking and feeling.

[NOVEMBER 1961]

THE KNACK *at the Theatre Royal, Bath*
Review by Michael Kustow

The curtain goes up on Ann Jellicoe's play, and Tom is sitting on a ladder, painting whorls on the walls of his big empty room. Colin, the landlord, comes in, and wants to move out his bed; he's buying a larger one, a four-foot, "just in case". Tolen, the third occupant of this house, climbs in from the street through the window, because the front door can't be opened, there's too much furniture in the passage. Every time a girl walks past the window, Tolen's after her, and back within ten minutes, with another victim added to the list of women he's going to make.

Nancy comes past the window. She's looking for the YWCA, and she's lost her way. The three boys invite her in. Tolen, who's got The Knack With Women, decides to demonstrate on Nancy for the benefit of poor Colin, who wants to learn how. The tempo gets faster and breaks into that tribal

free-wheeling which Ann Jellicoe has always done so well.
Only Nancy doesn't go the way of all Tolen's other women,
and the wild ballet ends with Tolen taking off from the house
in disgust, Colin kissing Nancy snatchily, and Tom trium-
phant over both of them.

What is important about this play is the freedom of its
style. The room changes aspect and colour before our eyes,
the bedstead is dismantled and trundled about, then becomes
a piano because that's how the characters want it, chairs get
hung on the walls, there's a regular Punch-and-Judy routine
through that window, and the Horst Wessel gets all mixed
up with tea-trays, carrier-bags and buckets. Theatre as pure
play. It's as carefree in style as a film like Godard's *Breathless*.

Which is what I said to Ann Jellicoe, and she replied, "Ah,
but, unlike Godard, I'm a moral artist." True, beneath its
exuberant playfulness, *The Knack* works towards a judgement.
Tolen, the lad with the Knack, says to Tom at one point,
"You get on my nerves when you're being childish." "Child-
like, Tolen," says Tom, and that's the point of all the high
jinks. The people who have the Knack in this world get
tangled up in their own self-seriousness, and the consequences are often grim. But Godard, too, is just as much a
moralist in this sense. The point of both *The Knack* and
Breathless lies not in the propounding of any New Order, but
in the playfulness of the work itself, the way it kids us, nudges
us in the ribs, and says, "Come on, get away with you, just
look at you." The creation in the theatre of this exhilarating
sense of release and potential which previously only the
cinema offered us, is new and valuable.

Both *Breathless* and *The Knack* are works of liberation
made for societies which are becoming gripped by a patho-
logical inability to look themselves in the face and take
themselves *un*seriously for a moment. The strange thing is
this: the more this ossified seriousness infects the society, the
more playful this kind of artist becomes. (How long can he
keep it up?) France at this moment has a slight lead over us
in the Collective Neurosis Stakes, and Godard's shrug in
Breathless becomes all the more studied. When both Authority and Opposition are locked in the easy postures of moral

indignation, a man like Godard feels he has to *tease*. He's not less moral than Ann Jellicoe: but the state of his country makes him tease more than she does. (How long will it hold up like this?)

Despite magistrates sermonizing over sit-downers, despite our Prime Minister accusing half Parliament of being subversive propagandists for the Soviet Union, we haven't quite caught up with France yet, and Ann Jellicoe can still manage to make her play open on to a wider world. With admirable lightness of touch, she succeeds in making the sexual shadow-boxing of four young people into a telling theatrical image for some of the woes that weigh down the world's headlines. The play races towards its end with Nancy crying "Rape!", Tolen and Colin screaming "Force!" and Tom pleading "Parley!" – a contrapuntal climax no audience can miss.

Except perhaps a Saturday matinee audience in the Theatre Royal, Bath. As the old ladies and gents who will soon be pleasured with *The Gazebo* and a panto manipulated their coffee-trays, the boys and girls of Bath were filling the aimless vacancy of a Saturday afternoon by wandering from Marks and Spencers towards a coffee-bar or even a tea-room. You've got to be young to get with this play. To get with the exuberance of Ann Jellicoe's writing and stage-sense, with Rita Tushingham, jumping and joyful and expectant as Nancy (see her flout Rape with a flared yellow skirt round her neck), with Terry Palmer, who has a great quiet activeness on stage as Hero Despite Himself (what he can't do with a bedstead is nobody's business), with David Sumner, sleek and cocky as Tolen (catch *him* standing so his 16-inch bottoms don't sit right on his black pointed boots), with Ronald Falk, a Colin who's always trying too hard (and whatever he does, he's somehow *akimbo*).

This is a play for people who are young. It's also the first result of the Royal Court/Cambridge Arts tie-up on a Gulbenkian grant for "raising the standards of drama, especially in the provinces". It's a shame that some of the money couldn't have been used to ensure that this play got to the audience it's made for. It's a greater shame that our theatre today offers so few ways by which *The Knack* could reach all the

kids who get such nasty labels pinned on them by the Press.
Everyone connected with the production hopes it gets to the
West End. It deserves to and, at the same time, it deserves
better.

[JANUARY 1962]

ARNOLD WESKER'S MISSION
by John Garforth

There is no development, no growth, no deepening of understanding, in the work of Arnold Wesker. He is a prophet, and
for a prophet to move on implies that he must have been
wrong. His prophetic purpose was stated by Wesker at the
very beginning of his career in a passionate article for *Encore*,[1]
and it is being maintained during the present pause in his
writing by the missionary activities of Centre 42. But the
message he brings is confused and the response he evokes often
disastrously unintentional. It is time somebody analysed
what Wesker is trying to do, what he is in fact doing, and
what it is about the theatre and the man which causes the
misunderstanding.

To consider the framework of the gospel we must go back
to that early article. Describing the life of a hypothetical
"ordinary man", Wesker said in effect that he was born
because if he hadn't been he wouldn't be here, he went to
school because he had no alternative, then he went into the
army because the law required it, he came out and found a
job because a man has to live; he went around with women
– well, everyone does, he married because you have to settle
down sometime, he had a couple of kids. . . . Well, that's life,
but he didn't know why. In the meantime before he died (it
comes to us all in the end) this ordinary man lived through
two world wars; he didn't know what they were about but
he did his bit, he lived through unemployment, elections and
social change, scientific progress, and it was all beyond him.
But it affected his life! "He didn't know why" is the recurring
phrase; this man lives a normal twentieth-century life and

[1] "Let Battle Commence", *Encore* 17. November–December 1958.

the whole thing is beyond his understanding. Arnold Wesker is trying to help him understand. This, he says, is what art is about.

We learn from *Roots* that what Wesker wishes for the "ordinary man" is that he should begin by thinking; not by reacting with mental conditioned reflexes, not by the repetition of fixed attitudes, and certainly not by learning new reflexes and attitudes to replace the old ones. To think one must react spontaneously and of oneself. Just how difficult this is the play sets out to illustrate.

The pivotal character in the whole Wesker trilogy, Ronnie Kahn, is obviously an autobiographical projection of the author, and before this play opens he has been teaching his girl friend to think. She goes home to Norfolk full of her newly learned reflexes and attitudes, to be met with both incomprehension and resentment by her family. They are hypothetical "ordinary people". Mere argument provokes only their rage, love or hardship only reinforce their values. Presumably it takes a severe shock to transform them into thinking beings, because Ronnie loses patience and jilts the girl, and her sudden isolation forces her to begin thinking for herself. When we last see her "Beatie stands alone articulate at last", although her family "will continue to live as before".

At this point Wesker's argument assumes a further dimension. For what Beatie says is that "there are millions of us, all over the country and no one, not one of us is asking questions . . . we might as well be dead". And their lazy incomprehension is being pandered to by the mass media and by commerce. "Anything's good enough for them 'cos they don't ask for no more!" It is a short step on to the idea that the ruling class is also exploiting their laziness and acceptance to maintain the social *status quo*. *Chips With Everything* takes this step.

We are presented with a picture of the men in the ranks as unthinking followers who accept the natural authority of the officer class. They will assert their independence as Beatie's family asserted theirs, but these airmen will never really rebel except under the leadership of another member of the officer class. And neither the ranks nor the officers can

5. "Roots"

6. "A Taste of Honey"

escape from this rigid division of society. If one tries to change sides it is merely a romantic gesture, if one runs away there is nowhere to go; tokens of independence are respected, for they are ineffectual. All this is realized by the officers and makes manipulation of the men so much easier.

In *The Kitchen* manipulation is scarcely necessary, because life proceeds under an inexorable logic of its own and any frustration is taken out on one's fellow workers. Here is a world in which things are valued above people. The waitress prefers her husband because he is buying a new house, and so her lover is rejected. So much for love, and Peter reacts in the expected way of Wesker's ordinary people: instead of understanding he goes berserk, because life is too much for him. The people in the kitchen have dreams, but they have no real control over what happens to them, any more than the Norfolk farmers or the airmen.

Obviously in such a world social change will be a very slow process and idealism will be doomed to disillusion. Optimism will degenerate rapidly into cynicism and lethargy. But the significant thing about social change in Wesker's work is that it occurs almost of itself, while his characters are talking about something else. Sarah Kahn believes passionately in communism and in humanity, not only as an idea which was fashionable in the 'thirties, but as a personal and family and human necessity. For she was a Jew in the East End of London when Mosley's blackshirts were marching outside her door, she had a husband constantly out of work, and she had a family to raise and feed and clothe. For her the Spanish civil war and the Cable Street blockade were vital battles in the struggle for a better world.

Well, all this idealism came to nothing. After the war we had a Labour government, a welfare state, Sarah had a council flat, and most people stopped caring very much about a classless society. A noticeably more comfortable world had been provided for ordinary people – by the ruling class. This is not enough for Sarah and she carries on fighting, but she carries on fighting for a rather strange reason: because "you've got to care or you'll die". Just as Beatie thinks to prove that she is alive.

This raises the question of what Wesker considers "ordinary people" should think about and what kind of lives they should want. Beatie Bryant, as we have seen, does not quite answer this point; she merely talks about the unthinking acceptance of her family, which takes us round in a circle. We must go back to her boy friend, Ronnie Kahn, for an answer.

Ronnie disapproved of Sarah's communism because of Russia's suppression of the Hungarian revolution. In *I'm Talking About Jerusalem* he approves. In this play Wesker shows us what people may care for and live for. He might almost have taken his text from Schweitzer, that civilization is in decay because we have lost contact with the roots of our existence: we do not produce any recognizable or personally necessary end product by our individual labour. For this reason, as Marx has said, man has become a slave to his own work. It is because of this condition that we have in our culture at the moment such a heavy strain of rural nostalgia. It would seem that man needs to express himself in his work, not necessarily as an artist nor as a man of power, but as a man who is manifestly useful to himself and to others, in order to enjoy real self-respect.

I'm Talking About Jerusalem is, as the title proclaims, Wesker's vision of heaven, and it is really a William Morris style reversal to a rural state of artisan self-sufficiency. Unfortunately, by the end of the play this reversal has been exposed as yet another romantic dream, and Dave Kahn packs up house to return to London. Again, the cause of his failure lies outside of Dave himself, for he is a fine craftsman; the cause is that the world doesn't want or recognize fine craftsmanship any more, it is quite content with mass produced goods. As a result Dave loses first his independence and then his ideals.

The nearest Wesker can come to optimism is in Ronnie's protests at his brother's acceptance. If he gives up then he might as well be dead: once more we hear the Arnold Wesker motif. But his brother does give up, and Ronnie remains on stage to affirm that there can be a Jerusalem in the future. We can only infer that man's need of a vision will guarantee that visions will occur and that while they occur Jerusalem will still be possible.

It is possible that the hopes for a better social order which Wesker is showing to his ordinary men are based on something more than British history. There is an interesting analogy between his Jerusalem and the kibbutz life of Israel. Although the kibbutzim were established as military outposts against the Arabs the community life is reputedly a splendid mixture of pride in working for a common aim and self-provided culture: there they have a small-scale Marxist way of life, and they have produced a spontaneous upsurge of folk song, theatre and so on.

The analogy can be pursued further, for the kibbutzim are now expanding into towns and movement from the land into commerce is becoming an inevitable aspiration; the idyll is ending: Israel's constant condition of military preparation and its jockeying for recognition as a world power is bringing the ideals on which it is based to nought, and when they have the H-bomb then we shall know that yet another splendid opportunity has been missed. Small wonder that Wesker is pessimistic about his ultimate success.

Sarah Kahn's belief in a classless society survived the suppression of Hungary in 1956, and Ronnie Kahn's belief in Jerusalem survived his brother's failure, because both have a faith that transcends the mistakes of others; yet neither ever acts in any real sense, they merely stand on the touch line and shout incentives to the players. Now that we have glanced briefly at the world Wesker is writing about we feel sadly that the struggle is all over bar the shouting.

The main irony of the plays is that Wesker is not shouting (or rather, directing his message) at the ordinary people whose sensibility he is concerned to awaken. Instead he is depicting those people and his ideas about them for a liberal, educated audience, and to communicate these Wesker depends on many shared attitudes. It was Alan Brien who pointed out that *Chips With Everything* reinforces the values of its audience.

At any moment in that play one expected the corporal to scream "Get your bleedin' 'air cut!" for the biggest laugh of the evening. For the audience received the picture of air force life in much the same spirit as they received *Reluctant Heroes* and *The Army Game*; it was what they were accustomed to. Beneath this form of service drama lies a sentimental respect, and occasionally in *Chips With Everything* we felt that this was a mystic celebration of manliness, the foundation of Britain's greatness, worked out in the ritual transference from mother to RSM.

In addition, plays about British service life can only show a rigidly immovable *status quo*, which is reassuring to a middle-class audience and enables them to feel safely liberal towards the working classes. Beneath their benignity, however, they must suspect that the working classes are not quite the simple folk of staunch and upright fibre that their liberalism requires; more probably they feel that uneducated airmen are rowdy, undisciplined and unthinking – in short, not quite up to our standard; Wesker clearly reinforces their feeling.

Wesker also shares the cultural snobbery of his audience. That folk music is better than rock 'n' roll by definition is a dubious assumption, but it fits with Beatie's tirade about the standards of mass entertainment. Perhaps there is a flattering assumption in this premise that because we are watching a Wesker play instead of sitting at home watching *Z Cars* we are superior beings. But the "popular equals bad" equation is a conditioned reflex of the intellectual and needs to be thought about.

There is nothing in *Chips With Everything* to shock anybody, although we feel a slight surprise at the end when we find that Wesker has after all demonstrated how degrading to everybody service life must be.

It is highly improbable that Wesker would consciously compromise so with his audience or with his own intentions, and it seems natural that at this stage of his career he should have announced a pause in his writing plays so that he could go out and work in the field. He forsook the "power houses" of Shaftesbury Avenue and took his message direct to the "ordinary people". He founded the Centre 42 movement.

In the actual programme that Wesker took to the five

festivals he organized, he made the same mistake as many well-intentioned middle-class idealists have in the past, the mistake which is perhaps implicit in his attitude to the "ordinary people". This mistake was to bring his own culture and values and try to impose them on his audience. He even brought them his romantic conception of their work in the form of a folk ballad opera, to show them, we suppose, the dignity of their labour. (Does Wesker honestly imagine that Arthur Seaton would be uplifted by a ballad opera on working his lathe, and did nobody explain that *Every Day Except Christmas* was aimed at the Everyman Cinema, Hampstead?) Quite a number of people who share Beatie's love of Beethoven would stay indoors when Wesker passes by with Stravinsky.

There is not merely one culture in this country, nor is there merely one true culture. And unless Wesker is to simply patronize the few who attend his Centre 42 festivals he will need to respect the values and psychology of his "ordinary men". He will only help them "understand" when he himself understands why football or pubs or *Coronation Street* or Elvis Presley form a part of their culture; to deplore them or to glorify them is equally to cut oneself off from them.

The case against the working classes is well presented in *Roots* and *Chicken Soup With Barley*, but it is not the whole case. There is enormous vitality in the Kahn family; why there should be virtually none in the airmen of *Chips* is strange, especially as we were convinced by Peter O'Toole when *The Long and the Short and the Tall* showed us a working-class Jimmy Porter in the Army. As for the people in *Roots*, we feel that Wesker deliberately didn't bring them to life; perhaps rightly, for we cannot imagine Beatie rampaging on about self-awareness through the pages of Zola's *Earth*.

The answer would seem to be to understand more clearly what working-class culture is, and to transform it from the reassurance of *Coronation Street* into something more dynamic, but from within. And when we have achieved this cultural vitality in the working class, when everybody is asking the questions Beatie requires, then a new Jerusalem may be inevitable. It will be unnecessary to go off into the Israeli desert or to isolated parts of England to found a dynamic society.

The truth of Wesker's fascination for us, of course, is simpler than any analysis of his thought would indicate. It is that in all his confusion, despair and impatient activity he becomes a kind of projection for those disaffiliated and liberal idealists all over England whom Jimmy Porter first brought to self-awareness. Of course Wesker brings no startling solutions to the problems of our time, and of course he can think of nothing much to put in the place of what is evil and corrupting in our society. Of course he is enraged at our increasing triviality as we move nearer to extinction. He has little idea of what we should do, but by God he cares! He cares enough to traipse around the country begging support from philistine trade unionists, he cares enough to go to gaol against nuclear diplomacy, to look naïve and perhaps look pompous, because it is the only thing to do. Maybe these things are grotesquely insufficient, as we all feel when we vote Labour and sit down in Trafalgar Square, but we have to do something, if only to show that we care. For when we stop caring we may as well be dead.

[MAY 1963]

LITTLEWOOD PAYS A DIVIDEND
by Charles Marowitz

"I do not believe in the supremacy of the director, designer, actor or even the writer. It is through collaboration that this knockabout art of theatre survives and kicks. . . . No one mind or imagination can foresee what a play will become until all the physical and intellectual stimuli which are crystallized in the poetry of the author, have been understood by a company, and then tried out in terms of mime, discussion and the precise music of grammar; words and movement allied and integrated."

The words are Joan Littlewood's; they describe, better than anything criticism might offer, the principle by which *Oh,*

What a Lovely War was brought into being. More ambitious than *The Hostage*, better integrated than *Taste of Honey*, more coherent than *Fings Ain't Wot They Used t'Be*, this is Littlewood's finest production and, ironically, the achievement of a company hastily reunited after a two-year separation which was thought to be its demise.

A panoramic view of the pathos and absurdity of the Kaiser's War, the production is a medley of disparate styles which the genius of Littlewood and the invention of the ensemble have welded into one. The music-hall score which accurately conveys the lace-trimmed romanticism of the early 1900s is interpolated with the brash, journalistic devices of a Living Newspaper – creating an effect which is at once epic and intimate, elegantly stylized and grimly realistic; comic and tragi-comic.

All the material was culled from authentic sources. The most preposterous dialogue is provided by Haig's speeches or extracts from pulpit oratory of the period. God is seen to be the rank immediately above Field Marshal, and war, particularly in the eyes of the British, becomes a test of Christian stamina founded on the assumption that victory belongs, as if by divine right, to well-heeled, white protestants with double-barrelled names and country estates.

The musical reduces the whole of that comic-opera fracas to its pathetic human elements and shows how behind every *miscalculation* and military blunder lay a lethal kind of patriotism and a murderous inefficiency. Like *Chips With Everything*, it stacks the cards against the "officers and gentlemen" who used men for cannon fodder, but unlike Wesker's, the Littlewood interpretation is supported by incontrovertible evidence and the verdict of history. For once in the theatre, an indictment against an entire class is not only justifiable, but inescapable.

It was the music which originally inspired the show (Gerry Raffles got the idea after hearing a Black and White Minstrel programme devoted to the songs of the First World War) and it is from the songs that one gets the full picture of an over-civilized society forced to cope with instincts of brutality it had almost rationalized out of existence. The songs have a unity and a drama all their own, and if they were lifted from the body of the production and performed by themselves, would still have a shattering impact and tell a terrible story.

Stylistically, the show is an astounding achievement, for it creates a context which accommodates – naturally and without strain – a number of different and often antithetical styles. The scene in which new recruits brandishing cane-weapons play at phallic squarebashing is pure vaudeville; this glides smoothly into naturalistic improvisations between foot-soldiers sharing Christmas rations with the enemy, or formal scenes of worship in which a canticle in praise of victory-in-the-field is answered by a chorus from a lewd barracks-ballad. No sooner has the production adopted one stance than it flips into another, but despite these endless modulations, there is no sense of contradiction. This is not merely the simplex two-dimensionalism of Black Comedy where laughter freezes up into menace, but the multi-dimensionalism of true Epic Theatre where styles appear in order to serve the nature of what is being said, and what is being said is constantly being varied.

A transfer of this play without the present company is unthinkable. Never before has there been such an umbilical connection between players and material. Charles Chilton probably provided certain basic materials; the company contributed shared social attitudes and a flair for improvisation, and Littlewood was the catalyst who compounded all. Here is a classic example of a company achievement. The Royal Shakespeare, in its present state, is incapable of such a fusion; the National Theatre Company, if it boasted Olivier, Richardson, Gielgud and O'Toole, could never bring off a comparable production. This is the end-product – not of four or five weeks' rehearsal – but of ten and twelve years of tension and discovery at Stratford East. The technique which produced this result grew out of the Living Newspaper productions of the 'thirties, the English Music Hall in its pre-war heyday, the satirical revues of the early Unity Theatre, the Pierrot tradition of the English seaside resorts, the socialistic convictions of the Manchester school (the city where Littlewood began), and the tardy influences of Piscator and Brecht.

It is, more so than anything now at the Old Vic or Stratford, a production which exemplifies an English tradition; the tradition that grew up alongside the more elegant one that today sustains Shaftesbury Avenue and the Shakespeare Establishment.

Of late, there has been a lot of gab about experiment in the theatre. I have heard the word bandied about by mouldy old West End managers describing square chat-plays which explore the stresses modern life places upon middle-class gentility. I have heard rep managers use it as a back-pat for inserting a Pinter play between a Christie and a Rattigan. And actors are always using it to describe plays, the point of which escapes them. The word needs a thorough overhaul for obviously it cannot be used as a synonym for *unfamiliar* or *chancy*, just as it is not the automatic antonym of *commercial* or *conventional*.

For me, experiment in the theatre is not simply a profession of faith in the off-beat or a short season at the Arts, but an involvement in new techniques and challenging craft-problems; a quest for new answers prompted by a distrust of old, standardized questions and the values they tend to confirm. By this definition, Joan Littlewood's company is the only experimental aggregation in the country. And it is the *healthiest* kind of experiment because it is not exploring, in the abstract, questions of technique and style, but devising forms to suit the practical need of conveying its intentions. Littlewood is finding the really creative way of saying things because, of all English producers, she is the one with most to say. The equation here is obvious, but it can never be said too often.

Although my admiration for Our Lady of Angel Lane will rival anyone's, I cannot join that chorus which chants: we need more Joan Littlewoods. What England needs is more companies as well-fibred and resilient as Theatre Workshop was in its heyday. Which is just another way of saying it needs an attitude to theatre which promotes the growth of living ensembles instead of the useless fragmentation of the present one-shot, commercial system in which Adamov and Genet are as sure to "flop" as Christie is to "run". At present, only the Royal Shakespeare Company has, by word and deed, affirmed those principles which foster permanent organisms in the theatre. But it is this approach more than expanded real estate or indiscriminate subsidy, that the English theatre needs. Not more theatres and more activity, but more concentration of resources and more encouragement of artistic discipline. More coherence to a fixed centre – be it in London or the provinces; less global rambling for the sake of a brand-image. Or am I perhaps saying what I set out to deny: that what we really need *is* more Littlewoods; more director-*animateurs*, goosing writers and mustering audiences, commanding group loyalties and creating solid mounds of earth and rock in an otherwise swampy and treacherous terrain.

[MAY 1963]

AFORE NIGHT COME *Review by Tom Milne*

Set in a pear-orchard in a rural pocket on the crust of the Black Country, the action of David Rudkin's play (Royal Shakespeare Company at the Arts) takes place – as one of the characters puts it – "on the dark side of the moon"; which is as good a way as any of describing this strange, unnerving play, unless one refers to a key passage in Golding's *Lord of the Flies*: ". . . and in front of Simon, the Lord of the Flies hung on his stick and grinned. At last Simon gave up and looked back; saw the white teeth and dim eyes, the blood – and his gaze was held by that ancient, inescapable recognition. In Simon's right temple, a pulse began to beat on the brain."

Right from the beginning of *Afore Night Come*, that pulse began to beat. John Bury's brilliant décor – three tall, leafy pear-trees set in a circle – is idyllic and summery. But in the long pause before anyone appears, and there is only the faint cawing of birds in the distance, the trees begin to lower threateningly against the black backcloth. Into this charged atmosphere, temporarily breaking the spell, wander three strangers: a delicately-spoken student; a Brummagem Ted, obsessed by the kicks to be had from tonning it on a motorbike; and an elderly Irish tramp, garrulous, stagey and weird, wearing dark glasses and a folded cloth on his head. Suddenly the orchard comes to life with noise and chatter as the new arrivals join the labourers already at work, all hurrying to complete an order, after which they will at last be put on piece-work. The boxes of pears mount up, but it soon becomes clear that the Irishman, endlessly talking and never doing a damn thing, is a dead loss. The atmosphere begins to tighten as he becomes the focus for all the fears and resentments that circulate. Spens, the foreman, casually plants a pitchfork in the centre of the circle. Drifting in, the men eye it warily. Gradually the scene is set for the killing. Knives appear, and are sharpened. One by one the onlookers disappear, leaving the four high-priests whetting their fury by ripping up bicycle-tyres, while the Irishman still sits in the circle end-lessly talking about the wonders he will perform. A question-ing, whispered "Spens?" from each of the four; the foreman vanishes, tacitly granting permission; then the climax of sheer horror when the four close in for the ritual murder as the sky grows dark, and a helicopter showers a spray of insecticide over the savage tableau in a moment of hallu-cinatory beauty. The orgasm over, the body and its severed head are borne away to burial, the sky lightens, the threads of work are picked up again, tools are put away, and every-one goes off home to tea. Once again the orchard is empty, tranquil now, as a motorbike roars up the road in the distance.

A simple enough, if gruesome tale, but what is remarkable about the play is the complexity of its structural web of cross-references. Basically, the theme is that of *Lord of the Flies* – the incredible, primitive savagery and blood-lust latent in mankind, so easily brought to the surface by fear or isolation. In *Afore Night Come* the blood-lust is fed by the country-man's instinctive fear of what is strange (it is worth noting that, as soon as the strangers appear, an attempt is made to rob them of their separate identity by deliberately mis-hearing their names, and rechristening them with nick-names) and by his deeply inbred superstition. No sooner has the Irishman appeared than he rambles on to the subject of magic, forecasting rain from a cloudless sky; Ginger, one of the locals, is furiously resentful at constant teasing by his mates about his impotence; the news about the arrival of the pest-control helicopter is accompanied by the joking warning that the insecticide will make their hair fall out and cause impotence. Gradually the superstitious fear focuses on the tramp – "Wisdom of the whole world they carry sometimes" – and he is blamed for everything that goes wrong; the cloth and dark glasses he wears as protection against the sun become the hood of power and evil-eye of the witch (hence the ritual in which he is held lying back facing the sky when he is stabbed: "Bend him over back ways and his eyes go out"); the fact that when they eat, the hungry Irishman follows their every move, at first a matter for casual pity, becomes a demonstration of his inhuman power of needing neither food nor drink.

This rich complexity is furthered by the way in which Rudkin handles the division of his characters into a natural hierarchy. The murder is a ritual purge of witchcraft, and is therefore committed by the three *local* labourers who have the deepest roots in the orchard, seconded by the Ted, merely out for kicks, who runs screaming from the actual horror: for him, unlike the others, there is no ritual justification. The foreman's permission, as local power, has to be obtained, and he acquiesces, partly because the work will otherwise suffer, partly because he has lost face by allowing the useless Irishman to talk him into giving him another chance in the orchard. The other two regular workers, a Welshman and an ex-commercial traveller, are divided from the locals by their worldly experience; they try to warn the tramp, but finally subscribe to the murder, partly through rationalization that it is none of their business, partly because they are fed by their own more sophisticated superstitions: what the hell did the Irish do in the war? (the commercial traveller); Irish girls riddle the country with prostitution (the Welshman). The only active protester is Johnny Hobnails, a gentle homosexual maniac released on sufferance from an asylum, who is more peripheral to the group as he works *outside* the orchard with his mate, Tiny, as its transport-driver. Johnny takes the suffering of the world on his shoulders (the Christ parallel here is probably the most questionable, though effective, part of the play), and tries to save the tramp, but is hamstrung by his fear of being sent back to the asylum. Tiny, whose whole world is Johnny, will accept anything provided he can be with Johnny. And the student, whose eyes Johnny tries to open to the horror, is almost caught up in belief, but makes an intellectual rejection of the situation ("Why do you want to make me afraid of something that isn't real?"). The terrifying quality of the play is thus that the killing takes place in a closed circle, it has happened before, it will certainly happen again, and nothing will be done about it.

Rudkin handles language with as much exactness as Harold Pinter but with a good deal more adventurousness. The rhythms of everyday speech are brilliantly caught, often used with devastatingly funny effect. But with the tramp's traditional Irish gift of the gab, the language begins to take a lift, and with Johnny, a step into biblical rhythms. Gradually it coalesces into a kind of wild, earthbound poetry, as in Ginger's denunciation of the tramp-witch: "I won't get my babby now . . . His hands are the hands of a dead man . . . don't eat nothing . . . don't drink nothing . . . grass do wither at his feet . . . why don't someone make him die then?" The play stands firmly on its own feet, and needs no explaining, but certain tantalizing references emerge, and the text would certainly repay close study of its language and symbolism. For instance: there are numerous references to the rain, forecast by the tramp and therefore linked with witchcraft; the foreman brings a tarpaulin to cover the fruit-boxes; the three locals don oilskins just before the murder; but the rain never actually comes (at least, one never hears it. In a production which handles its sound effects carefully, this is surely not an oversight). The oilskins are, in fact, used to wrap up the decapitated body, which is then rolled in the tarpaulin for burial. And the final line of the play comes when the foreman says to the student, "You s'll bring rubbers, tomorrow, boy": a reference back to his arrival in sandals when he is told that they are useless for working in long, damp grass, but possibly also, given the significance of oilskins and tarpaulin, a linking reference to the hint that he has either become an initiate of the group, or is the next chosen victim.

Like *Saint's Day*, *The Birthday Party* and *Serjeant Musgrave's Dance*, *Afore Night Come* caused considerable upset and found little enough favour during its brief stay at the Arts. But we have certainly not heard the last of David Rudkin.

[JULY 1962]

THE WORKHOUSE DONKEY
Review by Charles Marowitz

The curse of John Arden is that he simply won't play ball. After creating a picture of Welfare State slovenliness in the farcical *Live Like Pigs*, he switched gears and gave us the spare and chilling *Serjeant Musgrave's Dance*. Then, all set for more thought-provoking austerity, he trots out *The Happy Haven*, a Commedia dell' Arte zanni on old age.

Through all of this, reviewers who do not know how to react to a playwright who builds no consistent image and refuses to pander to an audience's signal-responses are being told by a fervent claque that this man Arden has got something. Not being able to define him with the clichés at their disposal, the critics cock a wary eye.

Along comes the much-heralded, long-awaited *Workhouse Donkey* and again Arden pulls a volte-face. The play turns out to be an ornery comedy of humours which is as opposed to quick sense as it is to pat conclusions, and the critics, now out of patience, smother it with indifference and cultivate their peevishness. T. C. Worsley raps the knuckles of those "young admirers" who have been hawking Arden round "on the basis of one failure and two rather interesting muck-ups". "Now," writes Worsley, "[Arden] has added an ambitious piece that is both a downright failure *and* a muck-up and is far, far from interesting. Perhaps his young fans will now stop ruining his chance of a career as a dramatist by turning off the praise until he has earned it." A sentiment whose subtext is: "I told you *Musgrave* was a dud, and to prove my point, I spit *The Workhouse Donkey* back in your face." But where, I wonder, would Wesker and Pinter be today if their "young fans" didn't reject the critics' assessment of their early work? And does Mr Worsley really believe Arden would have got as far as Chichester without an ardent clique pitting itself against the obtuse negativism of his critics? And would the re-assessment of *Serjeant Musgrave's Dance* ever have been made without their agit-prop voices in the background? Nowadays, as Mr Worsley ought by this time to understand, the only way to prevent the ruin of a new dramatist's career is to challenge the glib dismissals that deadline-pressure and closed-circuit thinking produce in the popular Press.

But putting to one side the reactions of our erudite (albeit pressured) drama critics, let us (with full recognition of our biases) examine the virtues of John Arden's new work.

– It is intelligent. There is a skill in the writing which breezily creates outsize characters and craftily develops a fanciful language to suit their dimensions.

– It is funny (not hilarious) and creates the sort of thoughtful laughter we expect from plays that do not set out to simply tickle our ribs.

– It is a generous play. It proliferates incidents; it tangles plot and sub-plot and, as it turns out, is generous to a fault. The play was conceived as a three-acter, and divided in two, the material does not properly resolve itself. One should either have scaled it down to the given time, or insisted on its natural full length.

– It is meaningfully complex. Beneath a bouncy exterior lies a maze of meaning. Municipal corruption is its amusing façade, but the play winds downward to connect with hard-boned ideas concerning law, justice and developments in social history. For me, the historical aspects are the most pertinent.

Councillor Butterthwaite, who runs a feather-bedded Yorkshire town like a family business, is a relic of a 1920s socialist idealism; the same idealism that spawned the English trade-union movement and turned labour solidarity into narrow-minded factionalism. He contains the ruins of pioneer Socialist principles and the contradictions of present-day Labour

Party. He is a glib and aggressive anachronism and stands as a valid symbol for what early twentieth-century idealism turned into.

With that inbred and relentless objectivity which makes Arden the writer least committed to sects and most committed to truth, he sketches in the other dominant forces. The Tories of his Yorkshire community have, what they take to be, their Establishment spokesman: a ramrod-straight pillar of Southern-law-enforcement who is as obsessed with the abstraction of Justice as Musgrave was with pacifism. He, like Musgrave, produces a result which is the exact opposite of his intentions. Although certain local corruptions (including Councillor Butterthwaite's theft of £500) are exposed, the pettifogging pattern of political expediency is restored – even as its most notorious exponent is destroyed. The Chief Constable, his principles intact, stands helpless in the face of it. No villains, no heroes, only varying degrees of grayness which in one light appear black, and in another, white.

About the high quality of the performances, the critics were largely unanimous. Frank Finlay's back-slapping Little Caesar is a great wheedling slut of a character who, for detail and verisimilitude, is equalled only by this same actor's Corporal Hill in *Chips With Everything*. Robert Stephens' knobbly goofiness beautifully suits the needs of the distraught Police Chief. Norman Rossington, in the second most persuasive role in the play, was too shallow; too much the peripheral chippy-chappy. Even a cartoon-character has got to have a certain black-and-white conviction. And Anthony Nicholls, with his Savile Row suits leaking integrity, could have stepped out of the pages of the *Sunday Times* Colour Supplement.

My only quibble with Stuart Burge's direction was that it concentrated too much on the play's superficies, and didn't direct the eye of the spectator to the line of the inner-action. Everything was as exuberant as everything else, and so one can understand the complaint of those people who saw the play simply as a Yorkshire version of *The Inspector General*. But the problem here is complicated by the fact that much of the material is diffuse. Several scenes seemed to be

7. "The Knack"

8. "Afore Night Come"

developed simply because they had been begun. Perhaps the author too, should have decided what was vital and what superfluous. On the basis of one performance and one reading, I feel the play can either be compressed into a workable two-acter (which at present it is not) or expanded into a true, rambling Jonsonian comedy. Anything in between cramps its intentions.

But the main point is that here Arden has given us a richness and a fulsomeness and I, for one, prefer a well-stocked buffet to a predictable round of fish and chips.

[SEPTEMBER 1963]

EXPERIMENT by Charles Marowitz

In fleeting moments of clarity, I suddenly see the contemporary theatre as a mouldy, gnarled and arthritic old man decked out in the latest Savile Row fashions. White, flabby, atrophied old limbs sheathed in Italian silk and the latest American check. No matter what shape it assumes, its stilted gait and tired old accent give it away. It thinks in old frames, moves in beaten paths and equates the cautious elevation of its right foot with a breath-taking pole-vault.

It is not only the crusty old playwrights, the Rattigans, Christies, Hunters and Duncans, but the entire diction of that theatre which no longer holds up; which begs to be annihilated. It is their insidious *influence* rather than themselves which is the real enemy; the language they have hardened, the patterns they cause to be repeated, the creaking stagecraft they have dignified and entrenched.

We haven't had even a glimmer of what the modern theatre is capable of. We are so fobbed off with *new writing* or *new stars* that we forget that the medium in which all of these novelties emerge is itself corroding. Why is Shakespeare so unflaggingly popular? Why do we continually nourish ourselves on the Elizabethans? Because there we can experience (albeit second-hand) a theatre bursting with variety, shifting freely into contrasting styles, astonishing us with richness of content and fluidity of form. We still rely on the motor-

power of the Elizabethan theatre to get our kicks; to experience the thrill of speed, the breadth of epic characters, the
jolt of intellectual audacity and the sheer fun of physical
actions. But the more we laud its riches, the more we accen-
tuate our own poverty.

The theatre, of all the arts, is the most complacent; the
most content to stew in its own juices. In painting, in dance,
in music – the search for new plateaux never ends. Every ten
years brings some kind of new discovery; some new development instigated by artistic boredom and the itch to find new
ways of saying things. The artist unearths new textures for
his canvas, new ways of applying them, new processes, new
instruments and (most important) new premises on which to
base the creative act. Modern dancers, harnessing the discoveries of Laban and the work of experimenters like Martha
Graham, Jean Erdman and Merce Cunningham, produce new
impulses and new ways of shaping the space of a stage.
Composers, having exhausted the obvious possibilities of
traditional notation, forage, with the aid of electronics and
tape, into the world of pure sound. But all the theatre can do
is fret its little head over whether plays should be staged in a
circle or on a square. When it wants to be really revolutionary,
it may create an "adaptable theatre" which is nothing more
than an elaborate device which has perfected three or four
different ways of slicing baloney.

The manic search for *new writers*, *new audiences* and *new
ways of staging* has obscured the real issue. What has to be
found in the theatre is a new urgency; a new imperative, a
new and better reason why thousands of people now glued
to the Box or snug in cinema seats should forsake these
diversions and attend to the live theatre. People must go to
the theatre today for the very same reasons that audiences of
old queued up for Athenian rocks or Elizabethan standing-
room: because the theatre, responding to irresistible urges, is
providing artistic provender without which men cannot keep
alive their image of the world and their understanding of its
meaning.

Anyone who compares the stream of our human experience and the rhythms of our theatre must be struck by the

appalling disparity. Our world is fragmented, discontinuous, erratic and uncertain; our theatre is pat, cohesive, arbitrary and consoling. The drawing-room playwrights tell us comforting white lies, and the social dramatists tell us disturbing half-truths, but nobody tries to correlate the tempi of our life with the clatter of its meaning. And no one *can* because it is not a question of content but of form. It would have been preposterous to ask Ibsen to express the streaming ambiguity of human consciousness within the limits of the problem-play; the convention simply would not permit it. Today, Ionesco dramatizes our fantasies and Beckett posits our anguish, but nobody attempts to dramatize the complexity of thought and feeling that produces both. We have a drama of *results* instead of a theatre of multi-layered action. It is as if our stages were fixated at 4/4 time and any attempt to introduce a more elaborate key signature fouled up the works. The theatre is not geared for complexity, but this is the nature of our present world and we must try to interpret this. As long as simple mechanisms regulate the art-form, every play will be reduced to what the medium can easily handle. But if new means can be perfected to cope with this complexity, there is a chance of creating a theatre which is existential and relevant instead of trying to modernize and make-do with an intrinsically eighteenth-century piece of claptrap.

The pockets of experiment in the modern theatre can be numbered on one hand – without even uncrooking the thumb or forefinger. The Becks of The Living Theatre in New York persevere in the face of what is best described as aggressive apathy. The American Establishment will not come to the aid of Peace Marchers and dubious patriots; the Foundations are not impressed by the bohemian aura which emanates from a theatre staging plays about junkies or Marine brutality. In Opole, Poland, judging by the report printed in this issue, a group of devoted actors are applying themselves to a problem that also preoccupies artists here in England; namely, how formal classics can be refurbished in order to speak more pertinently to a sensibility bred on discord and discontinuity. In New York (and now in France), artists and actors are trying to develop *Happenings* to become something more than art-school charades or Chelsea-party high-jinks which, judging by recent events in Paris, is all they still are.

In England, *experimental* remains the one word no two persons will agree upon. To most people, it still means mounting rashers of Ionesco and Adamov, or perhaps slivers from Saunders or Campton. Rarely does it mean depth-work on craft-problems seriously explored and adequately subsidized, but until it does mean that, the situation will not improve.

For over four years, In-Stage has attempted, with varying degrees of success, to be such a theatre. Although it has conducted a few experiments and threshed up a certain number of new plays, it has never had the stability (i.e. wherewithal) to pursue its work properly. Recently, Peter Bridgmont tried to create a workshop-theatre in Balham. The company presented two programmes of improvised work, but was hampered by economics and wobbly working conditions. In Edinburgh, the Traverse Theatre Club is gamely establishing a representative experimental theatre which, once the more obvious items are dispensed, may turn into something personal and valuable. Shortly, Peter Brook will be heading an experimental branch of the Royal Shakespeare Company working at the new LAMDA theatre. The Royal Court envisages a permanent experimental outlet in *its* refurbished premises. The National Theatre, thus far, has kept mum on the subject. The Arts Council is never very encouraging unless you are a floundering repertory company or trying to tour respectable bores through the provinces. The Society of West End Managers, which has most to gain from experimental activity, sees it either as a threat or a mutation although they are always ready to move in (as they did in the case of Theatre Workshop) if a project looks milkable.

The great irony in England today is the fervour that can be roused for a moribund art-form. It reminds me of that historical truism about empires appearing most confident just before they are due to collapse. I react badly to indiscriminate enthusiasm, and find it appalling for *theatre* to be madly approved of in the abstract and abominably practised in the particular. *More* theatre is not *better* theatre and better theatre does not necessarily mean highly-subsidized main-stream work. But without demeaning any of the activity that already exists, I would point out that the one sort of theatre which is practically non-existent in England is laboratory-theatre, studio-theatre, theatre peering intently into its own nature to discover something about its own chemistry. Until such theatre is (*a*) understood, (*b*) encouraged, (*c*) financed, the cause of theatre may be widely championed but the state of theatre will progressively disintegrate.

[SEPTEMBER 1963]

FROM ZERO TO THE INFINITE
A Letter from Peter Brook

I'd be delighted to write a piece for you about *The Connection*. The problem is purely one of time. You see, *The Connection* is interesting to me because of a vast number of questions it triggers off, so I don't see how to do a short article about it. However, once one starts on a long and serious article, then all sorts of literary vanities creep in. Style is really a bankrupt concern – one must attempt to say what one feels, and to hell with the adjectives. So the only way out is to just go on with this letter as long as I can.

To make a start. I suppose I found *The Connection* fascinating because it represented one of the few clear ways opening for our theatre. I think we agree that all forms of theatre are going through a deep crisis: where's the culprit? Is it the apathy of the audiences or is that in turn caused by the wrong shapes of the playhouses – or is it the commercializing influence of the impresarios – or is it the lack of daring of the authors – or is there suddenly no talent and no poetry around – or is this age of managers and technicians essentially untheatrical? Is the answer really to be found in song-and-dance: is it really to be found in a new form of naturalism? All we know is that the time-honoured forms have shrivelled and died in front of us.

We know that the first artistic wave after the war was a

tired attempt to reassert pre-1940 cultural values – and this was followed by a "putting into question" as the French call it, of everything. The English theatre revolution, like the similar movement in French films, has been a send-up of story, construction, technique, tempo, good curtains, effective moments, big scenes, climaxes – all of which simultaneously here became as suspect as the Royal Family, heroics, politics, morality and so on. Technically speaking, the revulsion has been away from "lying". What is lying? Well, all those grand-sounding, meaningless platitudes we learnt at school were lies – in one form or another. But also all that those older actors told us when we came into the theatre were lies of another sort. Why after all should the curtain come down at a "strong" moment, why should a good line be "pointed", why should a laugh be "got", why should we speak "up"? Against ordinary everyday standards of commonsense and truth, all rhetoric is a "lie". What once passed for language is now seen to be life-less and in no way expressive of what really goes on in human beings, what once passed for plot is now seen not to be plot at all, what once passed for character is now seen to be only a stereotyped set of masks.

You can thank the cinema and television for accelerating this process. The cinema degenerated because, like many a great empire, it stood still: it repeated its rituals identically again and again – but time passed and the meaning went out of them. Then television arrived at the very instant when the dramatic clichés of the cinema were being dished up for the nine millionth time. It began showing old movies – and rotten movie-like plays and enabled audiences to judge them in a completely new way. In the cinema the darkness, the vast screen, the loud music, the soft carpets added unquestionably to the hypnosis. On television the clichés are naked: the viewer is independent, he is walking about his room, he hasn't paid (which makes it easier to switch off), he can voice his disapproval out loud without being sssshed. Furthermore, he is forced to judge, to judge fast. He switches on the set and immediately judges from the face that he sees – (a) whether it's an actor or someone "real" – (b) whether he's nice or not, good or bad, what his class or background, etc. are – (c) when it's a fictional scene, he draws on his experience of dramatic clichés to guess at the part of the story he has missed (because, of course, he can't sit round the programme twice, as he used to do at the movies). So he learns to identify from the smallest gesture the villain, the adulteress and so on. The essential fact is that he has learned – from necessity – to observe, to judge for himself.

And this is where Brecht comes in. (There is so much of Brecht's work I admire, so much of his work with which I disagree totally.) I am convinced that almost all that Brecht was saying about the nature of illusion can be applied to the cinema – and only with many reservations to the theatre. Brecht claimed that audiences were in a state of trance, of sloppy dream-like surrender to illusion. I believe that this form of semi-drugged surrender did occur between audience and screen in the heyday of the movies. Being *moved* by a film was something for which one was ashamed – one had been *tricked*! I believe that the new cinema, unconsciously exploiting this new independence of the viewer that television has brought about is catering for an audience capable of judging an image. (I'd quote *Hiroshima Mon Amour* as the supreme example of this. The camera is no longer an eye – it does not track us into the geographical reality of Hiroshima as that famous tracking shot at the beginning of *La Bête Humaine* once sucked us out of our seats really into some French railway station. The camera in *Hiroshima* presents us with a succession of documents which bring us face to face with the whole vast historical, human and emotional reality of Hiroshima in a form that is only moving to us through the use of our own objective judgement. We go into it as it were with our eyes open.)

And this, surprisingly enough, gets me straight to *The Connection*. When you go to *The Connection* in New York you are aware, as you enter the building, of all the denial aspects of the evening. There is no proscenium – (illusion? Well, yes, in so far as the stage is arranged like a squalid room, but it is not like a set – it is more as though the theatre were an extension of this room) – no conventional playwrighting, no exposition, no development, no story, no characterization,

no construction, and above all, no tempo. This supreme artifice of the theatre – this one god whom we all serve – whether
in musicals or in melodramas or in the classics – that marvellous thing called pace – is here thrown right out of the window. So, with this collection of negative values, you have an
evening as boring as life must seem to a young Buddhist
sitting on the banks of the Ganges. And yet, no doubt like
Buddhism, if you persevere you are rewarded – from the zero
you get to the infinite.

How does this work? Well, the mental process is roughly
this. At first, you cannot believe that the reaction against the
"lies" of theatre can be total. After all, in Pinter, in Wesker,
in Delaney, there are new artifices to replace the old, even if
they seem for the moment to be closer to the "truth". In
Roots, we know the washing-up won't go on for ever, because
we sense the presence of a dramatist with purpose. In *A
Taste of Honey*, we know that a duologue will cease at the
moment when Shelagh Delaney's instinct tells her it was
played out. But in *The Connection*, the tempo is the tempo
of life itself. A man enters – for no reason – with a gramo-
phone. (Oh yes, there is a reason. He wants to plug it into the
light socket.) He wants (apparently – he doesn't say so) to
play a record. And as it's an LP, we have to wait for it to
finish – a quarter of an hour or so later. At first, our attitude
as audience is fouled by our expectations. We can't truly
savour the moment (enjoy the record for what it's worth, as
we would in a room) because years of theatre convention have
conditioned us to a different tempo – man puts on record,
story point made, now what? (Amazingly, we cannot enjoy a
record we would enjoy at home – because we have paid for
our seat . . .) We sit waiting for the next contrivance that
will – with seeming naturalness – interrupt the record and
let us get on with – with what? That's the point.

For, in *The Connection* there's nothing to get on with. And
as we sit there, baffled, irritated, and bored, suddenly we put
ourselves a question. Why are we baffled, why are we irritated, why are we bored? Because we are not being spoonfed.
Because we are not told what to look at, because we are not
having our emotional attitudes and judgements prepared for

us, because we are independent, adult, free. Then suddenly we realize what is actually in front of us. *The Connection* – as I should perhaps have said earlier – is a play about dope addicts. What we see is a roomful of junkies waiting for a fix. They are passing the time playing jazz, occasionally talking, mostly sitting. The actors who are portraying these characters have sunk themselves into a total, beyond Method, degree of saturated naturalism, so that they aren't *acting*, they are *being*. And then one realizes that the two criteria – boredom or interest – are not in this case possible criticisms of the play but criticisms of ourselves. Are we capable of looking at people we don't know, with a way of life different from our own, with interest? The stage is paying us the supreme compliment of treating us all as artists, as independent creative witnesses. And the evening is as interesting as we choose to make it. It is as though we were really taken into a room of far-gone drug addicts: we could be Rimbaud and spin our own fantasies from their attitudes: we could watch like a painter or a photographer the extraordinary beauty of their attitudes slumped in their chairs: or we could relate their behaviour to our own medical, psychological or political beliefs: but if we shrug our shoulders before this collection of warped, strange, miserable mankind, it's hard to feel that the lack is other than on our side. After all, *The Connection*, though "anti" in terms of stage convention, is supremely positive – it is assuming that man is passionately interested in man . . .

As I was saying earlier, we react against "lies" in the name of truth – but are in effect putting fresher conventions in the place of antiquated ones, and so long as they're fresh, they'll seem "truer". Now *The Connection* seems absolutely "real". Yet the fact that something *does* happen in *The Connection* – the man with the dope arrives and in the second act gives everyone a shot, and one character gets violent – is a form of plot. Equally, the choice of subject is in itself bizarre, theatrical, romantic. In twenty years, *The Connection* will seem plot-ridden and contrived. By then, we may be capable of watching a normal man in a normal state with equal interest. Maybe . . .

Note in passing that this is a Brechtian show in one particular sense – we look, we relate to our own prejudices, we judge. (And note also – for future talks about Brecht – the interesting corollary: the stage picture is a sort of illusion – it is a room and the actors try to pass themselves off as real people: it is the ultimate development of the utterly naturalistic theatre and yet we are completely "distanced" all through the evening. In fact, were a few Brechtian slogans to be hung up in front of us helping us to find our emotional attitude, then we might be caught up in illusion...)

The Connection proves to me that the development of the tradition of naturalism will be towards an ever greater focus on the person or the people, and an increasing ability to dispense with such props to our interest as story and dialogue. I think it shows that there is a supernaturalistic theatre ahead of us in which *pure behaviour* can exist in its own right, like pure movement in ballet, pure language in declamation, etc.

The film I've just made, *Moderato Cantabile*, is an experiment in this: it is an attempt to tell a story with a *minimum* of fictional devices by using and relying on the actor's powers of characterization in the *mediumistic* sense of the word. In other words, the actors were not instructed in the aspects of character that were useful for the story, they saturated themselves in the characters by rehearsing scenes which do not exist in the film. The actors *became* other people in *fictional* relationship – however, from then on we *observed* – the camera *recorded* their behaviour. The interest – if it's there – is in the eye of the beholder: the experiment is that the entire plot, exposition, narrative, exists in details of behaviour which we have to find and evaluate for ourself – as we do in life.

You see the subject is vast – and I really would like to move on from *The Connection*. I believe that the future of the theatre must lie in its transcending the surface of reality, and I believe that *The Connection* shows how naturalism can become so deep that it can – through the intensity of the performer (I'm sure *The Connection* is nothing much on paper) – transcend appearances. (Here it falls into place with the whole new school of French novel writing – Robbe-Grillet, Duras, Sarraute – which refutes analysis and puts con-

crete facts, i.e. objects or dialogues or relationships or behaviour, before you, without comment or explanation.)

But there are other ways of transcending appearances. I'm
interested in why the theatre today in its search for popular
forms ignores the fact that in painting the most popular form
in the world today has become abstract. Why did the Picasso
show fill the Tate with all manner of people who would not
go to the Royal Academy? Why do his abstractions seem
real, why do people sense that he is dealing with *concrete* vital
things? We know that the theatre lags behind the other arts
because its continual need for immediate success chains it to
the slowest members of its audience. But is there nothing in
the revolution that took place in painting fifty years ago that
applies to our own crisis today? Do we know where we stand
in relation to the real and the unreal, the face of life and its
hidden streams, the abstract and the concrete, the story and
the ritual? What are "facts" today? Are they *concrete*, like
prices and hours of work – or *abstract* like violence and loneliness? And are we sure that in relation to twentieth-century
living, the great abstractions – speed, strain, space, frenzy,
energy, brutality – aren't more concrete, more immediately
likely to affect our lives than the so-called concrete issues?
Mustn't we relate this to the actor and the ritual of acting to
find the pattern of the theatre we need?

[NOVEMBER 1960]

THE CONFESSIONS OF LENNY BRUCE
by Charles Marowitz

With the possible exceptions of Jack Gelber's *Connection* and
the Concept of the nuclear deterrent, no American import has
raised a greater stink than Leonard A. Schneider alias Lenny
Bruce.

The revulsions of *The People* ("He makes us sick") and *The
Daily Sketch* ("It stinks") are the stock reactions of the one-
celled mind. But apart from these predictable knocks, there
appeared a number of odd boosts. The word "moralist" was

prominent in most of these. *The New Statesman*, for instance, hailed Bruce as "the evangelist of the new morality" and the moralist tag was endorsed by a number of other approving critics. The tacit assumption seemed to be that anyone who dispensed social satire larded with obscenity must have an uplifting motive; must, in some referable way, be related to the Lawrence-Joyce-Miller ethos.

In my view, one has to give a very special definition to the word "moralist" before it will fit a *trumbanick* like Bruce. For me, Bruce is essentially a hedonist with sexual gratification as the basic pleasure-principle.

In an unsolicited testimonial, he expounds the virtues of marijuana – especially when compared to the evils of alcohol. He unequivocally advocates balling, indicting all obstacles, social and psychological, that stand in the way of sexual fulfilment. His advice to unmarried women: "Girls who are celibate wouldn't be that way long if they would only sell a bit." A pun which impugns that emotional stinginess which, on one level, withholds sex and, on another, love.

By his own admission he is a sensualist: "In an aesthetic sense if you could graph me, I'd be pretty shallow because I'm very concerned with the physical. First attraction is not intellectual, ever, with me."

That sex is not dirty seems to be marginal; that it is rabid, uncontrollable and desirable seems much more the point. In the midst of a fatal car-wreck (this is Bruce speaking) with only one male and one female survivor, horniness still rears its ugly head. Like Antonioni, Bruce reminds us of our inescapable animality. Like de Sade, he urges us to celebrate it. Like Norman Mailer, he sends us in search of the Big Orgasm and bids us not be ashamed to live for the wisdom our senses afford. All of which seems to be much closer to Wilde's hedonism than it is to any saint's concept of morality.

This is essential Bruce. Thankfully there are other layers or the man would be unbearable. There is, for instance, Bruce the Sham-Buster.

In demolishing the myth of The Lone Ranger, that legendary all-American paragon of justice, Bruce reminds us that a lie begins by enchanting the young and ends by warping the grown-ups. At our most impressionable age, the natural sex functions are stigmatized as indecent, death is fantasied as a shuttle-service between earth and heaven, and the public prints become a secular branch of the scriptures. In the Brucian recapitulation, all of these fictions wither. The Lone Ranger is revealed to be a selfish poof who no longer disappears when townsfolk try to thank him but who hangs around tallying up what he is owed. And Tonto (we should have guessed; it was far too early for integration) is exposed as a Comanche pederast.

Bruce shows us that our childhood has been a malicious fiction and what is more, that we are still trapped by it. That an imperceptible thread links the masked stranger on the white horse to a thousand other "masked men" of questionable virtue who hold political office, control newspaper combines, hear our confessions and mete out our punishments. Indicting, by unavoidable implication, that most heinous of all masked men, Jehova, Gutenyu, JC of the Head Office who, Bruce contends, has retained his popularity all these centuries simply because he has not been overexposed by publicity: "Nobody's seen the Cat's face!"

Bruce is the closest thing we have to a Zen comic; a direct descendant of the madcap monks whose lunacy is depicted in early Zen drawings. Out of an astonishing relaxation such as we find only in the finest jazz-musicians, Bruce pursues his riff to the furthest borders of rationalism and then wings across. Suddenly, we find ourselves in a world no longer confined by logical positivism or dulled with conventional associations. This is true Zen country where new frames are added to the mind and the Third Eye not only opens, but pops, rolls, swivels and boggles.

But classical allusions to one side, we should not lose sight of the fact that, before anything else, Bruce is a professional stick-comic, born into the business, son of a show-business mom. A man more concerned with comedy techniques than moral overtones. He is not a phenomenon but a highly-developed exponent of that loneliest of all art forms, stand-up comedy, and as such, is prone to all the usual occupational hazards.

In a New York interview, Bruce was once asked what he did on those nights when he didn't feel funny. His answer, "I bomb." (English translation: I fail.) "What I will do," Bruce went on to say, "is bare my soul and through this cathartic method achieve humour."

No one has described the Bruce method better than that. For this, fundamentally, is what a night with Bruce consists of: a confessional so relentlessly personal that the barriers of artificial communication are removed. A man telling the truth about himself and his world is, on the one hand, terrifying and on the other, hilarious. And the B-Effect (not that far removed from the A-Effect) commingles both terror and humour. The people who walked out on Bruce responded only to the terror.

As a performer, Bruce is essentially sloppy. So much so that some of his best material, because it is never shaped into a finished form, falls apart at the seams. (I have seen one bit overwhelm an audience on a night when Bruce was hot and firing nicely, and on the next, because he felt slightly under, wither into pointless drivel. Bruce himself seemed to have forgotten what the comic point had been.)

I pointed this out to him; that as an improvising comic, he was subject to the unpredictable highs and lows that beset all forms of improvisation. "If I go like clockwork, bang – one, two, three, four – I know I'm bad. Nobody's rhythm is like that. It's gotta be one, two, miss – pick up – three, four – otherwise it's not really there – on that night – for that audience."

The point is well taken. Certainly a comic whose genius lies in the fact that he brings a natural ease and candour to the strait-jacketed metres of public performance is going to shun the pat delivery. But when that easy-going, now-I-feel-it-now-I-don't rhythm subverts the comedic effect, isn't that a case of virtues cutting one's own throat? And yet, at the same time as I yearn for a greater economy of means, I realize that Bruce's skill lies elsewhere, and I grudgingly accept the fact that one must take Bruce on his own terms. It is fairly probable that a tidy, well-regulated Bruce would lose in *élan* what he gains in discipline.

One of the many summings-up of Bruce that appeared in the press was: "His fascination lies not in what he says but in what he is!" Which is all rather pointless unless one goes on to say *what* he is. I believe, if the laggard critic had pursued his thesis, he too would have come to the conclusion that Bruce is essentially a professional comedian. Certainly, this is how Bruce thinks of himself, and when he succeeds it is because all the skills that enliven the professional comedian are here being exercised on truer, more complicated and more arresting material. When asked how much of his act was autobiographical, Bruce admitted, "All of it", and so, in a sense, the fascination is as much in what he *says* as what he *is* and, to bring this boomeranging generalization finally to rest, because he uses comedy as confessional, he *is* what he *says*.

But not all of what he says is either interesting or comic, and it is a shamefully indiscriminate kind of approval that roundly accepts the man in all his trivia and aimlessness. If Bruce were a play, one wouldn't hesitate to say that its theme and content were magnificent even though some of the characters were a little confused and much of the dialogue needed tightening up. For in a lot of Bruce we are exposed to laxity and fuzziness. And much of the time we are being told simple home-truths that we can just as easily get from the bartender down the street or the personal page of a woman's magazine. A lot of the time he hedges about madly before making his leaps and often he mistakes banal impudence for original audacity.

Bruce, unlike other comics, is not concerned with the "house". He plays only for the handful of people who seem to dig him. The others either tag along or fall off depending on their make-up, but Bruce performs none of those desperate showbiz somersaults to "win" his audience. Although he worries about his technique, he also takes pride in his professional accomplishments, gauging his development in the only accurate way he feels he can, by tallying up the ever-increasing size of his audience and his earnings. He is today one of the highest-priced comedians in the business. He was incensed in London when someone suggested that anyone hopped-up could do what he did; rankled for hours at the

intimation that he was merely an eccentric and not a craftsman. Many think the same of Bruce and this, more than the
negative publicity, is grossly unfair. For though Bruce doesn't
prepare in the same way as a dancer – choreographing every
move and gesture – he is in a constant state of readiness,
always feeding his sensibility new ideas and watching them
take shape on the floor. Here again, the jazz parallel is very
apt. It is precisely what an improvising musician does, and
his success, like Bruce's, is determined by the quality of the
invention and the performing skill with which it gets developed. There is nothing easy about entertaining people for
two and three hours at a stretch – the usual duration of a
Bruce session. Most other comics reel off twenty or forty
minutes of set-pieces and think themselves very prolific to
sustain that much. Bruce figures that on the basis of per-
formance-time, he has put more years into the business than
many older comics (he mentioned Tommy Trinder) who
merely fill conventional spots. Judged on a *pro rata* basis, he
is probably right.

Although the categorizing British journalist tends to lump
Bruce with Mort Sahl and Shelley Berman, it is quite obvious
that there are no real chemical affinities. Sahl is the quick-
silver collegiate; a Bob Hope with political awareness. Shelley Berman, a hip, hard-centred Joyce Grenfell, but to place
Bruce, one must look beyond show business. He was fired in
the same crucible as Kerouac, Ginsberg, Mailer and many
of the other Beats; is like them in his middle thirties. His
delivery suggests the free-wheeling prose of *On the Road*;
his form, the deliberate discontinuity of William Burroughs;
his mordant satire finds parallels with Ginsberg's, and in his
psychotic drive, sexual preoccupation and ornery compul-
siveness, he could almost be Norman Mailer transplanted. All
of which is grossly misleading as Bruce is himself unsalvage-
ably non-intellectual and much less aware than any of the
gentlemen previously mentioned. But if we're going to play
the game of comparative analysis, at least let's bandy about
the right names.

Many British spectators commented on the prevalence of
homosexual references in Bruce. There are two reasons for

this. First of all, queer-jokes are part of any American comedian's stock-in-trade. It is a standard category like mother-in-
law jokes or talking-parrot jokes, and in this Bruce shows
himself very much part of the American comedy tradition.
But with Bruce, the homosexual reference is much more telling as it takes into account the subversive connotation of
homosexuality in America. (One of the biggest Eisenhower
Administration scandals was the discovery of homosexuals in
the State Department. In the Armed Services, suspected
homosexuals are frequently mustered out with a Dishonour-
able Discharge.) The homosexual and the Ideal American
stand in the same ratio as the War Hero and the Draft
Dodger. The homo is about as un-red-white-and-blue as you
can get. He doesn't take part in sports; he doesn't whore; he
doesn't eat Wheaties; he is never found in a painting by
Norman Rockwell. He is all arty and sensitive instead of
being practical and level-headed.

That is why the demasculinization of a character like The
Lone Ranger (prototype of the American He-Man; a kind of
Boy Scout Emeritus) is so devastating. In Bruce, the queer
is used to mock the brawny, heterosexual vision of the world
which, in America and elsewhere, is itself a desperately-
maintained fiction.

Bruce's homosexual preoccupation *and* sex-patter *and*
four-letter liberties, is by no means unique. Camp comics like
Ray Martine (who performs regularly at the Deuragon Pub
in Hackney) are just as blunt as Bruce and in the same areas.
Martine's routine is swamped in homosexual innuendo and
lavatorial allusions. There is also, as it happens, a strong
physical resemblance between them, though Martine hasn't
anything like Bruce's panache. Still it is well worth a visit
to Hackney simply to see a homebred comic playing easily
and well to a relaxed, exclusively proletarian coterie audience.
It is an atmosphere which is inconceivable at The Establishment.

One of the more notorious passages in Bruce's act is where he
assumes the guilt for the murder of Jesus. "Yes, we did it! I
did it! My family! They left me a note in the cellar. 'We killed
him.' Why? Because he didn't want to become a doctor!"

In the *Yorkshire Post* extract of this bit, Angus W. Murray, misquoting Bruce, rendered the tagline as "he didn't want to become a docker". Which, for me, only emphasized the fact that a good deal of Bruce is lost on English audiences.

What does not translate is the ethnic milieu; the cultural substructure on which a lot of the humour is based. How could Angus W. Murray be expected to know that in a good Jewish-American household, the promising son, to please his status-seeking parents, is encouraged to become a solid-square professional man, like a doctor?

Many of the allusions to early American motion pictures were lost. How many people, even in the hip Establishment audience, grasped the cornball significance of the Pat O'Brien-James Cagney-Charles Bickford prison films. How many understood Bruce's fleet reference to Joan Crawford when narrating the stag movies he advocated for the edification of the young. How many people have heard of Norman Vincent Peale or Sid Luft or dixiecups? Bruce was always on about his 'frame of reference' and one of the weaknesses of his act was that he didn't adequately research his British public for relevant parallels – although it was endearing to watch him do his homework in public by asking members of his audience if they could suggest counterparts to Clyde Beatty, Arthur Godfrey, Jack Paar, etc.

Of Bruce the Jew one could write a Torah.

Like many sophisticated American Jews, Bruce is more taken with the foibles than the suffering. (Although as Theodore Reik suggests in his essay on "The Nature of Jewish Wit", the great gift of the Jewish humorist has always been his ability to convert tragedies into comedy.)

The Jews, always quick to consolidate the successes of their brethren, have not fallen over themselves to endorse Bruce and his shmutzstories. ("A nice Yiddishe boy don't talk doity!") Many Jews protest that Bruce goes too far and echo the criticism of one American critic who said that no matter how sympathetic you are to Bruce, if you listen to him long enough, he's sure to offend you. (One of Bruce's funniest experiences in London was a backstage interview with a couple from a Jewish publication who, after expressing their admiration, proceeded to point out that the anti-Catholic remarks were really going too far. "People were embarrassed, you could see!" they admonished with effusive sympathy. Bruce, in a typical underhanded Brucian stratagem, secretly recorded the conversation and, characteristically, so bungled the job that nothing of it could be replayed. During his next performance, he spent twenty minutes trying to repair the tape-recorder while an incredibly tolerant audience bided its time.)

I am in no way qualified to analyse the phenomenology of Jewish humour through the ages, but it strikes me that one of its most consistent characteristics is its realism. It depicts types, attitudes, and subtleties of feeling which reveal a pose, a pomposity or a hidden set of circumstances – all of which correspond to our experience. It is a probing, penetrating and embarrassing kind of humour. ("Excuse me Mrs Cohen, I liked your apple tarts so much I had three of them." "You had five, but who counts?") It is a humour far removed from the shaggy dog story or the far-fetched absurdities we find in the routines of a gentile comedian like Bob Hope.

In this, Bruce can be said to be typically Jewish, and here perhaps one finds a link – tenuous but feasible – with Sahl and Berman. In each, the comedy can be traced back to some discernible, shared experience which then brings about a laughter of recognition. In Bruce, we often recognize life – not so much as it is lived but as it is experienced internally. This is what produces the nervous laughter and/or the outrage.

If we keep stripping off the many layers that constitute Bruce, we finally get down to the bedrock which is Leonard A. Schneider. Unspectacular pupil, farm-labourer, veteran US Navy, struggling comic, Hollywood scriptwriter (one credit), divorced (voluntarily pays maintenance), sex problems, harassed by police, malicious critics and vengeful prosecutors. Not as well adjusted as Richard Dimbleby, but then who is? The choice of the pseudonym is itself very indicative. For Americans, the name Bruce suggests brawn, self-confidence, acceptance, peerless white Protestantism. Bruce

Wayne alias Batman; Bruce the high school hero; President of the Class; star full-back; troop commander Bruce; conceivably, Bruce the astronaut. The helplessness which the name conceals is openly confessed by the man himself. One of the reasons why Bruce is both successful and adorable.

Lenny Bruce confirms the theory that the well-spring of comedy is the truth about oneself – if one is skilful enough to comprehend it. Cervantes, Shakespeare and Molière confirmed it just as strongly but what makes Bruce so remarkable is that he disclaims even the artifice of objective correlatives. He makes us a gift of his sensibility without any fancy wrappings. He reveals himself so directly and so thoroughly that he shames some of us and shocks others. After a session with the relative stranger named Bruce, we can rightly say we know the man. Can we say as much for our closest friends and most intimate relations?

[JULY 1962]

"HAPPENINGS" ON THE NEW YORK
SCENE *by Jill Johnston*

The term "happenings" was coined in 1959 after an event given in New York at the Reuben Gallery by Allan Kaprow titled "18 Happenings in 6 Parts".

In 1952 at Black Mountain College (North Carolina) John Cage gave an experimental performance with the audience seated in the middle of it. Cage lectured from a podium, David Tudor played the piano, Charles Olson talked or laughed on cue from the audience, Robert Rauschenberg the painter played a wind-up victrola, Merce Cunningham danced, and other activities took place more or less simultaneously. One might take this as a starting point for the recent flow of events, or Happenings, in this country, in Europe, in Japan.

John Cage was the most likely person to pioneer the new movement. His own experimental music, based on letting "sounds be themselves rather than vehicles for man-made theories or expressions of human sentiments", led him to a music in which sounds, like events in nature, would occur without premeditation. At any moment you might hear a number of sounds issuing from known or unknown sources, occurring in spontaneous continuities and combinations. To create an art based on this way of looking at things is to give oneself up to the possibility of anything; and this means at least a partial relinquishment of the artist's conscious intentions. It certainly means giving up the idea of Art as usually practised in the Western world. And in the end it leads inevitably to *theatre*: a field of action where anything may happen. Cage's *Water Walk* consists of three minutes of sound, but the sounds are made by so many objects and with so many actions by the performer that it is impossible to speak of the piece as music in any conventional sense. Nor is it a matter of art picking up where life leaves off, for the piece includes sounds and actions from mundane activities; and its start and finish is as arbitrary as anything that happens in it. It, like life, simply goes on.

It is difficult to make quick sense of the complex origins of any eventuality, but as for the immediate forerunners of Happenings, one might mention three sources.

In *The Theatre and its Double* (which the poet, Mary Caroline Richards, was translating in the early 'fifties, and from which she read a chapter each week to a group of interested friends), Antonin Artaud proclaimed the necessity of a theatre brought back to its *physical* essentials. Without pinpointing the exact forms these essentials should assume, Artaud was demanding a return to the primary function of a theatre: the exercise of magic through the combined force of all the physical properties that the stage in its decadence had relegated to the role of "support". He says:

> ... the theatre (must be) contained within the limits of everything that can happen on a stage, independently of the written text.
> ... to link the theatre to the expressive possibilities of forms, to everything in the domain of gestures, noises, colours, movements, etc., is to restore it to its original direction.

...the spectator is in the centre and the spectacle surrounds him.

...in this spectacle the sonorization is constant: sounds, noises, cries are chosen first for their vibratory quality, then for what they represent.

From the revolution in art posed by cubism and collage came the voice of Kurt Schwitters. Writing in 1920, Schwitters, who was associated with the Dadaists but who called his own theory of art "Merz", outlines a fantastic scenario for a stage event that would embrace all branches of art in one artistic unit. "Merz", he said, "stands for freedom from all fetters", and the Merz work of art *par excellence* would be the Merz drama in which all parts are inseparably bound up together. "It cannot be written, read, or listened to, it can only be produced in the theatre."

The Dada demonstrations, 1916–21, are the most obvious precedent for recent events. Georges Hugnet described a typical exhibition in Zurich:

On the stage of the cabaret tin cans and keys were jangled as music ... Serner placed a bunch of flowers at the feet of a dressmaker's dummy. Arp's poems were recited by a voice hidden in an enormous hat shaped like a sugar-loaf. Huelsenbeck roared his poems in a mighty crescendo, while Tzara beat time on a large packing case. Huelsenbeck and Tzara danced, yapping like bear cubs, or, in an exercise called "noir cacadou", they waddled about in a sack with their heads thrust in a pipe.

The Dada demonstrations were spontaneous and programmatic. The present Happenings, 1959–62, are more like serious extensions of paintings and construction. In 1956 Allan Kaprow converted an exhibition of collage into an environment, the *Penny Arcade*. Thereafter he experimented with environments, and with events as a natural result of the former. Then in 1957–8, along with several other artists (including a poet and a composer) he attended a class given by John Cage at the New School. Cage provided a new focus through the use of chance operations, stimulating the discovery of material and events through a liberation from personal habit.

But the painters, including Kaprow, who moved quickly to stage a series of events at the Judson and Reuben galleries in early 1960, were more interested in a new dimension for their constructions in the form of personal expressive images. They were, in other words, not so interested in *letting* things happen as in *making* things happen. The convergence, then, of several personalities from different places at more or less the same time and with similar tendencies produced the new outbreak of events.

Before meeting any of the above-mentioned, a young painter from Tennessee, Red Grooms, had done what he considered a "kind of play" in Provincetown, and later the same year (1959) gave *The Burning Building* at the Delancey St Museum. *The Burning Building* involved the action of a "pasty man", two firemen, a girl in a white box, and another girl in top hat, moustache and plastic covering. It was performed in front of and behind a curtain, which when pulled aside revealed a three-dimensional set of cardboard, canvas, sacks, cans, shoes, wires, etc., forming the image of a fireman, a door; and a building through which Grooms (pasty man) dived at the end. It concluded with a "grotesque" stomping dance by two real firemen, flashing lights, words yelled back and forth between Grooms and the girl in top hat, cries of "Fire" shouted through a slit, a chase, and a terrible racket.

By January 1960, Grooms was active at the Reuben Gallery, showing *The Magic Train Ride* along with Kaprow's *Big Laugh* and Robert Whitman's *Small Cannon*. And Claes Oldenburg and Jim Dine, two painters from the midwest, organized the Ray Gun Spex: three performances of six events by six artists at the Judson Gallery in February and March of 1960.

That same spring, out in California, La Monte Young and Dennis Johnson, two young composers, both students at UCLA, who had been giving simultaneous performances of music and poetry, staged *Avalanche Number 1*, a three-hour affair which included, among other things: several poems recited concurrently at different points in the audience;

electronic music; a thirteen-minute silence; and a *Poem for Tables, Chairs and Benches*, being the moaning and scraping music made by furniture being pushed across the floor.

The end of that year, 1960, Young came to New York where he joined other composers and artists of similar interests. Soon after he arranged a series of six concerts at Yoko Ono's loft, becoming deeply committed to the kind of event that devolved on a single action or sound. His aim was to entice the participant into an ever-increasing state of awareness of one particular sound or action so that he became *one* with it – which is what Young means when he says he likes "to get inside a sound".

He first did this in one composition when, for an hour he sustained the sound of a gong scraping over cement. At his last concert in Yoko Ono's loft he performed twenty-nine pieces, each one titled *Draw a Straight Line and Follow It*. Young thinks most artists are too busy trying to make their work interesting; to *make* something happen rather than to *let* it happen.

George Brecht is inclined to feel this way too. Brecht studied at the New School with Cage and became involved at the Reuben Gallery with Kaprow, Whitman and Lucas Samaras. However, because of his interest in Zen and aspects of Dada (Duchamp) as well as the music of Cage he continued, until recently, to use random operations and consequently did not make the kinds of Happenings the other painters were beginning to make. Before he came to do "less and less" he made several cabinets and "games" with "found" objects inviting manipulation and, by implication, removal or destruction. Thus he made participation in a work explicit, and again, the line between art and life dissolves. More recently he performed a *Comb Event* which consisted of engaging and releasing each prong of a comb with a finger-nail. In spring 1961, he presented an Environment: a small white room with a white chair in it. Brecht likes to make something out of ordinary things (door-bolts, coat-hooks) usually considered "uninteresting, boring, unlovable".

Once the original excitement subsided, Dine, Kaprow, Oldenburg and Whitman began to present their own respective Happenings at the New Reuben Gallery in the Winter season, 1960–1. The last evening at the old Reuben, in June 1960, was the end of the first flush. You could hardly move for all the people who jammed in to have a good time. The spirit was excellent. And Robert Whitman's *E.G. Opera* was a serious crazy mess that satisfied some of the craving for blood hell nonsense and purgation that people were expecting.

At the New Reuben, Whitman gave *The American Moon* and *Mouth*. Both were elaborately executed Environments: the first in the shape of nine cubicles for the spectators opening on to a central "play area" where the action took place; silent films were projected in each cubicle; the second, an enormous papiermâché mouth through which the spectators entered to sit inside. In *Mouth*, one event succeeded another in a quiet fantasy, ponderous and rhythmical, with a few scares. It might have been a forest scene. A large awkward shape of white cloth stretched on a frame of wire creaked side to side, as a pendulum, the heartbeat of the scene. A girl in heels came out running fast, staggering in a zigzag. She would start to fall, then catch herself and be off again. An arrow travelled slowly on a wire and pierced a cloth which made three people tumble out from behind it. A lovely "picnic car", a big paper and wood construction, drove patiently through the audience and disgorged two girls who sat down on the "ground" to eat a picnic lunch. A monster-like animal heaved slowly round from the back and nudged up to the girls. He left. One of the girls left too, got back in the car and drove it out. The other girl went to sleep near the pendulum. Four girls in costumes did a dance that had jumping and swaying in it. The girl in street clothes who had appeared first, as though escaping, climbed into the pendulum which turned into an elevator and rose, descended, rose again – and that was the end of the Scene.

Claes Oldenburg's events are also rich in the possibility of new experience through association. He likes to present objects from everyday life, and transmute them by abstraction or by placing them in some unexpected context. Fake food served at a real table; real food in a false situation (a suitcase full of lemons); a girl in man's clothes; parts of the body appearing in fragments, therefore as objects (or fetishistic substitutions); a collection of objects, like those drawn from the pockets of an inert man (whose clothes are paint-spattered so that he appears as an object himself), or those drawn and displayed from a suitcase: a yellowed book, fake rose, fake money, silver ware, work glove, beat-up shoe, red sponges, mallet, tin cans, rubber hose, mousetrap, etc.

Oldenburg also often transforms his sphere of action into an environmental mess – a calculated rubble of paper, cardboard, stuffed burlap bags, dirty mattresses, tin cans, paint-spattered walls and so on. He does this for several reasons. For one thing, he probably has a natural affinity for wrecks, the way most children do until they're "trained". For another, the use of found junk material is part of a contemporary tradition. Also, he lives in a proletarian neighbourhood.

Which brings us back to the hard reality of "the thing in itself". No matter what happens in this kind of contemporary art, it is the physical, palpable substance of a thing that is its primary reality. When a word is spoken it is like the sound a person makes when he speaks. Its meaning, whatever it is for each person, is secondary, and it does not appear in a rational context. It has a quality, a vibration, a physical substance. When you see a woman drying and stacking dishes, or two girls making eggs at a hot plate, you see, feel, the body (its bulk in space, its special shape), the movement of the body in this particular action, the sounds issuing from this particular action, or, as in the case of the eggs, their smell. What does a woman drying and stacking dishes mean? It means a woman drying and stacking dishes. It looks and sounds a certain way. It looks and sounds different ways to different people. A woman in her own kitchen will look a certain way too, if you choose to look. So now we are speaking of theatre (art) in general, or life in general. Where one begins and the other ends is one of the interesting questions posed by Happenings. John Cage has said that "theatre takes place all the time wherever one is and art simply facilitates persuading us this is the case".

[SEPTEMBER 1962]

THE BRIG *Review by Gordon Rogoff*

The Living Theatre here restates its presence as our most original, profoundly adventurous and persistently important theatre institution. The Brig *is a theatre piece realized with brilliant devotion.* Village Voice

Written with relentless fury, staged superbly, it crackles with electricity, brilliantly produced. Variety

An act of conscience, decency and moral revolt in the midst of apathy and mass inertia. If you can bring yourself to spend a night in The Brig, *you may start a jailbreak of your own.* The New Republic

Parallel actions: we are so revolted by our world, by its politic solutions that corrupt what art or humanity might remain in politics, by whatever retreats we have made in the name of practical realism, by the failures in memory from one generation to the next, by the clichés of democratic culture, breaking down form and feeling into one giant platitude signifying everything and, therefore, nothing; in short, we do not wish to be ciphers, things, numbers, mechanics, engineers of souls, physicists of feelings, a faceless, limbless, collective glut of hollow statistics more alienated from ourselves than from each other; and meanwhile, in this world of clear, present, daily existential nausea, we continue in the only madness that keeps us sane, the work of making art, in itself the action that contradicts the nullifying implications of our observation; yet, in so doing, there are some of us who are still naïvely surprised to find the world of art reflecting, in its corruptive behaviour, the politic world at large. These actions, not new so much as intensified, are more visible to the alienated eye in the work of the American theatre than in the work of the other arts. The poets, painters, novelists, and musicians have, at least in part, acknowledged the peculiar pressures of the century. Though the *business* of their art is no less corruptive, many of them have been aware of the parallel actions, and have maintained a standard of exploration that is, by now, almost unknown in our theatre.

I say "almost unknown" because our theatre has not yet separated itself wholly from the community of art. Indeed, it is misleading today to refer so casually to "our theatre", since appearances are so illusionary.

The American theatre only *seems* to be characterized by Broadway. That, no doubt, is the way most of our reviewers, producers, agents, and audiences would have it. But the rock of Broadway ages upon which they would build our theatrical lives has long since been shattered at its base, leaving only the chips and fragments of genuine impulse behind, fossils from a time of monumental indifference. Of "ideal" theatre we have none, neither on Broadway nor in any of the legendary decentralized corners of our country. Of "modern" theatre, however, we have one – a hard, persistent, nauseated biological quirk known, with remarkable aptness in this case, as The Living Theatre.

Formed, moulded, maintained, very timely ripped from the womb of off-Broadway by Julian Beck and his wife, Judith Malina, it is a theatre which manages, against more than customary odds, to demonstrate that an idea of theatre is still possible. The Becks do not know how to play the game of parallel actions as others play it. Following the useful distinction made by Erich Fromm between the *rebel* and the *revolutionary* – the first struggling against authority in order to become authority, the second simply fighting authority with no envy – the Becks can be described without hesitation as revolutionaries. They are, in the most positive sense, revolted. The only power they seek is power over their own work, the power available to those who are free enough to make choices unmoved by the attractive suggestiveness of convention. In this respect, they begin to be unique in America. But this uniqueness, and their special kind of power contribute, as pain follows pleasure, to their several weaknesses.

By working, in many senses, outside the system, they suffer from inevitable, continuous economic blight. Energies that might better be channelled into the making of plays and the education of a company are diverted into wars against the landlord, creditors, and the fundamental coolness of the

New York audience. This beleaguered stance comes easily to them, assuming a perverse logic in relation to their theatrical stance. Economic battles represent a very real engagement in real life for them, offering always a stern reminder that art cannot live by art alone. The struggle within to make a theatre that always mirrors struggle is matched, with sad naturalness, by the struggle without to keep the theatre alive.

Adding logic to logic, the Becks maintain still another struggle. As leaders in the non-violent fragments of our small, dispersed Peace Movement, they march, participate in sit-downs, and try not to get bashed over the head by our gentlemen police. On election day, they can be found near the polling booths in the upper west side of Manhattan, distributing a list of those few candidates for Congress who, by some generous stretch of the imagination, can be called "peace" candidates. During these moments, the theatre may well be running performances of Jack Gelber's *The Connection*, the one production in their repertory that always threatens to return its investment; but as the cause, with admirable consistency, takes first place in their passions, so must they "strike" for peace, thus closing the theatre, returning in time to an even greater economic pressure. Though they do not appear to exhaust themselves by their battles, they do exhaust the patience of their money-raisers, and at such times, try the patience of even their most devoted actors. The necessary connections between the Becks' theatre and the Becks' cause escape none of their admirers, but a little more of the one and a little less of the other might, so their friends suggest, make a happier balance. They are, after all, too far from the world of compromise to ever feel the danger. The only temptation they suffer is the temptation to fail, carrying anarchic logic too far.

Economic weakness may well be a chronic necessity for the Becks. But it would seem to contribute little to art and even less to their work. What they *might* do some day is build a theatre that is more than the most individual idea of a theatre that we have, a kind of starveling child at war with the elements, and form at last a *continuing* theatre based more on practice than theory. As it is today, their ideas are clear and their tenacity is awesome, but the standard of their work generally raises the question of an artist's first responsibility. It has seemed as if they were choosing art by default, saying what they have to say without caring half enough in how they say it. Yet we know this can't be the case. A suggestion of a personal aesthetic impulse resides in all their productions, an impulse touched by borrowings from sources that would, on the surface, appear irreconcilable. Artaud and Brecht, the first names that spring to mind, represent an apparently bizarre combination that can be understood only if you accept the limitless sympathies of the anarchist imagination. Nothing need be digested whole. Everything can be absorbed in fragments.

What, then, is the specific form of their default? One could point to several events as symbols, such as the fact that where once they ran some of their productions in rotating repertory (a lone defiance of American habits), they stopped doing so last year in favour of attempting a long run of their rival production of Brecht's *Mann ist Mann*, a little war they maintained against another off-Broadway production performed in a different translation. Not surprisingly, both productions succeeded in knocking out each other, an obvious embarrassment of dubious riches. But to cite such a symbol is only to describe an effect, not a cause.

The cause, until recently, runs deeper and along lines only partially related to their exterior wars. It is rooted in a particular deficiency, a laxness in fundamental craft, a relaxation of artistic principle just at the point where most theatres live or die; namely, the area of style marked by a standard of acting.

Everything has been constructed except a company of players. True, some of their personnel show remarkable loyalty, but this is only a tribute to the Becks' potential leadership, not to the actors' useful talents. The hard fact is that the good ideas in their productions have broken down in performance under the weightlessness of most of their actors. The demands of the texts, the real life in the bleak underbrush of their subtexts, the development of character, the flashes of individuality that lift performance from the grey plains of observation into the dazzling reaches of perception – these have been largely absent at The Living Theatre. The laziness of the Becks in this respect is their most unforgivable weakness, and it forces one to wonder what conditions are finally necessary in the United States for the creation and maintenance of genuine group theatre. Other attempts have failed on the quicksands of commerce and personal compromise. The Becks, however, are belligerently uncommercial, working, as I have said, persistently outside the system. They retain their individuality, it seems, at the cost of failing as an ensemble. Where, if anywhere, we have asked, is the anarchist's middle ground?

Some clues to an answer have emerged at last in their latest production. *The Brig* is the first produced play by a young man named Kenneth H. Brown; and its production, under Miss Malina's direction, with the set designed by Mr Beck, suddenly makes sense out of all the doubts and agonies in the past. It does so because it is a theatrical existence by itself, drawing its life not from any single participating element, but from all the elements available to performed drama. Any one factor alone would be reduced to virtual meaninglessness away from the presence of the other factors. Mr Brown, undoubtedly, wrote his words and his directions on paper, and even without judging those words in terms of our accustomed literary standards, it is clear that they might well make striking patterns on the page, suggesting – but only suggesting – their life in the theatre. But the words surrender completely to the ritual demands of theatrical experience. They join with the lighting, setting, and acting into an occasion that is inconceivable outside of a theatre. The physical fact of theatre, regardless of shape, justifies the event. Neither film nor any other medium could contain the work: the script breathes into the theatre and the theatre breathes in the play.

We have become so inured to the corruptions of theatre – the endless adaptations from one medium into another, the active contradictions between contemplative, written prose and poetry, and the prose or poetry written to be expressed *only* on the stage – that we are none of us well equipped today for recognizing the theatrical event that is indigenous. Here, distinctions must be made. There have been, lately, various kinds of "acted" performances known as "happenings", sympathetically related to the extreme abstract painters who do "action painting". *The Brig*, inspired by similar indignation, is nevertheless a highly ordered organism. It would be misleading to think of it in terms of something that is simply allowed to *happen*. More accurately, it might be called a *becoming*, in the existential sense of truth – both theatrical and contextual – as something that emerges.

Sartre, indeed, might once have been describing the subject that *The Brig* makes into a theatre metaphor:

> Nothing (he wrote) – neither wild beasts nor microbes – can be more terrible for man than a cruel, intelligent, flesh-eating species which could understand and thwart human intelligence and whose aim would be precisely the destruction of man. This species is obviously our own . . . in a milieu of scarcity.

The Brig's metaphor for this essential, *present* condition, its particular "milieu of scarcity", is the prison of a United States Marine Corps base in Japan. It is not, as some prefer to think, a simple social document about a simple national scandal. Indeed, the plea implicit in its presentation is that we recognize, for once, that the elimination of the obvious social scandal would be no more than a token action, a symbol of the thorough eliminating process that must begin if we are ever to cease our merciless reduction of one another into so many unhuman things. The Marine Corps brig represents a useful, intensified location for a general action in which we are participants and witnesses everywhere in our lives. The scandal is the mockery we make of our brief chance to seize life and make it bend to our will; for in the brig, what little will anybody has – either guard or prisoner – has been totally perverted to the uses of hiding man from himself.

The forms we know in western theatre might have been chosen by Mr Brown and the Becks, and if they had done so, we might have had a more acceptable, formal play; but it would then have been what several of its critics call it now –

a documentary about one forgivably awful part of Marine Corps life. The story they tell – the eventless events of one day in the brig – is essentially a tale of reduced feeling, a tale in which the brutalism we use to alienate ourselves *must be felt* to be believed. The old ways – presenting a problem in the beginning that is fundamentally soluble by the end – would not be adequate to the special challenge of the theme. Nothing less would do than *physically* forcing the audience to endure, and therefore feel, exactly what the prisoners – and, indeed, the guards – feel as they enact their brutal ballet of mechanized screams and pain.

The play, therefore, though it is clearly a written work, is more a notation for an action, a symphonic scoring, a preparation for the plastic realization of an idea about our wounded indifference. Feeling is the play; the play is a feeling; the set is an actor; the actors are – horribly – walking, running, jumping, hitting, humiliated furniture on the set; and the words, sharp, denatured, constantly played in counterpoint, because a litany to what ought to be our active, involved fury. The old, more comfortable forms – and this, surprisingly, must include the innovations of Ibsen, Chekhov, Brecht and Beckett – will not serve us today *as well* as this startling theatrical incantation. This, at least, is what the Becks and Brown seem to be saying through their work. If the solution seems either absurd or merely strange, it is, I suggest, a very temporary one; not an innovation so much as a necessary outrage, a moment in American theatrical time in which all our surrenders are suddenly called into urgent question.

Years ago, Stark Young in *The Theatre* wrote some words that accurately place The Living Theatre and *The Brig* today:

Life, the energy, the living essence – Pirandello's "stream of life", Bergson's "vital urge" – goes on, finding itself bodies or forms to contain and express it. Behind whatever is dramatic lies the movement of the soul outward toward forms of action, the movement from perception toward patterns of desire, and the passionate struggle to and from the deed or the event in which it can manifest its nature.

Behind any work of art is this living idea, this soul that moves its right body, this content that must achieve form that will be inseparable from it. A perfect example in any art arrives not through standards but when the essential or informing idea has been completely expressed in terms of this art, and comes into existence entirely through the medium of it. This is perfection, though we may speak of a perfection large or small.

The perfection here is small. But in the framework of our lives and our theatre, this small perfection assumes heroic proportions. The Becks, failing still to match some of our severe, historical standards, have shown us how momentarily obsolete those standards can be at a time when anguish and disgust cry out for new forms. They have moved their own parallel actions into one, relentlessly straight line, pointing the way to what is always possible in any theatre at any time: an aesthetic choice that does not surrender to the corrupting forces of the milieu of scarcity, a choice that clings to the perceptive life of art rather than to the deceptive trap of craft alone. In the end, their victory is greater than that of the "realists" who capitulate because, through the emergence to truth in their own stubborn way, they have also emerged into a triumph of craft, a craft which has finally revealed itself, not through talk and training, but through the logical rhythms of action.

[SEPTEMBER 1963]

TALK WITH TYNAN *by Charles Marowitz*

Two years ago you said that despite Osborne and the New Wave, little had changed in the English theatre. Do you still believe this?

I was talking of what was being performed at the moment I wrote that. Apart from Wesker's *Chips With Everything*, the sort of plays being presented were much the same as they had been in 1951. And that was still more or less true a few months ago. A different aspect of this: I was looking at the playbills just two months ago, and I discovered that there were only two plays being shown in London that were written more than ten years ago. That meant that all links with the past had been severed. There was a Shakespeare at the Old Vic, a revival of *Misalliance* at the Royal Court, and that was all. So that nobody coming to London could get any sense of the whole spectrum of world drama, English drama, or even English drama before 1950. Apart from the two classics that I've named, *The Mousetrap* was the oldest play on in the whole of the metropolis. And that seemed to me ridiculous.

Isn't it more a matter of significant plays opening at certain periods of time, having their runs and then closing? Isn't it simply the way the commercial system works?

Obviously that's a great deal to do with it. But at the same time we do have the Aldwych, and we do have the Old Vic, which is supposed to do new plays occasionally but hasn't done one for about nine or ten years. The Aldwych had a Pinter play in its repertoire for a short period, but even if there were two more Aldwyches, you still wouldn't be able to sustain a large repertoire of world theatre and contemporary plays. Even on the present subsidy allotted to the National Theatre that will not be possible. It isn't enough money.

Should one throw the whole of this problem into the hands of government? Don't you think that with a combination of government subsidy and independent management, there should be enough going on to be representative of what the English theatre's got to offer? My question is based on your own assumption that the theatre is a minority art-form and only caters to one per cent of the population.

More government subsidy, more enlightened private management, more use of the LCC, more use of rates by provincial corporations – these could all help. But the fact is that ten years ago, and in the 'thirties and 'forties, the West End managements inclined toward the elegant and the mannered, and had a strong feeling for the past. A great deal of good West End management between 1930 and 1950 was essentially nostalgic in its bias. They did put on a surprising number of good revivals of eighteenth-century plays, restoration plays, and minor Elizabethans. Since the decline of that sort of management and that kind of actor, the Gielgud era actor, that gap has never been really filled. The Royal Court has done the odd Restoration play, Middleton, etc., and so has the Royal Shakespeare. But there's been no steady flow of the plays of Congreve, Wycherley, Dryden, Sheridan, Goldsmith, Webster and so on. Instead, we've had short runs by new playwrights, which are important, but not representative.

Do you see the subsidized theatres undertaking the flow of this sort of middle classics and the independent managers concentrating on new plays, or do you see the commercial managements widening their orbit to include classical revivals? Should government subsidy be doing one thing and independent managements another, or do you think there should be traffic between the two?

Ideally, they should both be competing. But obviously the point of a National Theatre is to have a permanent library of plays which can do the work of subsidized theatres *and* commercial theatres. A kind of central warehouse where there ought, as Granville Barker said, to be about forty or fifty plays, permanently available in two theatres, every season. In the heyday of the 'thirties and 'forties, the Gielgud period, the West End managements, particularly H. M. Tennent, and their star actors – your Gielguds, Richardsons and so forth, had a common attitude towards the sort of plays they considered were good for prestige and for their acting style, and these plays obviously had to be slightly artificial.

Our new actors nowadays are not so interested in that sort of classic it seems, nor perhaps equipped for it. Because their bent isn't essentially nostalgic. It isn't an accident that the same actors who were so good in Chekhov under Michel Saint-Denis in 1938, were equally good in Restoration comedy; both demand an essentially nostalgic attitude towards theatre which our actors today haven't got. I didn't see Tom Courtenay in *The Seagull* – I'm told he was excellent; if so he must be an exception. I don't see the new wave of actors as being good for the minor classics. Though they are good for the more gutsy, thunderous parts of Marlowe and Shakespeare, and they are very interested in the big heroic parts. Albert Finney recently played an enormous part in Glasgow[1] and Richard Harris gave a big solo performance in Gogol. They

[1] *Henry IV*, by Pirandello.

adore the big outburst. But I would not like to have to cast *The Importance of Being Earnest* out of a cast of New Wave actors.

But when the National Theatre starts up, plays like these will have to be included in the repertoire. What exactly does that portend . . . ?

A great problem. I don't know. I think there are two big problems in any company attempting as large a repertoire as the National Theatre eventually hopes to have. One will be this question of period style, by which I don't mean lace and silver-headed canes and elaborate wigs, but developing a sense of comic style within a period of the past. That will be a big problem. The other problem, which I find even harder to explain, is the fact that there are very few solid actors of weight between, say forty and sixty – the essential middle order of actors. The example, I suppose, is Alan Webb in one style, Michael Hordern in another. They are very few, and these actors are in great demand. Why there should be this age gap I don't know. It can't be because of the war, there was no cutting off of the prime of the nation's acting talent like there was in the First World War. But these actors, who are the backbone of the German Theatre and the Russian Theatre, simply don't seem to exist in England. We have our one or two stars – Gielgud, Richardson, Olivier – but where are the people who are automatic casting for, let's say, Gloucester in *Lear*. After Alan Webb, where do you go?

There is a general fear that the National Theatre may turn out to be a sort of an extended version of Chichester. Do you think it will present the works of the new dramatists?

I hope so. Some, a great many in fact, are committed to the Royal Court, or to Peter Hall and, obviously, one can't attempt to poach. But one can say, for instance, to a play-wright like Osborne, if you have a play on the stocks which demands larger staging than the Royal Court can provide, and if George Devine won't object, we will commission it instead. That kind of commission is certainly very much in my mind.

Do you think a National Theatre should take some sort of new cue for its development? . . . Isn't there a danger that it may just become a larger and more Establishment version of theatres like The Royal Shakespeare and The Old Vic?

There is no theatre in this country, so far, that has been able to do the job that Granville Barker and Archer envisaged for a National Theatre. The money hasn't been there. Peter Hall now has two plays in his repertoire at the Aldwych. Well, this is splendid, they are both excellent productions, but they aren't forty-nine plays and Peter Hall will never have forty-nine plays in his repertoire. And probably the National Theatre won't have built up to that number for about five or six years. But once that number's reached it'll be constant, with some productions being scrapped every year and new ones coming in to replace them. Also the National Theatre has to do certain dull but basic jobs, which are essentially educational. It's got to, for instance, make it possible for somebody who comes to London for a week, to be able to see about six different plays from different periods of international and English drama. That isn't part of Peter Hall's job. Peter Hall's job is to do plays that attract him or Peter Brook or any of his other directors. The National Theatre has a much more general purpose.

It is precisely that which worries a lot of people, the fear that a National Theatre will, in a dry and official way, discharge a national obligation. Most of the arguments put forward for the National Theatre are based on sociological considerations, that it would be good for the country; that it would create an official precedent for subsidy which would benefit local communities; that it would create a more widespread interest in theatre. But don't you think a National Theatre should have an artistic purpose quite distinct from its sociological benefits?

It isn't a sociological benefit. There is a purely theatrical and artistic benefit in seeing these plays – assuming that they aren't done badly or drably. But I am not persuaded that in the absence of an absolutely great director . . . or father-figure like Stanislavsky – that it is the function of a National Theatre to have a very highly recognizable style. We shall be using a number of different directors. But to attempt to impose a National Theatre style on every production isn't, I think, part of our job. I think we have to be a little more anonymous than that. Peter Hall can do the other job – of evolving a specific Shakespeare style. That's splendid. The TNP is, in some ways, the equivalent of Peter Hall's company, and has its own attitude; its own staging style and acting style. I would like our relationship to be like that of the TNP with the Comédie Française – hoping of course that we shan't have had time to ossify like the Comédie Française.

But the Comédie Française too has a very discernible style.

Quite, and I think *that* is its weakness. By insisting on the quality of this particular declamatory style, and paying less attention to the substance of the plays or the variety of the repertoire, the Comédie Française became a shell housing *only* a style and lost the flexibility and variety of a real National Theatre.

But in the case of practically every theatre I can think of that amounted to anything, there has been some kind of an artistic premise which has concerned itself with ideas about style.

I'll be concerned mainly with the repertoire side, the literary side, and that's all I can really talk about. The aesthetic shape that the company takes on will depend mostly on its directors, and the directors that Sir Laurence is talking to now to become his associates are people with very definite and recognizable directorial styles. And attitudes. The sort of company that these associates will want to shape will definitely have its own approach. All I'm saying is that it should not be as recognizable as, let's say, the approach of the Berliner Ensemble, which is a great company but only equipped to do plays by Brecht in the Brechtian style. I don't think it is any part of the aim or ambition of a National Theatre to have a style as rigidly prefabricated as that.

At a discussion a few months ago, you said that a theatrical style is very often the product of a shared attitude. Could you enlarge on that? The impression I got was of a social and political attitude being shared, is that right?

That would be to define it too closely. It seems to me that all the great companies have had – not always consciously, sometimes unconsciously – a shared attitude towards life, that is to say that the members of the company would not, in broad principles, disagree with the way in which their

world – at that time – was being run; or, in the case of a
revolutionary or a rebellious company, they would be in
broad agreement about the things they did *not* like about the
way their world was being run. It occurs to me, for instance,
that the actors who created the Racine style must have been
in broad sympathy with the world of Louis Quatorze; a
world of power, of elevated passion and great formality. This
must have appealed to and attracted them all. Just as, I
suggest, the world of high comedy, of artificial, mannered
elegance, had an enormous appeal to English actors of the
1930s. It responded to a deep chord in all their temperaments
and created what someone at that discussion called an
English ensemble style, which one could see in productions
like John Gielgud's *Love for Love*, which, I suppose, is one
of the peaks of that achievement; its decadence can be found
in a production like *The Chalk Garden*. The female emblem of
that style is Edith Evans and the male emblem, I suppose, is
John Gielgud. Now of course they didn't all sit down and say
we are all interested in Tory elegance. They didn't, and probably don't, think politically, but the unconscious agreement
is there. Similarly, you find a conscious agreement on political
principles in Joan Littlewood's Theatre Workshop. That was
what held it together for so long, this shared conviction that
it was the business of drama to reflect life in a certain way
and to celebrate certain aspects of life at the expense of others.
Similarly you find that in the Roger Planchon company – a
shared attitude which is, also in their case, political; it is a
workers' theatre and there is a deliberate policy of reshaping
the classics to fit the Planchon plan. You find it even more
consciously in the Brechtian productions. You found it, I
suggest, although not so politically apparent, in the Stanislavsky productions.

*In present-day terms, could one say of those actors associated
with the typical Shaftesbury Avenue frame of mind that they have
a common attitude which one might define as a Tory attitude to
life?*

I'd hate to pin it down so precisely to Tory. They have a
sense of glamour attached to formal behaviour, which I suppose is more common amongst the Tories than amongst the

Socialists. I simply think it is very hard to talk about a developing style if you don't have a company of actors with more or less the same viewpoint.

But this is not the case with the Royal Shakespeare Company where some kind of style is now definitely emerging. There are great disparities in the attitudes of these actors.

It emerged only in a few productions, and then only with Shakespeare. I think it has been mainly in productions like William Gaskill's *Cymbeline*; the lead played by Vanessa Redgrave, herself a rebel; herself interested in Brecht; Gaskill himself a rebel, interested in Brecht and the left wing.

It seems to me that in Cymbeline *what produced the effect of that production was an aesthetic concern on the part of Gaskill and his designer, René Allio (who happens also to be Planchon's designer); that it was the result of an enthusiasm for a certain kind of stagecraft, and that it does not really reflect anything more than that.*

What I perhaps mean, is that Gaskill's approach to a play of that sort is anti-Romantic and anti-heroic. Temperamentally he isn't a hero worshipper, nor is he an intense romantic, whereas those two qualities go together in a right winger far more often than in a left winger. And the conventional Imogen as a sort of a beautiful young flower is very far from Vanessa Redgrave's conception. And the approach to verse speaking also reflects social attitudes. Gaskill is much more interested in teaching his actors to get over a precise concrete meaning from the lines, whereas the more romantic, the more, let us say, Tory attitude, is to go for the decorative aspects of the sound. These are the aesthetic results of what I think is an inner attitude that can only be described as a social one; an attitude towards people.

Do you think this attitude is just as legitimate, just as original, if it comes about in a second-hand way? By which I mean, if this attitude is expressed in a production mainly because the production is modelled on Brechtian stagecraft, doesn't that produce a kind of accidental commitment? What, for instance, would Gaskill have done if he'd had to find a completely new and personal form. Doesn't the Brechtian approach itself contain certain built-in social connotations?

It depends on the sort of person who'd be attracted to the Brechtian style. It would be almost inconceivable for – one hates to keep coming back to John Gielgud and using him as a whipping boy, I don't mean to – but it would never occur to him to use that approach to a production. It isn't only the relationship of the actors to the director or the actors to the play or the actors to each other which reflects how they feel about society in general, it's an attitude towards the audience. You find that the romantic heroic actor of the old school either tries to charm the audience or to overpower them. That is to say he is either temperamentally servile to them, coaxing and cajoling them in comedy, or he thunders them into submission in tragedy. And this can produce marvellous effects. Wolfit's *Lear* at its best, was a performance like that. It was shattering – it was like being run over by a train. The left wing actor will tend to take another attitude, of talking directly to the audience on equal terms, no matter whether he is speaking verse or prose – treating them as equals in a sort of a dialectic, rather than people to be sweetened, or flattened.

So you think there is a natural gravitation to Brecht because Brecht happened to –

. . . have those kinds of virtues, yes. I don't think John Gielgud would be capable of that kind of attitude. The interesting thing will be to see what style Sir Laurence – he's the most pliable, I should have thought, of all our great actors and will try anything – it will be interesting to see if his acting style, as it develops in the National Theatre, has been affected by the events of the last ten years.

Do you think it is possible for somebody at his stage of development to alter his style? Isn't Olivier very much of a given quantity?

One hopes that he'll be acting in a lot of parts he hasn't played before and in styles that he hasn't attempted before . . . I think he is the most protean of them all, temperamentally. I certainly would find him the hardest to describe to anyone who had not met him. It would be very easy to convey the essence of Richardson or Gielgud to an outsider, but there is something curiously elusive about Olivier which gives one grounds to believe that he is capable of almost any kind of shift.

In 1958 you said that you thought there was perhaps too much emphasis on style and that you were much more interested in what was being said rather than how. But is it really possible, with Brecht or Beckett or anyone for that matter, to make a hard and fast distinction between what is content and what is style?

No, obviously they are simply two words. In fact, when you *can* tell the difference, then you have bad style. If you can look at a production and say, oh yes, that is the production style, and that is what the play is saying – two separate things – then it's a bad production and bad style. But what the Brecht company has achieved is such a paring-down, such a reduction to essentials, that it takes on an aesthetic quality of its own. Anything that will fulfil an aesthetic job effortlessly is good style. And the great thing about the Brecht company is the absence of effort; it communicates without raising its voice. That is really one of the definitions of style.

Do you find a beneficial Brechtian influence on contemporary English writers? Would you say that a play like Osborne's Luther *was better than a play like* Epitaph for George Dillon *because it was influenced by a Brechtian sense of form?*

I don't think it was. I wouldn't have said that was a Brechtian play. It may have been that reading Brecht and seeing Brecht turned Osborne's mind towards the German subject, I don't know. But I should have thought what attracted him about *Luther* was a temperamental affinity with the man himself.

Do you see any traces of Brechtian influence on English writers?

Very little. I think it has had much more influence on the directors, and I think its effects would be much more rapidly seen in productions of the classics . . . I would very much like to see directors applying that technique to fields other than Elizabethan drama, which is the most obviously Brechtian. I can imagine the Brecht treatment being given to Restoration plays as he himself did with *The Recruiting Officer*. What this really means is a director and a company looking at plays as bits of historical evidence rather than as separate "works of art".

When you saw Planchon's Georges Dandin, *I remember you saying you didn't think that was a successful experiment, but wasn't Planchon doing with Molière exactly what you are talking about?*

Absolutely. And also what Planchon's done to the plays of Marivaux: as one French critic said, we shall never be able to see Marivaux for our generation except through Planchon's eyes. He treats them not as exercises in style for splendid high comedy actors who pirouette, but brings in the whole household, the servants, the stable, the gardener. He gives you a picture of the society which is hidden beneath the text. The subtext in Stanislavsky is psychological; in a Brechtian production the subtext is social. What this means is that in Shakespearian tragedies, the Brechtian approach is to look at the plays as histories instead of tragedies, and in comedies (Restoration included) to look at the plays not as exercises in verbal style or physical rhetoric, but as evidence on which to recreate a whole society.

But if the playwright himself didn't intend such evidence to be visible, to manifest itself in the play, isn't there a danger here that it will become a highly elaborate, terribly impressive irrelevancy?

I think it can only help the play. Now let me be quite clear. I don't mean that one should apply Marxist interpretations to Congreve, I don't mean that at all. I merely say that the background, the underside of Restoration life, which was familiar to every Restoration playgoer and is not to us, ought to be made available to contemporary audiences. It is simply helping them to see the play in a context.

But in filling in the social context of these plays, won't the original intentions be altered?

One hasn't seen it tried. I would certainly not advocate changing *The Recruiting Officer*, as Brecht did, putting it in the period of the American War of Independence. That really is a radical change and a completely new play. That I don't mean. What I really mean is that I should like to see Restoration plays done as if the people in them had worn their costumes more than once before. I see no necessity for a glittering verbal style to be accompanied by glittering new costumes. We should get a feeling that this was *every* day not just gala-occasion wit.

But there was a great deal of flourish during the Restoration, and its concepts and behaviour were different from our own. Is it wise to apply a historical-realistic approach to material which was rather artificial and mannered?

I don't think it is the *only* approach. It would simply be a very useful corrective to what is now the tradition. And I do feel that the dialogue, particularly in Farquhar, but even in Wycherley and Congreve, is far nearer to realism than we customarily think.

In order to achieve this kind of result, one would have to overcome something like fifty to a hundred years of bad acting-training, which has placed an enormous emphasis on literary felicities and the external shape of the text. Even if a director was inclined to approach a play in this way, would he be able to find a quorum of English actors equipped to produce such a result?

Again, that's an experiment that hasn't been tried. That's called forming a company, and that's something we've had very little experience of. Peter Hall is doing marvellously, but he's only been at it for a few years and the number of actors who have stayed with him since he began is a very tiny handful. He has very wisely started an acting studio, and I hope there will be one eventually with the National Theatre. I don't see how you can preserve a style without that sort of constant practice in a sort of acting gym. But an even greater problem is the one of preserving any continuity when actors are so frequently tempted into films and TV. An actor has a success – say he goes straight from the Royal Court to a lead in a new film, well after that he thinks not of joining somebody else's company for a period of years, but of forming his own. The danger is we shall have too many talents acting centrifugally instead of coming to a common centre. There are enough first-rate young actors in England to form two or perhaps three large permanent companies. But will they?

Would this activity be more useful if these actors could be

persuaded to create these companies outside the realm of tempta-
tion, which is what London is . . . If, for instance, they started
up in the Midlands or Scotland?

No, because even in Scotland cables are delivered and a
sudden request from Sam Spiegel to play Lawrence is more
than most actors can resist.

You mean then, the system can't be outwitted?

Well it's a financial problem. The great thing about the
German theatre, what has made it able to hold large groups
of actors in one place over a period of years, is that the German film industry is a trifling consideration to an actor. It
isn't worth an actor's while to give up playing lots of good
parts in a permanent company just to make one German
film, for which he will not be all that well paid. This is not so
with the English-speaking film industry. But this isn't a new
problem here. It happened ten, twelve years ago, with an
actor like Richard Burton, who suddenly appeared at Stratford as a first-rate Shakespearean actor. One prophesied
great things for him, but of course he went to Hollywood –
saying, oh, I'll come back to the Old Vic. He did come back
to the Old Vic in 1953, but it was more in the nature of a star
bestowing a boon; coming back to salve his conscience. You
didn't feel during that season – at least I didn't – that the
theatre was any longer Burton's life. And the same thing is
true to an extent of O'Toole, and it may be true of Richard
Harris and even of Albert Finney. But unless you can produce
a system of financial incentive strong enough to keep an actor
in a permanent company and at the same time allow him to
make, say, one film every two years, you're just not going to
hold him. And our subsidies at present are just not high
enough.

You think then it is a matter of a certain kind of compromise
whereby actors can be permitted to go and make a film and then
come back to the theatre, and not feel they are slumming because
the salary difference won't be that great.

Yes, it oughtn't to be that great. You see as it is the
National Theatre subsidy is £150,000, which is less than twice
as much as the Old Vic now gets a year. And that won't permit any stratospheric rise in salaries. Nor can it offer the sort

of permanent security, as yet, that the Moscow Arts Theatre can: steadily rising salaries, official recognition, Honoured Artist to the Soviet Union, a guaranteed pension, pension for your wife – all that. It can't guarantee those things yet. . . .

In an interview you had with Sartre several years ago, Sartre was quoted as saying that he couldn't conceive of a play being written now that was right wing and good. Left wing and right wing are rather arbitrary, all-encompassing classifications. Do you believe literature can be divided into these two broad political categories?

No. No more than you can divide literature into classic and romantic. But they do reflect a cast of mind which we more or less understand. It's clear that, as I said, a sense of hierarchy, a respect for tradition and the traditional virtues are more or less right wing concepts, whereas a spirit of scepticism and equality, a mistrust of heroes and a belief in the infinite potentiality of every human being, these are more or less left wing concepts. But I wouldn't restrict it to politics – I think there are left wing lovers and right wing lovers.

With a play like The Caretaker, *with certain of Ionesco's plays, if one wanted to define their cast of mind using these very loose left wing, right wing labels. . . .*

. . . It would be very difficult. If one wanted to call Ionesco anything one would call him a right wing anarchist. But I would hate to use that sort of classification. Ionesco thinks that the results that can be achieved by men banding together to change a social or political system are very limited. He believes they cannot solve the basic human problem that we all have to die. And this problem apparently is out in the open in the new play, *Le Roi Se Meurt*, where he is obviously considering the fact of his own mortality. As for Pinter, he is certainly not classifiable as left wing or right wing, though I doubt whether an author of Tory background would have the incredible instinct for lower-class behaviour and speech that Pinter has.

Pinter has said in a discussion somewhere that he is opposed to propaganda in the theatre, even propaganda for life. I take it from what you said and what you've written, that this would not be your attitude.

It depends what you mean by propaganda. Obviously crude poster propaganda is always bad art but some good poster propaganda can be good art. *Everyman* is propaganda for God – one can't deny that – but that doesn't affect its quality as a play. There are a great many plays which are propaganda for causes I believe in which I wouldn't hesitate in attacking – because they were ill-written, ill-built, ill-conceived. On the whole I would agree with Adamov on this question. Adamov said when he changed from being an Absurdist to a conscious Marxist writer that he thought it was a luxury to indulge in introspection and fantasy, until everybody in the world had an equal chance to be equally despairing; that there were certain priorities – that without an equitably governed and organized world it was a bit of a luxury for the isolated western middle-class writer to contemplate his own despair and generalize from it.

A lot of great social plays tend to come out of periods of social upheaval. Do you think the present period, in England, is capable of producing great social Theatre? It seems to me that a large percentage of Brecht-worship is due to a craving on the part of certain English theatregoers, to have a social-orientated, politically-concerned theatre expressing convictions – which unfortunately are not truly felt in England. Reproducing Brecht plays of the 'twenties and the 'thirties seems to confer a vicarious sense of commitment. I question whether or not that is a worthwhile craving in a contemporary audience.

There are two things here. I don't necessarily think that a period of great social upheaval does produce great plays. Chekhov wrote *before* a period of great social upheaval and produced better plays than actually came out of the upheaval.

I should really qualify that. By social upheaval I don't mean plays actually written during stress times, like the Depression or the Russian Revolution, but obviously when something like the Russian Revolution erupts, there are many many years of fermentation – everything building up to that one climactic moment in history. In The Cherry Orchard, *for instance, and many of Chekhov's plays, you get the feeling of the new world which was rapidly evolving.*

In England, social change, particularly since our civil war, has always been a gradualist affair. It tends to be a slow ground-swell producing the fall of a monument at the same time as somebody else builds a housing estate. Old landmarks tend to crumble rather than get blown up. And of course this cannot be treated with intense dramatic impact because it's a slow process and it does require much more subtle seismographical charting by playwrights than the major earthquakes do. It is much easier to write an effective play about the Russian Revolution or the Kronstadt Mutiny than it is about the Education Act. Although the repercussions of the Education Act may, over a period of time, be just as potent. It's a harder job, but not necessarily less worth doing.

You see, since about 1900, all the arts have been reflecting a sort of social fragmentation. A lot of people were expecting, especially in the 'thirties, some sort of apocalyptic vision – the end of capitalism – but one factor prevented that. The existence of the atom bomb and the H-bomb make it unlikely that there will be a great sudden dramatic political and social change in the foreseeable future. After the Chinese Revolution, there won't be any more enormous ones because neither side will allow the balance of power to alter that much. So it will be harder for playwrights who are looking for that sort of immediate brash journalistic impact. But it is still basically true that all plays written up to, let's say, the end of the seventeenth century, the end of the period of heroic plays, are more or less about power. But all plays written in the Bourgeois period tend to be about money and social status, however concealed. Nearly every Restoration play is about how a penniless aristocrat can get married to the merchant's wealthy daughter. It's always a question of dowries and wedding portions; Molière is concerned with it constantly. So we got the drama of power and status achieved through money. Now we have got the new twentieth-century drama, which is concerned with political or social change to produce a new sort of society, which is not based on power or money. And because this change is gradual, the plays have to be tentative.

And it's certainly true that Brecht's plays of the 'thirties,

T

when he envisaged the triumph of world wide socialism in the
near future are not particularly relevant to our condition
now.

But there are still certain parallels . . . ?

Yes, you see, it's still true. I mean the playwrights of the
United States are falling down on their job in this respect.
They are not, especially now that Arthur Miller has apparently chosen silence, they are simply not aware of a whole
strata of society in the United States which is submerged and
unrecorded in books, plays or films. There was a recent long
piece in the *New Yorker* by Dwight MacDonald whom nobody
could accuse now of being a flaming red; he was reviewing
four recent surveys of poverty in the United States which
happened to come out more or less at the same time. In these
four books, two of which I believe were inquiries set up by
universities, the lowest estimate of people living on the poverty
line or below it in the United States was 25 per cent of the
population. The highest estimate in the four books was 49
per cent. This is a shocking fact and a proof that that sort of
capitalism is just not working in terms of people. This submerged 25 per cent, which was written about by people like
John Steinbeck in *The Grapes of Wrath* is simply not being
dealt with in American drama at all, and it should be. When
we say that affluence leaves one little to write about, I think
there's *plenty* for a social playwright to get very worked up
about in the United States. I think it's a pity that nobody is.

*What seems to be frustrating most Americans today is not the
overt social situation but this kind of secret tyranny that goes on
all the time in America. You have a state of affairs where there
is a strong power-control over people and yet one is unable to pinpoint the forces or how they operate. And, of course, it is all
terribly chummy, which is very deceptive because it conceals great
anguish and misery. I believe Edward Albee has begun to deal
with these subjects – started to mine certain veins opened up by
Norman Mailer.*

From what I've read of Albee, I wouldn't say that he had
the sort of passionate subterranean violence of temperament
that Mailer has. I mean Mailer is really "the revolutionary"
who thinks that history has dammed up the revolutionary

impulse and turned it into cancer, and that the only answer
is a return to a completely instinctive life ungoverned by any
concepts of morality. I don't think Albee is as revolutionary
as Mailer. It seems to me he simply tears the scabs off middle-
class guilt and unease. I don't think he, or any American
playwright, has much interest in or sympathy with the submerged 25 per cent for whom the ads are not written, for
whom the products are not made, to whom newspapers
aren't sold – and who are unrepresented on TV and the screen.
There is of course one safe subject of political protest and that
is the colour problem . . . but that's only one of dozens, the
others are never touched.

*There is today in England a discernible disgust with modern
satire. The charge is that it never gets out of the undergraduate
stage, that it's merely offensive, and doesn't stem from any conviction – that, in the long run, it's innocuous. I am wondering
whether or not the same things which take the bite out of satire
today are also responsible for a certain vapidity in the drama.
Do you think there is a tie-up there?*

I think . . . yes.

Do you agree that modern satire IS innocuous?

I think there has always been a place for innocuous satire.
Nobody would say that Goldsmith was a biting, savage
satirist, yet there is a place for a Goldsmith. There is also
room for a Sheridan – whom nobody would say was lacerating
the ills of society as Juvenal did, for instance. There is a place,
and a valuable place, for satire that does not actually conduct an operation on the living body of the audience. One
cannot judge satire by its intensity. One cannot say that the
satire contained in *The Importance of Being Earnest* is of less
value than other more savage kinds – simply because it
doesn't conduct an all-out assault on the most cherished prejudices of society. That is point one.

Point two is: in general, the twentieth century has been an
age of either positive iconoclasm which has deliberately set
out to topple idols and has succeeded, or one in which the
idols themselves have been eroded by history. We feel we
have been had by convictions and we want no part in them.
As Brecht said, scepticism moves mountains. And the post-

war generation, even more than the one after the First World War, is convinced that almost all general convictions about morality and politics are to be taken with a grain of salt. And on the whole one can't blame them. I have a cherished corner reserved for Socialism as an answer to the most immediate problems of human intercourse, but one obviously can't ask all satirists to have this attitude. And even those who have it are not necessarily better writers.

But shouldn't they have some kind of attitude?

Well, what was Oscar Wilde's attitude?

Wilde – if one takes him at his own word, believed in pleasure and aesthetics. That sense of pleasure and that enormous respect for aesthetics can be derived from all his plays. There is a certain consistency of attitude in all of his work which stems from the temperament of the man rather than an external set of beliefs. It doesn't, in my opinion, connect back to any social principles or political credos. . . .

Oh but it does. I would say Wilde was much more positive than you make him sound, even though I seem to be arguing against myself. He thought of himself as a Socialist.

Well there have been grave doubts about that. The Soul of Man Under Socialism *is a piece of artistic rhetoric rather than a finely reasoned political tract.*

I don't think he was an active Socialist, but I think because of homosexual inclinations which could more easily be satisfied with working-class partners, that may have been partly the temperamental root of it, but he believed in a kind of aesthetic socialism; that aesthetic experiences were possible in everybody and it was the duty of the artist to teach people how to use their aesthetic responses. . . . Although that idea does not come out in his plays, you could construct, and people *have* constructed a pretty elaborate indictment of the English upper class from Oscar Wilde's plays.

It's open to interpretation. I wouldn't have looked at it in quite that way, but granting your point you are saying that Wilde does have a positive attitude?

In a very submerged way, yes – in his actual work. But on stage, what comes over is this sheer delight in conjuring tricks and paradox. Which is splendid and just as valid though less an intense an emotion, as the one that one gets from seeing a more bitterly and venomously aimed satire; since we have had two generations or more brought up on the aftermath of world wars and the collapse of any ideals beyond individual ones, the collapse of Religion, the collapse of Victorian morality – all this sort of thing – you are likely to get an absolute rash, as we have now, of satirists. There are so many targets now that there is a great temptation to become a satirist. When there are few targets, and the act of attacking them is regarded with suspicion and hostility by the great majority of the people, then it's a much more difficult thing. Now everything is fair game, and the fact that it's open season on all targets, naturally produces people who come out with the guns and pop away at them.

There seems to be a uniformity in English satire. One finds the same targets appearing over and over again; it becomes fashionable to knock certain prescribed institutions.

But if you list the number of available targets, there aren't all that many. They are really the established ethos and the established organization of a country or of one's world. Well, what does that mean? The government, the civil service, the church, the monarchy, the class system, the universities, sexual hypocrisy. A remark I am always quoting of Cyril Connolly's is from an essay where he is pointing out that all satire must necessarily be, what prevailing opinion at the time will consider, left wing. He says all Tory satire is doomed to ultimate peevishness because it is directed from a stationary staircase to a moving staircase. Hence the peevishness of the later Evelyn Waugh. This is the kind of satire which is now directed by the Establishment at the less ossified parts of society; it is necessarily peevish and a little squalid. But I don't blame the satirists for not achieving social change. I don't think any work of art can be expected to trigger off any sort of direct social change. The social change is probably happening, because of root causes which are the same as that which produced the satire.

You can make jokes about established targets in such a way that everyone admires your cleverness, or you can make jokes about it in such a way that it expresses a genuine attitude on your part to change the status quo. The conventional mechanics of comedy can be applied to satirical subjects very simply, and in this way, one could call someone like Bob Hope one of America's leading satirists – which of course he isn't. It's the absence of conviction that seems to bother people.

Yes, I think it's true, just as when the English drama discovered that it was successful to write plays in blank verse, and the proper subject of a tragedy was a king or hero – a lot of bloody awful writers sat down and turned out blank verse plays about heroes, and they went on doing it until well into the nineteenth century. And the twentieth century even. Of course, anything that is easily imitated will be imitated, and blank verse plays about heroes are just as imitable as prose-knocks at heroes. Now we live in the age of the prose-knock rather than the verse-inflation, but it's the same thing. I don't think one ought to be surprised at this. I feel that the really serious satirists who have the convictions which you rightly feel are missing from a lot of facile satire, the real ones, are moved by a conviction that the essential thing about life is people and human relationships, living together, eating and dying. Any body or organization which is pompous enough or highfalutin enough to set anything above that, to say that pomp and ceremony, that abstract morality, that abstract principles, are more important than people, is a target for the genuine satirist; anyone who says that the book of rules is more important than the person who reads it; that the letter of the law is more important than the health and well-being and adjustment of the criminal. Anyone who puts the *form* of life above the substance always draws the aim of the real satirist – your Swift, for instance, who is deeply concerned about people's starving in Ireland because this is a basic human failure while people in England are talking about Ireland as if it was simply an experiment in killing off people for a generally Socialist, desirable aim of reducing the population – people who talk in those abstract terms about people who are starving aroused Swift's deepest fury and produced his greatest work. I would like to feel that there were satirists in England or Europe or the United States now who had that same conviction: that the importance of human relationships, of food, shelter, birth and death, must take precedence over everything else.

Is it for this reason that you think of Lenny Bruce as being a social satirist?

Yes, quite. His great failing is a certain lack of intellect. He simply hasn't read enough. He goes bull-headed with rage at a subject that he simply hasn't done his homework on. But his guiding principle is to look at a situation and say, is this helping or corrupting the way people get on with each other? If it's corrupting, then I'll attack it. And he does. Because an abstract morality holds that sexual intercourse before marriage is evil, perverts people, turns them into guilt-ridden messes, this must be attacked, and attack it he will.

I'd like to leave this and go on to the subject of acting. Peter Hall and Peter Brook, at the Royal Shakespeare Company, continually talk about a tendency in Shakespearian production towards neutrality.

I talked to Peter Brook about this question a little bit, and what I thought he meant by it was that actors – and he seemed to think it was a good thing – actors no longer pass moral judgement on the characters they are playing. Which is the easiest thing for an actor to do. If he's playing an unsympathetic part, it's a great temptation to show to the audience by the way he acts the part that he disapproves of the character or wants the audience to disapprove of him.

This tendency is particularly visible in Brook's production of *Lear*, although it isn't all that new. You can see it in the way Iago is played. Iago is conventionally played as a sort of lip-licking Italianate villain that the audience is invited to giggle at with a sort of horrified glee, but they are to disapprove of him and think of him as something monstrous. Now, Richard Burton played Iago as a completely honest NCO with a genuine grudge, who believed passionately that he was justified in what he was doing. That was a neutral attitude towards the character. Similarly, when Alec Clunes played Claudius in Peter Brook's otherwise rather bad production of *Hamlet* in 1956, instead of playing Claudius as a villain inviting the audience's contempt or disapproval, he played Claudius as a man who had committed murder in the heat of passion – a *crime passionel* – and found himself with all his gains crumbling; a figure almost to be sympathized with, certainly not to be despised.

Do you connect this kind of neutrality in Shakespearian acting with the Brechtian idea of objectivity, allowing the audience to draw its own conclusions?

No, I think the Brecht system in some ways almost works against this, because Brecht *does* ask the actors to express attitudes towards the characters they are playing, to show in the performance that this character should have made another choice from the one he did. And to invite the audience to be critical of what the characters are doing. This man acted badly, he could have acted better. The approach I mean in Shakespeare is almost the reverse of that. It is seeing every character from the character's point of view, not from what the author may have thought of the character.

But in Shakespeare there are many places where, looking at it from the character's point of view, the character confesses to his own villainy, accepts his own blackness.

You see that in a play like *Richard III*, where the hero is constantly exulting in and announcing his own horrific acts. The way to do that is to be found in a performance which in many ways was the first of what you might call modern Shakespeare performances, which was Olivier's in 1949. He gave you a man, not a great blustering monster of horror, not a toad or viper or hog or any of those things, but an immensely sophisticated man with a sense of humour and a great sense of other people's weaknesses – and of his own – with no self-pity and no pity for others. These are compensating qualities; 'I myself can have no pity on myself', this is almost a virtue by making this immensely shrewd, crafty person, who's ready to confess his Machiavellianism, not to be ashamed of it. Instead of hating him or fearing him, one understood him, and one could accept him as the sort of person you might meet at a Party meeting. And not be as terrified of him as you would have been of a Stalin.

Isn't this part of the general Method trend of removing the indicational and obvious traits of characters? Of resisting the

temptation to play stock characters in easily definable, often
banal, terms?

It is all part of the search for valid motives, which certainly
began with Stanislavsky – that there are no actions without
causes and if you look for the cause without sympathy you
will never find it, and if you look for the cause with sympathy
you will play that sympathy into the performance. That is
what Olivier did and is what I think actors are more and
more doing with Shakespeare. It is often impossible. And at
certain points of Peter Brook's *Lear* it ceases to work, and
you find that if you start giving a little sympathy to Goneril
and Regan and Oswald, you must take away the sympathy
which normally goes wholly to Kent. And the scene between
Kent and Oswald, where normally it is made clear by the
actor that Oswald is an uppish little fop who deserves all he
gets while Kent is being treated appallingly, with the equal
balance of sympathy, that scene definitely counters the playwright's intention. A different sort of clarity comes out of it,
but not what the author had in mind.

Lastly, I want to talk a bit about drama criticism. Peter
Brook has suggested in a recent issue of Encore *that criticism*
ought to free itself from journalism and that, ideally, the critic
should be somebody inside the theatre. Brook says: "Anybody
working inside a theatre movement, whether it's a writer or
director or actor, is working towards an idea of theatre, which
means that you are working today towards something which you
hope is getting better; is reaching cumulatively better goals,
better targets than the one you have behind you, the one that you
have today. The critic who, however sympathetic, however intel-
ligent and however experienced, is simply recording, is recording
without being involved himself in this process of pushing the
theatre towards something better"; and he talks about this sort of
critic "moving something towards something".

In an article some time ago, you put forward the view that the
critic should try to record what actually happens in a particular
theatre on a particular night, so that it would exist almost as a
document. Do you still feel this?

Yes, I think that is the basic job, but of course he can do
many others. The real job is to write interestingly about what

you have seen, whether you are a novelist or a sporting journalist. But beyond that you can do a great deal more. Whether
you ought to have personal knowledge of how a play is produced and the workings of a theatre from the other side of
the footlights, I'm by no means convinced. The old analogy
is true, that the ideal gourmet isn't necessarily a chef.

*But Brook's point is that the critic should be involved in
theatrical aspirations; should be part of a theatre movement.*

That's certainly one kind of critic. Shaw was that kind of
critic. But it isn't the only kind or necessarily the best kind.
I don't think Hazlitt was that kind of critic and I think he
was a great critic. Hazlitt wasn't concerned with changing
the course of world drama. As a judge of plays he was lamentable quite often. But he did respond to the living phenomenon with all of his senses, and if you do that and can set
down what your senses tell you, then you can be a great critic
even if you are quite content with the theatre as it is.

*The same distaste a lot of people feel with satire, is perhaps
more strongly directed against drama criticism. The charge is
that critics are woefully unqualified, make snap judgements,
simply describe physiological symptoms and let that pass for
criticism.*

Playwrights write bad plays, but that is no argument for
the abolition of playwrights. Critics occasionally are ill-
equipped for their jobs, but that is no argument against the
function of a good critic. I happen to have a streak of exhortation in me which quite often obtrudes in what I write, and
sometimes overbalances my judgement. A tendency to tell
the theatre which way it ought to be going. But there are
equally good critics who are content with the *status quo*, who
are, one might say, passionately content with it. I think the
critic who argues against change is just as justified as the
critic who argues for it.

Wouldn't such a critic personify the Tory state of mind?

Yes, surely; I would hotly contest it but I don't see any
reason to proscribe it. Take a critic like Philip Hope Wallace,
who probably knows more about the variety of experiences
that one can get from a stage than any other English critic in
that he also reviews opera and ballet and is immensely

authoritative on both subjects; he is much more skilled as a connoisseur than any other English critic. On the whole, with a few exceptions, he's fairly content with the bourgeois theatre and isn't easily impressed by experiment. He tends to say things like – 'one saw this when the Compagnie des Quinze came over in the 'thirties', or 'one saw this in Berlin in the 'twenties' – and tends to stifle a yawn when people claim to be revolutionary. This attitude of the wittily-stifled yawn often drives me mad in his reviewing, but it's a price I'm quite happy to pay, for his experience and the deliberate detachment which can, in a person like him, be a positive virtue.

Isn't it rather a relative virtue? Such a critic becomes diverting perhaps, after one has already read the more committed, more involved critics, but if there were, let's say, twelve such genteel palates delicately tasting a theatrical bill-of-fare, it would be unbearable.

Of course, absolutely. But I suppose the larger one's experience of different sorts of theatre, the more one tends to get slightly suspicious of anyone's claims to novelty. These two things may be inseparable – the wider your knowledge, perhaps the less your tendency to advocate revolution.

What about the view that the critic is not really representative of the theatre-going public, because no average member of an audience goes to the theatre four or five times a week? Don't a critic's senses get a little tarnished by the fact that he is constantly being exposed to all sorts of stuff whereas the average playgoer is carefully selective. Do you think this affects the sensibility of a critic?

Oh yes. It should.

I mean affects badly.

No. To quote from George Jean Nathan; he said, the ideal critic must be blasé; only to be really moved by the first-rate. It is only the theatrical innocent who is capable of taking a completely open mind to each play. The critic must be much more sagacious, much more wily and much more blasé. He must only be impressed by that which is *really* impressive. The sign of the very young critic is his tendency to hail every new play as either a masterpiece or a disaster. Only the truly blasé critic, who has been at it for – how long have I been at it now? – twelve years? – can ever hope to arrive at a balanced judgement.

Do you think there ought to be some sort of appeal against drama criticism? A place where artists who feel they have been badly criticized can answer back? Very often people in the theatre feel they have been unfairly reviewed and that the source of the unfairness stems from ignorance on the critic's part, but they refrain from expressing their opinion publicly because they feel – well, I'll be reviewed by this critic again in some other play – and so I'd better play safe. Should there be some kind of check against harmfully ignorant criticism?

But, ignorance of what? If you mean the fact that an actor took over a part at four days' notice, and the critic is ignorant of this fact and gives him a bad notice, when in fact he ought to have said, "in view of the fact that this actor only had four days he did quite well" . . .

No, I mean more the case of a critic who can't distinguish between the work of a director and the work of an actor; between the deficiencies of text and the distortions of production; the critic who, not having that fundamental knowledge to know what each person is supposed to be doing, might say of a new writer that this play is tripe, whereas what he really means is the performance was so badly acted he actually didn't get to see the play.

I think it would be an excellent thing if sometimes critics who requested it were allowed to read the text of new plays. Then one might be able to distinguish between direction and text. Which, the better the production, the harder that distinction is to make. It is only obvious in a bad production; well only blatant, let's say.

That seems to be inclining towards Brook's position, that the critic should be someone more involved in the theatre, at least to the extent of reading the script beforehand.

Nineteenth-century critics nearly all did. The managements distributed scripts to Archer and Shaw as a matter of course, so that they were familiar with what they were going to see. Nowadays managements prefer to take us by surprise.

As far as relations with management are concerned; don't you find that they think of themselves as being on one side of the fence with the critics on the other? There is a sort of natural animosity between managements and critics.

It's only natural because of economics. There is far less animosity between actors and critics in a non-commercial theatre. This is a very important point. A fruitful discussion can take place between critics and management where the critics are not going to be able to ruin a production commercially. In a well-subsidized theatre both critics and management are concerned only with the artistic value of the product. In our society, the managements are concerned with its commercial chances and the critics with its artistic ones. Therefore they are always bound to be at cross-purposes. But this is an economic thing. It is not inherent in the relationship.

Secondly, about actors having some sort of kick-back. Of course I am incorruptible, and I think a surprising number of critics are. And if an actor wrote an angry letter to the *Observer*, it would never occur to me, I hope not even subconsciously, to hold it against him. As long as it was clear we were both talking the same language and not entering into a sort of slanging match. I think more actors ought to do that. On occasion, actors writing to one to thank one for an appreciative notice, say, "I know this isn't the custom and I hope you will forgive me for doing this" – well, that shouldn't be the attitude. If they feel pleased with a review that's been perceptive about them and they want to say so, one is delighted. I think this animosity is partly a by-product of the commercial theatre. You find it very much less, for instance, in the German theatre, where, also significantly, the idea of civic theatre activity was born, and in one of its early manifestations, the Deutsches Schauspielhaus at Hamburg had a critic – Lessing – a *Dramaturg* on the permanent staff. That kind of intimate relationship, where Lessing was writing plays for the company, was employed by it and also reviewing it, is possible only when critics *and* management *and* actors *and* playwrights are all working towards a common artistic end.

[JULY 1963]

A LONDON DIARY

Letters after play titles indicate theatres: A—Arts, Ald—Aldwych, BDL—BDL Practice Theatre, Ca—Cambridge, C—Comedy, Ch—Chichester Festival Theatre, F—Fortune, G—Globe, H—Haymarket, HTC—Hampstead Theatre Club, LOH—Lyric Opera House, M—Mermaid, NL—New Lindsey, P—Palace, Q—Queen's, RC—Royal Court, RCs—Royal Court (Sunday), S—Saville, TW—Theatre Workshop.

	PLAY	AUTHOR	DIRECTOR	DESIGNER
1956				
May 8	Look Back in Anger (RC)	John Osborne	Tony Richardson	Alan Tagg
May 24	The Quare Fellow (TW)	Brendan Behan	Joan Littlewood	John Bury
June 26	Cards of Identity (RC)	Nigel Dennis	Tony Richardson	Alan Tagg
July 25	Don't Destroy Me (NL)	Michael Hastings	Robert Peake	Jefferson Strong
1957				
April 10	The Entertainer (RC)	John Osborne	Tony Richardson	Alan Tagg
June 9	Yes – And After (RCs)	Michael Hastings	John Dexter	Jocelyn Herbert
June 25	The Making of Moo (RC)	Nigel Dennis	Tony Richardson	Audrey Cruddas
June 30	The Waiting of Lester Abbs (RCs)	Kathleen Sully	Lindsay Anderson	—
Oct. 20	The Waters of Babylon (RCs)	John Arden	Graham Evans	—
Nov. 21	Flowering Cherry (H)	Robert Bolt	Frith Banbury	Reece Pemberton
Dec. 1	A Resounding Tinkle (RCs)	N. F. Simpson	William Gaskill	—
1958				
Feb. 11	Epitaph for George Dillon (RC)	John Osborne	William Gaskill	Stephen Doncaster
Feb. 25	Sport of My Mad Mother (RC)	Ann Jellicoe	George Devine & Ann Jellicoe	Jocelyn Herbert
Mar. 23	Each His Own Wilderness (RCs)	Doris Lessing	John Dexter	—
April 2	The Hole (RC)	N. F. Simpsou	Will am Gaskill	Stanley Rixon
Apr l 9	The Dock Brief & What Shall We Tell Caroline? (LOH)	John Mortimer	Stuart Burge	Disley Jones
May 19	The Birthday Party (LOH)	Harold Pinter	Peter Wood	Hutchinson Scott
May 27	A Taste of Honey (TW)	Shelagh Delaney	Joan Littlewood	John Bury
July 14	Chicken Soup With Barley (RC)	Arnold Wesker	John Dexter	Michael Richardson
July 14	Hamlet of Stepney Green (LOH)	Bernard Kops	Frank Hauser	Michael Richardson
July 16	Five Finger Exercise (C)	Peter Shaffer	John Gielgud	Timothy O'Brien
Sept. 30	Live Like Pigs (RC)	John Arden	George Devine & Anthony Page	Alan Tagg
Oct. 14	The Hostage (TW)	Brendan Behan	Joan Littlewood	Sean Kenny
1959				
Jan. 7	The Long and the Short and the Tall (RC)	Willis Hall	Lindsay Anderson	Alan Tagg
Feb. 8	Progress to the Park (RCs)	Alun Owen	Lindsay Anderson	Sean Kenny
Feb. 15	Fings Ain't Wot They Used T'Be (TW)	Frank Norman	Joan Littlewood	John Bury
May 5	The World of Paul Slickey (P)	John Osborne	John Osborne	Hugh Casson
June 1	The Rough and Ready Lot (LOH)	Alun Owen	Casper Wrede	Malcolm Pride
June 30	Roots (RC)	Arnold Wesker	John Dexter	Jocelyn Herbert
Sept. 6	The Kitchen (RCs)	Arnold Wesker	John Dexter	Jocelyn Herbert
Oct. 22	Serjeant Musgrave's Dance (RC)	John Arden	Lindsay Anderson	Jocelyn Herbert
Dec. 22	One Way Pendulum (RC)	N. F. Simpson	William Gaskill	Stephen Doncaster
1960				
Jan. 21	The Room and The Dumb Waiter (HTC)	Harold Pinter	Harold Pinter & Roose Evans	Michael Young

PLAY	AUTHOR	DIRECTOR	DESIGNER
1960			
Jan. 27 The Lily White Boys (RC)	Christopher Logue, etc.	Lindsay Anderson	Sean Kenny
Mar. 1 Change for the Angel (A)	Bernard Kops	David de Keyser	Yolanda Sonnabend
April 27 The Caretaker (A)	Harold Pinter	Donald McWhinnie	Brian Currah
July 1 A Man for all Seasons (G)	Robert Bolt	Noel Willman	Motley
July 27 I'm Talking About Jerusalem (RC)	Arnold Wesker	John Dexter	Jocelyn Herbert
Aug. 24 The Tiger and the Horse (Q)	Robert Bolt	Frith Banbury	Sam Lock
Aug. 24 Sparrers Can't Sing (TW)	Stephen Lewis	Joan Littlewood	John Bury
Sept. 13 Billy Liar (Ca)	Keith Waterhouse & Willis Hall	Lindsay Anderson	Alan Tagg
Sept. 14 The Happy Haven (RC)	John Arden	William Gaskill	Michael Ackland
Nov. 23 Trials By Logue (RC)	Christopher Logue	Lindsay Anderson	Jocelyn Herbert
Dec. 7 The Tinker (C)	Laurence Dobie & Robert Sloman	John Hale	Jane Graham
Dec. 29 The Lion in Love (RC)	Shelagh Delaney	Clive Barker	Una Collins
1961			
Jan. 18 A Slight Ache (A)	Harold Pinter	Donald McWhinnie	Brian Currah
Jan. 18 The Form (A)	N. F. Simpson	Donald McWhinnie	Brian Currah
Jan. 18 Lunch Hour (A)	John Mortimer	Donald McWhinnie	Brian Currah
Feb. 15 Stop It, Whoever You Are (A)	Henry Livings	Vida Hope	Brian Currah
Feb. 20 The Devils (Ald)	John Whiting	Peter Wood	Sean Kenny
May 10 Beyond The Fringe (F)	Peter Cook et al	Eleanor Fazan	John Wyckham
July 27 Luther (RC)	John Osborne	Tony Richardson	Jocelyn Herbert
Sept. 12 August For The People (RC)	Nigel Dennis	George Devine	Stephen Doncaster
Oct. 2 Counterpoint (C):			
Soldier From The Wars Returning	David Campton	Leila Blake	Brian Currah
Barnstable	James Saunders	Leila Blake	Brian Currah
A Night Out	Harold Pinter	Leila Blake	Brian Currah
Nov. 13 That's Us (RC)	Henry Chapman	William Gaskill	Stephen Doncaster
Nov. 22 The Keep (RC)	Gwyn Thomas	John Dexter	Ken Calder
Nov. 28 Big Soft Nellie (TW)	Henry Livings	Abraham Asseo	Brian Currah
1962			
Mar. 13 Everything in The Garden (A)	Giles Cooper	Donald McWhinnie	Henry Bardon
Mar. 27 The Knack (RC)	Ann Jellicoe	Ann Jellicoe & Keith Johnstone	Alan Tagg
April 12 Nil Carborundum (A)	Henry Livings	Anthony Page	Michael Knight
April 27 Chips With Everything (RC)	Arnold Wesker	John Dexter	Jocelyn Herbert
June 7 Afore Night Come (A)	David Rudkin	Clifford Williams	John Bury
June 18 The Collection (Ald)	Harold Pinter	Peter Hall & Harold Pinter	Paul Anstey & John Bury
July 19 Plays For England (RC):	John Osborne		
The Blood of The Bambergs		John Dexter	Alan Tagg
Under Plain Cover		Jonathan Miller	Alan Tagg
Aug. 29 Infanticide in the House of Fred Ginger (A)	Fred Watson	William Gaskill	Stephen Doncaster
Sept. 23 Day of The Prince (RCs)	Frank Hilton	Keith Johnstone	—
Dec. 5 Semi-Detached (S)	David Turner	Tony Richardson	Loudon Sainthill
1963			
Jan. 23 Next Time I'll Sing To You (A)	James Saunders	Shirley Butler	Timothy O'Brien
Jan. 31 The Bed-Sitting Room (M)	John Atrobus & Spike Milligan	John Antrobus & Spike Milligan	John Antrobus & Spike Milligan
Feb. 1 Jackie The Jumper (RC)	Gwyn Thomas	John Dexter	Michael Annals
Mar. 19 Oh What a Lovely War (TW)	Charles Chilton, etc.	Joan Littlewood	John Bury
April 18 The Trigon (BDL)	J. Broom Lynne	Charles Marowitz	Frank Phelan
June 12 Kelly's Eye (RC)	Henry Livings	David Scase	Alan Tagg
July 8 The Workhouse Donkey (Ch)	John Arden	Stuart Burge	Roger Furse
Sept. 18 The Lover			
The Dwarfs (A)	Harold Pinter	Harold Pinter	Brian Currah
Oct. 16 Cockade (A):			
Prisoner & Escort			
John Thomas	Charles Wood	Patrick Dromgoole	Alan Barrett
Spare			
Nov. 28 Gentle Jack (Q)	Robert Bolt	Noel Willman	Desmond Heeley

INDEX

References to the authors of articles in the text are in **bold type**